TVh 1

PENGUIN BOOKS

THE STING MAN

ROBERT W. GREENE was a veteran reporter for more than twenty-seven years, a senior staff investigator for the New York City Anti-Crime Committee, and an investigator for the U.S. Senate. As a reporter for *Newsday*, he headed investigative teams that twice won the Pulitzer Prize gold medal. He was also president of the Investigative Reporters and Editors Group. He died in 2008.

516 – 234 – 1420
585 – 3399

Telex: 941359

Mel Weinberg

London • Paris • Zurich • New York

Financial Consultant

ABDUL ENTERPRISES LTD.
4250 Veterans Memorial Highway
Holbrook, L.I., N.Y. 11741

THE STING MAN

★ ★ ★ ★ ★

INSIDE ABSCAM

———

ROBERT W. GREENE

PENGUIN BOOKS

PENGUIN BOOKS

Published by the Penguin Group
Penguin Books Ltd, 80 Strand, London WC2R 0RL, England
Penguin Group (USA) Inc., 375 Hudson Street, New York, New York 10014, USA
Penguin Group (Canada), 90 Eglinton Avenue East, Suite 700, Toronto, Ontario, Canada M4P 2Y3
(a division of Pearson Penguin Canada Inc.)
Penguin Ireland, 25 St Stephen's Green, Dublin 2, Ireland (a division of Penguin Books Ltd)
Penguin Group (Australia), 707 Collins Street, Melbourne, Victoria 3008, Australia
(a division of Pearson Australia Group Pty Ltd)
Penguin Books India Pvt Ltd, 11 Community Centre, Panchsheel Park, New Delhi – 110 017, India
Penguin Group (NZ), 67 Apollo Drive, Rosedale, Auckland 0632, New Zealand
(a division of Pearson New Zealand Ltd)
Penguin Books (South Africa) (Pty) Ltd, Block D, Rosebank Office Park,
181 Jan Smuts Avenue, Parktown North, Gauteng 2193, South Africa

Penguin Books Ltd, Registered Offices: 80 Strand, London WC2R 0RL, England

www.penguin.com

First published in the United States of America by Elsevier-Dutton Publishing Co, Inc., 1981
This edition with a new chapter published in Penguin Books 2013
001

Printed in Great Britain by Clays Ltd, St Ives plc

ISBN: 978–0–241–97047–8

www.greenpenguin.co.uk

To
KATHY
Who urged me to reach higher.
My love and gratitude

Kings Park, New York
January 29, 1981

CONTENTS

PREFACE

This is the story of Mel Weinberg, certified hustler and swindler, and Abscam as seen through his eyes, based in part on 237 interviews with Weinberg beginning in March 1980 and ending January 29, 1981. I also had access to many of the FBI Abscam tapes and the official transcripts of six trials and two special court hearings on the subject. For information on his early life, I have relied on Weinberg and his relatives. Other independent evidence is available to document Weinberg's years as a swindler. This includes the files of his company, London Investors, Ltd., police reports, and interviews with Weinberg's wife, Marie, and others. His Abscam years are documented in the FBI tapes, court records and numerous interviews. A few names and the exact nature of certain personal relationships have been slightly altered, but all of those relating to Abscam are accurate. The most significant change is the name of Weinberg's mistress; he prefers that I call her Diane and I have respected his wishes. I like Mel Weinberg. He is different. But, in many ways, he is more honest than many of the people I know. And when he lies, he does it with verve.

I wish to acknowledge the help of Tony Insolia, Tom Renner, Joe Demma, Carole Agus, Tony Marro, Susan Page and Pete Bowles, all of

Newsday; Hank Messick, author and teacher; Gail Meadows of the *Miami Herald*, Mary Neiswender of the Long Beach, California, *Independent-Press Telegram*, and countless others who have made this book possible. My special thanks to Attorney Andrew L. Hughes for his patient and constructive criticism, to my erudite editor, Chuck Corn, and to my enduring secretary, Pat Byrne.

THE STING MAN

1

THE MAN AND THE SCAM

... I have nothin' to hide. I'm an open book; if I can make a buck, I make a buck. —MEL WEINBERG, 1979

The United States Courthouse for the Eastern District of New York is a white, concrete rectangle in what is known as downtown Brooklyn. It is a clean, efficient but graceless building, with a shabbily kept park fringed with maple trees opposite the main entrance, a cool haven from the hot summer sun and a nighttime refuge for muggers and perverts. A few blocks away, over the gargoyled façades of turn-of-the-century office buildings, the pillars of the Brooklyn Bridge spear the sky, dimly visible through a blue haze of exhaust fumes.

Motorists fight for parking spaces on the narrow street fronting the courthouse amid a confusion of signs warning that the block has been reserved for the parking convenience of government bureaucrats.

It was the shank of August 1980; at 9:00 A.M. on this day it was characteristically hot and humid in Brooklyn, and Federal workers raced the last few steps to reach the air-conditioned coolness of the lobby.

Despite the humidity the air was electric with anticipation. Television newsmen with their camera crews were assembling on the sidewalks, and press photographers congregated against the row of parked cars at the curb. It was during this preparatory moment of relative calm that a non-descript car with government plates eased down the street and abruptly nosed into a reserved parking spot.

The driver, a modishly slim FBI agent, quickly exited and walked around to the passenger side, glancing up and down the street as he moved. The agent nodded quickly and the passenger door sprang open. Out stepped Melvin (no middle initial) Weinberg.

Blinking owlishly in the sun despite his tinted, aviator-style sunglasses, Mel Weinberg snipped the end from a huge Te-Amo Toros cigar, jammed it into the corner of his mouth and scanned the sidewalk running to the courthouse door. "Photographers," he said to his companion, FBI Agent Tony Amoroso. Weinberg spoke softly. The only visual indication that he was talking was a slight up-and-down jiggle of the Churchillian cigar.

"Walk like we belong and they'll think we're part of the scenery," said Amoroso. Weinberg grinned agreement and the two men moved down the street, past the idle photographers and into the courthouse. They took the elevator up to the third-floor offices of the Eastern District Federal Strike Force.

When the two men strolled into the large, nearly empty ready-room, several agents murmured automatic greetings before returning to their gin-rummy game. Weinberg and Amoroso slumped into easy chairs and sat quietly. They had worked together for nearly two years and felt no need to fill comfortable silence with useless words. Each was deep in his own thoughts.

Mel Weinberg took stock of himself. For a fifty-five-year-old confidence man, swindler, avid hustler of the fast buck, the avenues of life seemed to be merging this morning at the Brooklyn Federal Courthouse. He couldn't complain. For a runny-nosed kid who had barely graduated from grammar school, he hadn't done badly. Learning, always learning, he had progressed through a thirty-five-year career in white-collar crime—from hustling phony gold contracts over Formica-topped tables at all-night diners to lavish office suites on Long Island, a staff of 500 franchised salesmen and an annual cash income of more than $500,000.

He had worked North America and five other continents, fleecing public officials, movie stars, dictators, generals, mobsters, political terrorists and ordinary businessmen with democratic impartiality. His enemies regarded him as a conniving crook; neutrals called him a rogue, and a small army of underworld admirers and incredulous cops added to the legend daily as they swapped Weinberg stories in the world's bars, jails, cafés, courtrooms and whorehouses.

The money was good and, through the years, Weinberg had developed an appetite for first-class living. But, as he readily admits to himself and his few close friends, the real reward of scamming is the fun of the game. Each new "mark," or potential victim, was a new mind to be wrestled to the ground in a one-on-one battle of wits.

For a bright, agile-minded person like Weinberg, who compensates for his lack of education by sneering at books and passionately embracing the argot of the New York streets, there was heady satisfaction in skinning the powerful, well-educated elite of the business and government world. And he was able to quiet his few moral scruples by remembering an adage that had always been operational in the world of confidence games. The adage goes: You can't con an honest man.

Weinberg puffed on his cigar and gazed absently around the still quiet ready-room. Thoughts flowed through his mind in vagrant order. He pictured his mother, still going strong in her late seventies, by now up and about in her Miami condo. He was generous to his mother, as he had been to all the women in his life. He visited her often and was considerate about helping with matters important to her happiness. She in turn had a special affection for him despite her vocal reservations about the way he made his living.

He grinned as he recalled a recent telephone conversation between his mother and his sister Sylvia on Long Island. It was occasioned by headlined accounts of his career as a confidence man. "Nobody else in the family ever did things like Mel," she exclaimed. "I don't know where he gets it from. But Mel is basically a good boy."

All in all, thought Weinberg, he was satisfied with his life. There had been a few moments of pure terror, terror that turns legs to jelly and, as Weinberg would put it, makes "the asshole so tight it can't pass a mustard seed." There was, for example, the time he fleeced a young Miami lawyer out of $8,000 and afterward checked into the high-rise Holiday Inn in Hallandale to relax for a few days.

A few hours later he answered a knock on the door. In barged a New York hoodlum with a small band of helpers. The hoodlum, it seemed, was the mark's uncle, and he took the swindle as a gesture of personal disrespect. The thugs calmly opened a window and proceeded to push Weinberg out as he frantically tried to fast-talk his way back into the world of the living.

As he later recounted: "I kept throwin' the names of big hoodlums at this guy and telling him that I was connected with them and they'd be mad at him if he killed me. They kept inchin' me outta the window and I kept tryin' for the magic name. I finally said it just before I grew wings."

But mostly he remembered the good times: Julie Podel ushering him to an upfront table on opening night at the Copa; the white flash of camera bulbs as the Lieutenant Governor of Texas made him an honorary citizen, blissfully unaware that he had just hustled some of the state's leading citizens for a quarter-million in cold cash; the respect he saw in the eyes of the lesser primates when the listing "Herring with Sour Cream Weinberg" appeared on the menu at Orlando's, a popular Long Island watering spot.

And then there were the girls and the money. Lots of them and lots of it. Good times.

It was all coming together, probably ending, here and now. The United States Government, in a rare flash of wisdom, had hired the considerable talents of Mel Weinberg, con man. He had cast his net and hauled in a heavy catch of corruptible Congressmen and public officials.

Already defense lawyers were bellowing that the government, in hiring Weinberg, had assumed an unsporting advantage in the war against greed.

Weinberg was scheduled to take the stand as a government witness today. Defense lawyers had already announced to the press that they regarded Weinberg as the heart of the government's case. They said that they were going to have the case thrown out by destroying Weinberg on the stand.

Wreathed in cigar smoke, Weinberg contemplated the battle and enjoyed the idea. Lawyers. More smart guys with college educations, offshore tax shelters, pot-head kids and bony wives who talked like they were biting on marbles and always got headaches when they climbed into the sack. He'd had a lifetime of lawyers. Their meters were always running.

Today lawyers were the enemy. He would follow his own advice: "Play stupider than them and sooner or later ya always get 'em by the short hairs." The lawyers could be had, but nothing was going to kill the headlines. And when a con man's face and name get too well known, he'd better find a new line of work, particularly if he's been doubling as a government agent.

Mel Weinberg does not look like the smooth, prototypical con man. He is squat, resembling a gray-bearded fireplug; a few strands of carefully arranged brown hair tenuously bridge his bald pate. He speaks with a gravelly voice in the rich accents of his native Bronx and he talks in the slang of the underworld. He wears $200-designer sweaters and Christian Dior socks, but they don't affect him. He admires luxury, but its nuances escape him.

He ruefully recalls the time that he was trying to impress a mark in a swank French restaurant on his first foray into Europe. Weinberg was paying and trying to act suave. He ran his finger down the wine list pretending comprehension and ordered a bottle of red listed at $45. A few minutes later, the waiter returned and with a suitable flourish poured a small amount into Weinberg's glass to be tasted. "Fill it up, ya fuck,"

Weinberg barked. "Whaddya think I'm payin' for?" He has since absorbed a rudiment of sophistication, and a style that is unique.

He had come to testify that day in a cream-colored Pierre Cardin suit with matching vest, and a shirt and tie in shades of yellow. He wore a gold bracelet on one wrist and gold rings with diamond chips on each pinkie finger. This ensemble, combined with the tinted sunglasses, gave him the look of a retired mobster on opening day at Santa Anita.

Tony Amoroso looked at Weinberg speculatively and broke his silence. "The Pooch [Eastern District Strike Force Director Thomas Puccio] is sure gonna love your uniform," he said. Both men grinned at the thought of the ultraconservative Federal prosecutor. "Screw 'im," replied Weinberg. "He ain't got no taste."

The excitement in the courthouse had been building for a week ever since the start of the bribery trial of Philadelphia Congressman Michael J. (Ozzie) Myers and three codefendants—Angelo J. Errichetti, Mayor of Camden, New Jersey, Philadelphia City Councilman Louis C. Johanson and Howard L. Criden, a Philadelphia lawyer.

The trial was the first in a series, all involving brand-name Congressmen and public officials, which had resulted from an audacious FBI undercover operation dubbed Abscam (short for Abdul scam). The two-year investigation, starting in the murky world of white-collar crime, had burgeoned into a massive corruption probe reaching from the city halls of the East Coast to the United States Senate and, maybe, even higher.

At the core of Abscam was Mel Weinberg, the sting man. The government had paired Weinberg with Amoroso and a series of other FBI agents to pose as the American representatives of two imaginary Arab sheikhs, Kambir Abdul Rahman and Yassir Habib. Operating behind a dummy corporation on Long Island called Abdul Enterprises, Ltd., Weinberg and Amoroso laid out the bait: The two sheikhs wanted to invest their OPEC-swollen billions in the U.S. and eventually—after they had completed the rape of their national treasuries—find permanent asylum in this country.

A small tribe of hustlers, middlemen, con men and influence brokers, that mysterious breed that seems to emerge from nowhere when there is the scent of big money, swarmed over the bait like flies. They brought in the Congressmen and public officials. And Abscam grew.

The list of indictments in Abscam was impressive. Besides Myers and his spear carriers, Federal grand juries had already returned bribery counts against Representative Raymond F. Lederer (D-Pa.), a member of the House Ways and Means Committee; Representative Frank Thompson, Jr. (D-N.J.), Chairman of the House Administration Committee and the powerful subcommittee on Labor-Management Relations; Representative John M. Murphy (D-N.Y.), Chairman of the House Merchant Marine and Fisheries Committee and Chairman of the Select Committee on the Outer Continental Shelf; Representative John W. Jenrette, Jr. (D-S.C.), a member of the House Appropriations Committee, and Representative Richard Kelly (R-Fla.), the only Republican in the batch.

Another Congressman, Representative John P. Murtha (D-Pa.), a member of the House Ethics Committee, had dodged possible indictment and agreed to become a Federal witness in the Thompson and Murphy cases. And even now, according to office scuttlebutt, Strike Force attorneys were presenting Abscam evidence on U.S. Senator Harrison A. Williams, Jr., to another Federal grand jury. As Chairman of the Senate Labor and Public Welfare Committee, Williams exerted a strong influence on the domestic policies of President Jimmy Carter.

With predictable media focus on the easily understood issue of corruption, an even more chilling thesis of the Abscam case went unnoticed: the fact that supposed agents of a foreign nation could so easily bribe some of the most powerful members of the United States Congress. Some of these very Congressmen had been at the forefront of the battle to win greater Congressional control over the day-to-day activities of the Central Intelligence Agency.

Almost from the beginning of the case, the government taped everything: telephone calls, hotel room meetings, casual conversations. A tape recorder with a suction-cup telephone attachment had become as much a part of Weinberg's everyday accoutrements as his cigar snipper or the brown plastic box in which he carried his high-blood-pressure and heart pills.

Every major meeting between the government agents and Congressmen, mobsters or middlemen was videotaped—particularly those meetings where actual payoffs were made. Video cameras equipped with special lenses were aimed through the screens of dummy TV sets, ceiling light fixtures, keyholes and even needle-thin holes drilled into doors and walls. The film, combined with the recorded phone conversations and audiotapes of the bugged meetings, provided the government with devastating evidence.

Throughout the investigation, platoons of FBI agents and secretaries worked late into the night transcribing more than a thousand tapes, some of which ran 150 typed pages. At times the mounds of transcripts threatened to engulf the modest Strike Force office. They were stacked on the floor against walls, heaped on desk tops and piled on most of the vacant chairs.

The attention devoted to massing this overkill of evidence went far beyond that devoted to the ordinary criminal case. And it was prompted by more than investigative fascination with electronics. Both the Justice Department (the prosecutors) and the FBI (the investigators) were emulating the pragmatism of a former Miami Strike Force director, who, when asked why he hadn't indicted a close friend of President Richard Nixon's for security fraud, replied, "You don't jump on a king unless you can kill him."

In the Abscam case, Congress was king. Congress controls the budgets of both the Justice Department and the FBI. Congress can hamstring government agencies, remove functions, eliminate departments and skewer key government officials in front of its committees. Congress has the power to subpoena and to hold in contempt. Congress has done some noble things, and it has done some contemptible things. But

Congress has one enduring characteristic: it tends to regard attacks on its members as threats against the institution itself. Revenge is often swift and undiscriminating.

Right now, Congress was in a cantankerous mood. Opinion polls showed that it stood even lower than the legal profession in the public's respect. With increasing frequency its members were embroiling themselves in scandal. Koreagate lingered like a bad dream. There was a widespread perception that Congress had become so beholden to competing special interests that it was no longer capable of operating in the national interest. Now there was Abscam. What had been public contempt for Congress now verged on hostility.

For the once legendary FBI, Abscam promised to be the benchmark of its new beginning. Sullied by Watergate, demoralized by the pettiness of J. Edgar Hoover in his waning years as Director, and harassed by charges of illegal procedures, the Bureau had been revamped, rekindled and aimed in new directions by a series of able directors. If the Abscam cases were successful in the courts, the courage and professionalism shown by the FBI in taking on Congressional corruption could restore public confidence in the agency.

Caught in the middle was the Justice Department. The Attorney General is appointed by the President. He is publicly charged with enforcing Federal laws and privately expected to be as benign as possible toward the President and the President's friends and political supporters. This spirit of benevolence has sometimes involved the outright squelching of a criminal case, whispered warnings to FBI targets, or carefully orchestrated bumbling. There are also more subtle forms of prosecutorial avoidance, including the demand for excessive evidence, bureaucratic delays, cost-paring and the catch-all excuse: legal technicalities.

There were two successive Attorneys General during the Abscam investigation, both of whom monitored every step in the various cases. They were Griffin Bell and Benjamin R. Civiletti, both professional Democrats and close friends of President Carter. Both would appear to have acted properly, although, as the tapes poured in, they evidently had some extremely squeamish moments.

On one tape, a politically connected New Jersey garbage racketeer, who candidly talked about bribing Newark Mayor Kenneth Gibson, confided that Attorney General Bell, apparently at President Carter's request, arranged for the United States Attorney in Newark to quash an income-tax evasion case against Gibson. Other tapes detail arrangements made to bribe U.S. Senator Herman E. Talmadge of Georgia and Atlanta Congressman Wyche Fowler, Jr., both strong supporters of the President and close associates of Bell's in the Georgia Democratic organization. Both Talmadge and Fowler, who have denied knowledge of any bribe negotiations, lost interest in the deal rather abruptly, according to an account given by a middleman who was arranging the meetings.

In still another tape, South Carolina Congressman John W. Jenrette, Jr., who said he left a White House party early so that he could meet with Abscam agents to discuss his bribe, boasted that the White House had promised him help in squelching a proposed Justice Department investigation of his part in a scandal-tainted South Carolina real estate deal. He later told the agents that his attorney had talked with Civiletti and the investigation had been killed.

There were also party considerations. Almost all of the Congressmen in the Abscam net were Democrats. They were concentrated in New Jersey and Pennsylvania, heavily populated northeastern industrial states important to the President in the 1980 elections. Although some of those indicted were strong supporters of President Carter's primary opponent, Senator Edward (Ted) Kennedy (D-Mass.), many of the tapes involved Senators, Congressmen, city mayors, state legislators and party officials who were ardently behind the President. And all of them, Democratic friends and foes, would be needed after the convention when the party closed ranks for November.

Furthermore, hundreds of pages of still secret tapes, including an hour-long session with Alvin Malnik, top money-mover for mobster

Meyer Lansky, bared inside details of how the mob, working with bought public officials and politicians, controlled the casino gambling industry in both Las Vegas and Atlantic City. If this information were made public, it could wreck casino gambling in Atlantic City and block it in New York and Florida. Leading Democratic politicians were closely associated with pro-casino gambling interests in all three states.

Abscam was a political burden to the Attorney General, not only because leading Democratic Congressmen faced sure indictment but also because the tapes were larded with the names of even more prominent Democrats. Among them were House Speaker Thomas P. (Tip) O'Neill, Jr. (D-Mass.), House Majority Leader James C. Wright, Jr. (D-Tex.), House Majority Whip John Brademas (D-Ind.) and Representative Peter W. Rodino, Jr. (D-N.J.), Chairman of the powerful House Committee on the Judiciary. One middleman even offered to produce Senator Ted Kennedy.

On the Republican side of the ledger, besides Representative Kelly of Florida, the only names mentioned on the tapes were those of Senator Strom Thurmond (R-S.C.), Senator Jacob K. Javits (R-N.Y.), Representative Norman F. Lent (R-N.Y.), and Steven Stockmeyer, executive director of the Republican Congressional Committee. In the case of Thurmond, who has said that he was never approached with any bribe offer, it was Jenrette, a Democratic Congressman from the same state, who offered to make the contact. And in the case of Javits and Lent, it was clearly stated by the middleman that neither one would take any money personally for assisting the mythical Arabs. Instead, said the middleman, Javits suggested contributions be made to the GOP committee through Stockmeyer.

Many of these names, Democratic and Republican, may have represented nothing more than the fond pipe dreams of middlemen anxious to impress the undercover agents. But these same middlemen did produce a number of Congressmen, almost all of them Democrats, who did take bribes. And, if the Abscam cases were prosecuted and the names of the other Congressmen were revealed, the sheer number of Democratic names might foster a public impression that the party was totally corrupt.

Nonetheless, Civiletti eventually endorsed the Abscam indictments and did so despite a ready-made excuse not to prosecute any of the Abscam cases. The excuse arrived on his desk while the investigation was still in progress. It came in the form of a lengthy memorandum arguing that the government—particularly hired swindler Mel Weinberg—had gone too far in enticing some of the defendants.

The memo was sent to Civiletti by Robert J. Del Tufo, the United States Attorney in Newark, who was charged with the investigation and prosecution of Federal crime in New Jersey. Del Tufo, a Democrat, had been nominated for his post by Senator Williams. Through the course of the Abscam investigation, Del Tufo had been routinely briefed on its progress and the contents of the tapes as they applied to New Jersey politics and politicians, including Senator Williams.

The memo was the final shot in a behind-the-scenes battle for control of the investigation between Eastern District Strike Force Director Tom Puccio and Del Tufo. The feud had developed as Weinberg and FBI undercover agents penetrated deeper and deeper into the corruption that permeated New Jersey politics and government.

Del Tufo, who had been named on two of the tapes as the official designated by Attorney General Bell to kill the income tax case against Mayor Gibson, resigned, citing "financial reasons" shortly after the first Abscam indictments were returned. But not before his chief assistant told members of Puccio's staff that he hoped the Abscam probers would "fall flat on their faces."

Congress, the Justice Department, the FBI, all stood to be affected for better or worse by Abscam. So did many as yet unnamed Senators, Congressmen, public and party officials, businessmen, union executives and underworld figures. Abscam itself, or the hundreds of investigations that would be spawned from information contained in the mountains of Abscam transcripts, could threaten a billion-dollar investment in

Atlantic City, reverse the eastward migration of casino gambling, tumble powerful political organizations and even provide a margin of difference in a presidential race.

Credit for Abscam belongs to only a few people. John Good, the tireless, streetwise FBI supervisor, started Abscam and supervised it from beginning to end. Tom Puccio gave it case craft and unstinting support. And FBI Agent Tony Amoroso and a small platoon of dedicated fellow agents provided it with day-to-day professionalism. But it was Mel Weinberg who styled Abscam, wrote the investigative scenario, shaped the bait and planted the sting. As Good will quickly admit, without Mel Weinberg there would have been no Abscam.

Abscam, after all, was a massive confidence game. The United States Government was running the swindle and the marks were streetwise hoodlums and public officials. All of them had survived by being careful and it took an extraordinarily gifted swindler to catch them.

Weinberg's touch in the Abscam investigation was as obvious to his FBI pupils as a hammerhead shark in the kitchen sink. The budget-conscious government investigator simply cannot think in terms of Dom Pérignon refreshment, rented Lear jets, leased Lincoln Continentals and authentic Louis XIV furniture. The government mind tends more to Sears, Roebuck suits, dinner meetings at Howard Johnson's and discount rooms at the local Holiday Inn.

Weinberg was the difference. He had run every con game in the business for more than thirty-five years and been arrested only once. He was a master of the *sine qua non* of the confidence world: the plausible story. He could talk his way into and out of any situation. He knew how to stall, cajole, inveigle and entice. And he knew that props were vital to the game. Weinberg had to create a lure so irresistible that the targets would come to it. That lure was the aura of easy, big money. And Weinberg was able to marshal all of his skills as an experienced con man to build that aura replete with chauffeur-driven limousines.

James West, former U.S. Attorney in Pittsburgh, who nailed Weinberg with his only conviction in 1977, recognized something familiar about Abscam from the first news reports. "I said, 'Damn, that must be Weinberg,'" West told a reporter for the New York *Daily News*. "He's a very unusual person. He's very persuasive and convincing. He's heavyset; he's balding; he doesn't dress well; he's not very smooth or suave. But he's the best talker I ever heard . . . this guy Weinberg is very good. He may be the best."

SCENE

A private plane flying at night over New York State's lower Hudson River Valley. At Weinberg's feet is a suitcase supposedly containing $750,000. It actually holds torn-up phone books. Next to him in the plane sits a 320-pound hoodlum who is leading Weinberg to a remote country airport where he and his waiting confederates plan to exchange more than a million dollars' worth of art treasures for the suitcase. The pilot and Weinberg's "art expert" are both undercover FBI agents. Weinberg's idea for the fly-in exchange has finally convinced the nervous art thieves to deal. He got the idea from a television movie.

SCENE

A suite at New York City's swank Plaza Hotel. An FBI agent in the head-dress of an Arab sheikh waits to receive an attorney who wants to sell the Abscam agents more stolen art. Other FBI agents are posing as the sheikh's assistants. There is a small problem. Weinberg insists that Arabs always serve food to guests, but he is told that the Abscam budget at this stage of the investigation cannot afford Plaza-priced hors d'oeuvres. A fuming Weinberg storms out of the room and returns a short time later with his own favorite snacks—kosher corned beef, potato salad and coleslaw. The agents question whether a real Arab sheikh would be serving Jewish delicatessen to an honored guest. "Don't worry," says Weinberg. "We'll tell this guy that the sheikh admires Jews so much, he only eats Jewish food when he's outta his own country." The attorney, who is Jewish, arrives, swallows the story—and the corned beef.

SCENE

A sixty-five-foot yacht named the *Left Hand* sits at Fort Lauderdale's famed Pier 66 under a full spring moon. Aboard the yacht, Weinberg, assisted by undercover FBI agents, is throwing a party in honor of Camden Mayor Angelo Errichetti. The carefully selected guests include swindlers, politicians, mobsters, narcotics smugglers, contractors and at least one murder-fugitive. A hush falls over the crowd as a robed Arab sheikh steps forward, embraces the Mayor and presents him with a gleaming "tribal" dagger. Errichetti, eyes glistening, promises his friendship and aid to the sheikh. The sheikh is an FBI agent. Weinberg had purchased the dagger at an Athens flea market for $2.75.

Sitting in the Strike Force ready-room at the Brooklyn Federal Courthouse, Weinberg gave little thought to the effect of Abscam on national politics and the institutions of government. He could care less. As he had told Philadelphia lawyer Howard Criden in one taped conversation: "I don't get into politics, because, uh, politics you can go nuts with. They're all a buncha humps as far as I'm concerned."

Abscam was a highly personal thing to Weinberg. For the last two years he had mustered every skill and used every trick he had ever learned as a con man. To Weinberg, Abscam was what victory over the Persians was to Alexander, the Sistine Chapel was to Michelangelo, Mount Everest to Hillary. It was both the fruition and the valedictory of his career in crime.

The Abscam trials (including the Myers case already underway in a courtroom just overhead on the fourth floor) were the crucibles in which Weinberg's ultimate scam would be tested. Successive batteries of the nation's most skilled defense lawyers over the next year would be paid millions of dollars to rip Abscam to shreds and nullify Weinberg's testimony.

Weinberg was determined this would not happen. And he knew that the Myers case was the most important one of all. Already some of the other defendants were exploring the possibility of pleas if Myers were found to be guilty. Each of these defendants would in turn become a government witness, shoring up some of the weaker cases. But if Myers and his codefendants were found innocent, Weinberg was certain that the Justice Department would rush to quash the rest of the Abscam cases before the November election.

Since early in February 1980, when details of the Abscam investigation were first revealed in the Long Island newspaper *Newsday* and the *New York Times,* Weinberg had led a hectic life. Attorney General Civiletti, who lost all his options on Abscam when the newspapers published the names of the Congressmen and details of the actual bribes, had ordered a massive internal investigation to fix blame for the news leaks.

Despite the unflagging loyalty of the FBI, Weinberg quickly realized that he was not exactly popular at the higher political levels of the Justice Department. Twice he had been visited at his new Florida home by Department investigators who insisted that he admit that *he* was the source of the news leaks. Without any advance notice or preparation, he was flown to Philadelphia on Justice Department orders and shoved onto a Federal Court witness stand where he was questioned by defense lawyers who also hoped to blame him for the news leaks.

He was called to Washington by Attorney General Civiletti's top aides and told that they did not want him involved in any book about Abscam. He refused and angrily countered he had heard that Neil J. Welch, who had had no part in Abscam, had already resigned as an Assistant Director of the FBI to write a book about it. He refused Justice Department instructions to cooperate with the United States Attorney's office in Newark, claiming that the office was more interested in trapping him than in prosecuting corrupt politicians in New Jersey.

During this time FBI Agents John Good and Tony Amoroso stayed almost constantly with Weinberg, sympathizing, supporting and, where possible, trying to rationalize Washington's heavy hand. At one point, Weinberg grew so incredulous of the Justice Department's attitude that he complained to Good: "All my life I've been movin' careful; I was always lookin' over my shoulder for the law. If I knew then what kinda schmucks you guys got runnin' things in Washington, I coulda made another five million bucks."

But now the first trial had begun. The nation and, it was to be hoped, the jury had been shocked as Puccio turned the courtroom into a literal theater of corruption. The jurors and spectators watched enthralled as videotapes played over thirteen television sets showed Myers taking a $50,000 bribe from Amoroso and Weinberg in a motel room at New York's Kennedy Airport. In return for the money, the Congressman promised to introduce legislation to provide permanent asylum for a mythical Arab sheikh.

And the country was given a chilling civics lesson on the screen as Myers took the money from Amoroso and said, "Tony, you're going—let me just say this to you—you're going about this the right way. I'm gonna tell you something real simple and short. Money talks in this business and bullshit walks. And it works the same way down in Washington."

In still another taped court exhibit, Myers was seen in a Philadelphia hotel room, complaining to another undercover FBI agent that he had only gotten $15,000 of the $50,000 handed to him by Amoroso and Weinberg. He asked for another $85,000 for himself and to take care of various Philadelphia City Councilmen and unspecified mobsters. Other tapes and witnesses revealed how Myers's three codefendants, Mayor Errichetti, lawyer Criden and City Councilman Johanson, had divided the balance of the $50,000 bribe to Myers among themselves—their commission as middlemen for putting the bribe deal together.

And in what *Newsday*'s Pete Bowles described as "pure Marx brothers," the government showed a tape in which Criden and Errichetti unsuccessfully tried a reverse con on Amoroso and Weinberg, introducing a junior member of Criden's law firm as Mario Noto, Deputy Director of the U.S. Bureau of Immigration and Naturalization. The courtroom howled with laughter as a suspicious Weinberg asked the poorly coached ringer to repeat his name and the fake Noto replied, "Mario Nopo. N-O-P-O."

Even the Democratic Convention, which was going on in New York City that week, couldn't push Abscam off the front pages and the defense took a heavy mauling in the newspapers and on TV and radio. Weinberg was scheduled to take the stand as a government witness as the trial began its second week and defense attorneys confidently assured the press that the entire case would turn around once they finished beating up Weinberg on the witness stand.

It was 9:50 A.M. when John Good walked into the now busy ready-room, went over to Weinberg and Amoroso and deadpanned: "Always sitting around. Don't you guys ever do any work?" Both men groaned and Amoroso extended his hands palms up in the ageless Italian gesture of helplessness in the face of injustice. Good smiled encouragement at Weinberg and said, "They're going to try to get you to lose your temper on the stand, Mel. Just tell it like it is and don't let them get to you."

"Hey, John," said Weinberg, his cigar at a jaunty angle. "Don't worry about a thing."

"Okay," Good said, glancing at his watch. "Why don't we get on upstairs so you can see what it looks like before things get started. All the pretty girls want your autograph."

The three men went out to the elevator, Weinberg stroking his beard in the same automatic way and for the same reason that a woman unconsciously pats her hair when she hears she is about to meet a member of the opposite sex. The elevator disgorged them into the crowded fourth-floor hallway. Lawyers, reporters, defendants, friends of defendants, spectators, marshals and court attendants milled in front of the courtroom door. "Over there," said Good, indicating a doorway opposite the courtroom with a nod of his head, "is the marshal's office. When you're not on the stand, wait there."

Weinberg stood unnoticed in the doorway of the marshal's office for several minutes, looking curiously at the defendants as Good and Amoroso went into the courtroom. Errichetti, expensively dressed, gray hair modishly swept back, machine-gunned conversation at his statuesque blond wife and his lawyer Ray Brown. The Mayor's wife noticed Weinberg and she quickly bit on the knuckle of her right index finger—the ancient Sicilian sign of a vendetta.

A few feet away, Criden peered owlishly through his horn-rimmed glasses at Weinberg over the shoulder of his bantam-sized attorney Richard Ben-Veniste. Myers, his handsome Irish face set in the look of contrition affected by small boys as they enter the confessional, and Johanson, a forgettable man, huddled down the hallway with their lawyers Plato Cacheris and John J. Duffy.

A bustle of movement inside the courtroom signaled that the Honorable Judge George C. Pratt had taken the bench and the trial was ready to resume. The defendants and their lawyers, followed by assistants toting large black trial bags, scurried into the courtroom. The huge doors swung shut and Weinberg was alone in the hallway with his thoughts.

A few minutes later, the courtroom door cracked open slightly and a blue-uniformed court attendant peered out at the man in the hallway. "Weinberg?" he asked. Weinberg nodded slowly. "You're on."

2

HEADSTART

I'm no more a thief than the guy who pockets a quarter he finds in the phone booth. Stealing is stealing. He took a quarter; I took a coupla million. He just doesn't have the balls to take a million. I respect people who won't even take an ashtray from a hotel room. Most of them kinda people, though, are a pain in the ass.
— MEL WEINBERG

Mel Weinberg's first scam occurred in 1931. It was also the first time he was caught. He was six years old. On the last week of school he returned home to his family's apartment in the Bronx, at Webb Avenue and 195th Street.

Since the start of the school year he had been swiping gold stars from his teacher's desk when her back was turned and bringing them home every day to his mother. His teacher had never missed the stars; they made his mother happy, and he thoroughly enjoyed the praise they earned from the family.

His mother answered his knock on the door.

"You're late. How did it go in school today?" she asked.

"Not so good," answered the boy.

"What happened?"

"I got left back," he replied.

His mother stared at him. The message short-circuited her ability to comprehend, much less believe.

"You must be mistaken," she said, clearly aware that something was amiss. "Nobody gets left back in the first grade. Besides, you bring home all those gold stars every day. That means you are doing wonderful work in school. Why would they leave you back?"

"Because I'm Jewish," he sighed, fixing his mother with his most earnest look.

"Because you're Jewish," she replied in a voice that took on a slightly hysterical edge. "How can that be? This is the Bronx, in New York, not Poland. Your teacher is Jewish! Why were you left back?"

"That's why," he persisted, head bowed and hands thrust deeply into the pockets of his knickers.

The next day, head still bowed, hands still in pockets, he stood with his mother in the hallway of P.S. 86 while his teacher listed his transgressions in minute detail and his classmates strained to listen through the partly opened door.

"But," Mel's mother interrupted, "if he acts this way, why does he bring home four or five gold stars every day?"

"Mrs. Weinberg," the teacher replied tartly, "I give Melvin one gold star at the beginning of every day because he comes to school dressed neatly. But, by nine-thirty every morning, I have taken that star back. If Melvin is bringing home gold stars, I can assure you that he doesn't get them from me!"

Even at the age of six, the gold-star incident taught him a valuable lesson. "I learned two things," he recalls. "Always have a good excuse and always split the scene if you see two of your marks getting together."

The event was the first of many in Weinberg's early life pointing to the person he would become, but he could never blame his childhood environment for what happened later. From the day he was born on

December 4, 1924, Weinberg grew up in a family that was marked by love, laughter, good example and firmly held ethical values.

Because his father worked long hours, it was a family dominated by women. There was his mother, Helen, a gentile of Swiss descent who embraced Judaism when she married and adopted the role of Jewish mother with an enthusiasm that only converts can bring to their cause. There was his maternal grandmother, Martha, adored by the family, who lived nearby and visited frequently. And, finally, there were his two sisters, Sylvia and Lynn.

His father, Harry, was an easygoing man who liked to talk, play cards and take his family on Sunday outings to places like Peach Lake in suburban Westchester County.

But it was the early female influence that obviously had a profound effect on Weinberg's personality. In conversation with other men he affects the basic underworld posture toward women. He calls them broads and describes them only in terms of their real or imagined sexual performance. But he is a changed man in the actual company of women. His face lights; he becomes animated; his stories take on extra sparkle; he softens his profanity; he is attentive, almost courtly. "Most of them are okay," he grudgingly admits.

It was in the seventh grade that Mel Weinberg became fascinated with a subject that was to dominate his thoughts for the next forty-seven years: wealth, with its attendant position and power. The process began innocently enough as he wandered farther from home each day, exploring his neighborhood in ever-widening circles.

Four blocks down Webb Avenue the six-story wall of cheek-to-cheek apartment houses abruptly ended, giving way to a vista of gracious single-family homes surrounded by broad, neatly kept green lawns. Tall trees arched toward one another from both sides of the avenue and flowers bloomed from window boxes and meticulously arranged gardens. Walking past these houses for the first time, Weinberg saw a dream come to life.

Older boys in his neighborhood described this area of private homes as "down where the rich kids live." And he quickly determined that if he couldn't be a rich kid, he was going to live as much like one as he could. Each day, as soon as school ended, he beelined down Webb Avenue to the suburblike setting.

Within a few weeks, he was accepted by the other boys in the area, an accomplishment achieved by deceit. He told his new friends about his father's thriving glass business, the endless family discussions over financial investments, his mother's family ties to Swiss bankers.

When asked where he lived, he would point vaguely down the avenue. His friends invited him into their homes. He was dazzled at what he saw. He joined the Bruins, their sandlot football team. He was enjoying himself immensely. Suddenly, reality smacked him in the face when his family's meager circumstances wouldn't allow him to attend a summer camp upstate with his friends. At stake was Weinberg's continued acceptance by a group of boys who represented a way of life that had become almost an obsession to him. To fit in, he had used his fertile imagination to weave a web of deception and then had half convinced himself that his rewritten life story was true. Circumstances had called his bluff and forced him to fold his cards. He couldn't face his new friends with the truth. His days of running with the rich kids were over. But the dream remained. "That's when I decided," he recalled, "that when I grew up, I would never want for anything and neither would any of my kids—no matter what I hadda do."

His first opportunity came quickly. He had taken a part-time job at the corner grocery store delivering orders and was paid a nickle an order plus tips. As was usual in the 1930s, everyone in the neighborhood had a charge account at the grocery store and settled bills at the end of the month. Weinberg habitually stole milk, butter and cheese out of the packages he was delivering and took them home for the family. He told his mother that the food items were part of his pay and she accepted his story without question.

As each customer ordered, the grocer would spike the bill on a hook hanging from the wall. Weinberg always arranged to be in the store when his mother ordered the family's weekly groceries. As soon as the grocer busied himself with another customer, Weinberg would tear his family's bill from the stack on the hook and rip it up.

He suspected that his mother knew, but times were desperately hard and he knew that a truthful answer would compel her to march down to the grocery and pay the bill.

"I never thought about getting caught," Weinberg remembers. "We all think we're too smart to get caught. The kids I was hanging out with, we all stole in them days. It was part of the American way of growing up when you didn't have too much money. After a while, it felt natural. We didn't regard taking as stealing, just getting."

Weinberg continued to struggle in school. He was nearly fifteen years old, only in the eighth grade, and found himself with other problem students. They moved in a group through the neighborhood, cutting classes, picking fights, experimenting with beer. They mimicked the argot and mannerisms of other outcasts, local hoods, numbers runners, and movie wise guys like James Cagney, Edward G. Robinson and George Raft, whom they applauded at the local movie theater popularly known as The Dumps. Then came Weinberg's first arrest. He recalls it as a bum rap. Accused of shooting birds with a BB gun while playing hooky from school, he remembers, "The cops kicked my ass—it wasn't like it is today with all this civil rights shit—took me down to the station house and called my mother. She hadda come for me."

At the police station, Helen Weinberg surrendered any lingering hope that her son would still make it as a scholar. Alternating between tears and tirades on the long walk home from the police station, she told Weinberg that he was to drop out of school, get working papers and find a job immediately. "Maybe a full day's work will make you too tired to get into trouble," she added uncertainly.

At the moment, Weinberg viewed his mother's orders to quit school as triumph snatched from tragedy. He hated school. The idea of a job where he could make—and spend—real money was hugely attractive. As he grew older, however, he privately regretted and resented his lack of education while ridiculing education in general and gloating when he was able to outwit well-educated marks.

But in moments of candor, he talks wistfully about what he could have been with an education, while reflexively knocking the idea. "I never liked school," he said. "And, sometimes, I think that if I'd gone for an education, I wouldn't have it as good, because a lot of things is just streetwise. Out in the world it's the greatest thing when you're streetwise."

He got his working papers the next day and went to work at $12 a week for an electric company. He still moved with the same neighborhood crowd at night drinking beer and sampling local nonvirgins, but he was honest on the job. "I was never a petty-ante thief," he explains.

After Pearl Harbor he volunteered for the Seabees, was trained to operate landing craft and quickly shipped to the South Pacific, where he stayed for the next four years of the war.

SCENE

A captain's gig pulls smartly into the pier at an Australian port. At the helm is navy coxswain Mel Weinberg. An officer leaves the gig, instructing Weinberg to wait for his return. An Australian loitering on the pier offers to sell Weinberg homemade wine in a fifty-gallon drum labeled as oil. Weinberg, hungry for the fortune he can make selling the forbidden wine to thirsty sailors aboard ship, pays the Australian $100. The pair hook the metal drum of wine to a crane and raise it into the air to clear the pier and lower it into the gig. At its apex, the crane suddenly lets the drum fall and it holes the gig. The gig sinks in fifty feet of water. The officer returns and asks Weinberg where he has put the gig. "You wouldn't believe it, sir," Weinberg replies crisply. "But one of our Flying Fortresses dropped something as it was flying over the harbor and it sank the gig." The officer doesn't believe it. Weinberg is in trouble.

SCENE

The invasion of the Philippines. A navy landing craft is ferrying troops onto a beachhead on Mindanao. Once again, Weinberg is at the helm. Suddenly the troops on shore are bracketed with withering mortar fire. An officer orders Weinberg to bring the soldiers back from the beach. "You don't wanna do that, sir," Weinberg answers, mustering what he regards as his most winning smile. "We could get killed doing something like that!" The officer pulls his gun and barks: "If you don't follow orders, I'll shoot you on the spot." Weinberg shrugs and heads to shore. He makes twenty-eight trips under fire before everyone is out. He is recommended for the Silver Star.

SCENE

Behind Japanese lines in the steamy jungles of Mindanao Mel Weinberg, in navy uniform, pushes his way on foot through giant ferns. He has been searching for a native whorehouse that fellow sailors assured him was just the other side of a mountain that could be seen from shore. Now he is lost, soggy, insect-bitten, exhausted and a little bit scared. He is also unarmed and still horny. He pushes his way into a small clearing and pauses momentarily to get his bearings. He is startled by a sound on the opposite side of the clearing thirty feet away. Two Japanese soldiers, also unarmed, emerge from the ferns. Weinberg stares at the Japanese soldiers. The Japanese soldiers stare at Weinberg. Ever so slowly, Weinberg steps backward into the fern cover on his side of the clearing. Ever so slowly, the Japanese soldiers do the same. They must be looking for the same whorehouse, thinks Weinberg. He reports back for duty six hours AWOL. He is in trouble again.

Weinberg emerged from the navy in 1946 with several battle stars and skills that are never listed on the recruiting posters. He had, among other things, learned how to steal boldly and systematically. It was a time when the theft of military supplies was benevolently defined as "liberating" or "scrounging." The rationale was that since the government owned everything, taking supplies destined for another military unit wasn't really stealing, just transferring the items from one unit of the government to another. This definition delighted Weinberg and he was soon known as the most dedicated scrounger in the First Seabee Battalion.

"I learned a lot about human nature in the service," said Weinberg, "and that's the name of the game in the con business. In the service, I met people from all over the world, all kinds, and I got to know what makes people tick. For example, I learned that just as long as you march into some supply house with a buncha guys and look like you know what you're doing, you can march out with your arms full and nobody's gonna ask you a question. That's not just true in the military; it's true every place in life."

The navy with its infrequent liberty ports sharpened Weinberg's appetite for women, as well.

A psychologist recently suggested that Weinberg's enormous sexual appetite is just another expression of his attraction to females in general. When queried on this point, Weinberg characteristically gets to the heart of the matter: "I get laid because it feels good."

The reluctance of one young woman to accommodate him led to his first marriage to Mary O'Connor two weeks after they met and eventually to their three children. The couple settled on Long Island, and Weinberg went to work for his father in the family glass business, founded by Weinberg's Russian immigrant grandfather near the turn of the century, and occupying premises on Second Avenue in the East Eighties in Manhattan.

Glass installation in New York City was a tough, highly competitive business. Operators who paid bribes for jobs, greased union officials' palms and cheated their customers were successful. Honest people only succeeded by luck or accident. Weinberg saw that things improved quickly for his father's firm after he met Irving, the tough, resolute official of the glaziers' union. Irving needed someone to roam the city at night breaking store windows of shopowners who dealt with nonunion glaziers. Weinberg obliged.

The union teamed him with another glazier, named Izzie, and the two men became close friends. With Izzie at the wheel, the pair would slowly cruise the city streets after midnight. As they approached a targeted storefront, the car would slow to a crawl, Weinberg would wind down the window, aim a slingshot, send a metal bolt through the display window, and they were on the way to their next target.

The money flowed in, from his regular salary, from the union and from weekend jobs for other contractors that the union threw his way. But as fast as it came in, it went out. Weinberg was moving in a fast crowd and an expensive one. His world abounded in bribe-laden union delegates and upcoming young mobsters like James (Jimmy Nap) Napolitano and Augie (Red Prince) Carfano of the Bronx, a hoodlum who some people said would soon rival his downtown Manhattan namesake in underworld status.

Hoodlums in Weinberg's vernacular were "wise guys" and he sought out their company, did them favors and aped their expensive habits and attire. But these men were making much more money than Weinberg. As a result, he was always short, no matter how much money he made in any given week. And, like most gamblers, his disasters heavily outweighed his triumphs. Except in his penchant for one-night stands.

At this time Weinberg took all of his conquests to the LaGuardia Motel, just across the busy Grand Central Parkway from the airport in Queens. It was convenient to the city and the hotel management discounted rooms to New York City cops. Weinberg had a police shield that he had gotten from one of his underworld friends. He would flash the shield at the front desk and get a $15 room for $5.

During one such encounter Weinberg and his stunning redheaded partner were interrupted by a pounding on the door. An ashen-faced bellhop sputtered that a holdup was in progress at the main desk, and would the officer intercede? Authoritatively, Weinberg bolted from the room, slipped out a side door to his car, and drove home alone.

On at least one occasion, discovery by his wife of his extramarital affairs was avoided by what would become Weinberg's stock-in-trade years later during Abscam: a combination of quick answer and quarter stall. Entertaining the wife of a Long Island neighbor one summer day at home when his wife and children were to be gone until early evening, Weinberg had the foresight to take the lady to the seclusion of the attic. Engaged in the activity at hand, Weinberg froze at the sound of his wife's voice downstairs. For reasons long since forgotten, she had come home early. Panicking, he stepped off the wooden walkway of the unfinished attic and plunged stark naked through the plasterboard ceiling into the bedroom, miraculously unhurt. Pleading the heat, Weinberg explained that he had stripped to take a cold shower, then climbed to the attic to open the vent. Startled by her unexpected call downstairs, he misstepped. "Why don't we go out for hamburgers," he suggested. Mary agreed. For her part the woman in the attic remained discreetly silent until the proper time for her leave-taking.

By the fall of 1952 his father's glass business, always precarious, was going under. Weinberg had even more pressing problems: his gambling debts were mounting and the bookies were turning nasty. Driving a secondhand car, he moved his family to Florida for a fresh start; but after a series of accounting mishaps, they moved across the country to Los Angeles. Near Santa Monica Weinberg found quarters and a livable wage as a janitor for two apartment buildings, whose owner was a homesick Jewish New Yorker delighting in his new employee's nonstop recitation of his janitorial skills. Service for the buildings was, of course, another matter.

SCENE

The first-floor apartment in a complex near Santa Monica. Weinberg sits at the window grumbling. In three months, he has broken as many things as he has fixed as janitor. Maintenance calls from tenants are interfering with several outside jobs he has taken for side money. Mentally, he ticks off the list of the most demanding tenants. He spots one of the offenders coming out the apartment-house door and starting down the grass-bordered walk that leads out to the street between two long sections of the U-shaped building. Weinberg runs into his kitchen, briskly turns a valve, and races back to the window. Jets of water from sunken irrigation pipes spray the lawn and sidewalk. The tenant, trapped midway between door and street, is forced to run the water gauntlet. Sopping, he reaches the street and glares back in the direction of Weinberg's apartment. Weinberg smiles and waves. He later tells his wife. "When someone crosses me, I never say a word. But sooner or later, I always get even."

Weinberg was practicing old skills and learning new ones in California while hardly taking his duties as a janitor seriously. Equipped with a reference from his old employer in New York, he got occasional work smashing windows for a local glaziers' union. He also quickly got to know most of the hustlers and fast-money operators in the area.

Through this quick-buck grapevine, Weinberg challenged his ingenuity. He learned that because of a machine malfunction, a local manufacturer of men's socks had produced thousands of socks that had no feet. Each sock in the batch began just below the ankle and ran midway up the calf. An employee of the company had salvaged the semisocks and was trying to hustle them at a dime a hundred to anyone who could figure out what to do with them.

Weinberg told the sock hustler that he would buy the 5,000 pairs of socks if the hustler would provide him with 5,000 of the manufacturer's size labels in the standard men's sizes. He got the socks and the labels. Carefully tucking under the bottom of each sock, he folded them in half and bound them together with several twists of Scotch tape into bunches of six pairs. Then he jotted down a list of Los Angeles manufacturing firms that employed more than 200 people.

The next morning, as workers poured into the first factory on his list, Weinberg stood at the gate hawking the socks at a dollar for a six-pair batch. He did a landslide business and the customers were pleased that he had socks in every size.

That evening, he moved to another factory and once again it was a sellout. He noted that the people on their way out of the factory were more prone to examine the socks closely. They obviously had more time than people rushing to work. He goosed the overly careful buyers by shooting a look over his shoulder and whispering, "Is that a cop over there?" The buyers, convinced that they were getting hot merchandise, quickly pocketed the socks, handed over their money and furtively walked away. After that he only sold his footless socks to morning shifts.

Each day, Weinberg would travel to a factory far removed from the one he had hit the day before. "I figured that people who worked in the same neighborhood probably drank together in the same bars and they would tell each other how they were stung by this guy selling socks without feet," he explained. "I wanted to make sure I was in virgin territory every day because if the people ever knew what I was really doing when I showed up with my socks, they'd beat the shit outta me."

Eventually, Weinberg ran out of socks, new factories and patience with his opportunities to make it big in California.

He thought about the triple-decker sandwiches, pastrami, salami and corned beef with Russian on Jewish rye, which he used to enjoy with a bottle of Dr. Brown's Cel-Ray at Katz's delicatessen on New York's Houston Street. He wondered whether some of his wise-guy friends had moved up in the underworld pecking order. He thought about some of the really big hustles he had heard about from his old drinking buddies. He remembered the pained look on his bookie's face when he had scored a $100 bet on the daily double at Aqueduct. And he could almost taste his mother's chicken soup with mandles.

"Mary," he said late one evening, "the West is for Indians, snakes and losers. We're going back to New York. If I can't make it big there, I can't make it big anywhere."

Off they drove into the sunrise.

Eighteen months. That was the span between good times and bad: the difference between the heap Weinberg had driven back from California and the sleek Cadillac he now steered through the city streets; the margin between a cramped apartment in Far Rockaway and the spacious new split-level in the Long Island suburb of Plainview—the progression from broke to flush.

All it took, Weinberg reflected, was a little luck and a lot of hustle. But his sudden change in fortune also stemmed from a personal trait that would play a vital role years later in the Abscam investigation: his unique ability to snatch advantage from the jaws of catastrophe. What happened after Weinberg returned from California to New York was a case in point.

He renewed his acquaintance with old pals in the fast-buck confraternity, people like himself who spent most of their waking hours scheming business deals, legal, illegal, and somewhere in between, all of them willing to believe any story, no matter how exaggerated, about fellow dreamers who had made huge financial killings overnight.

From the ranks of these people come some of the nation's most successful swindlers and spectacular victims. The same consuming ambition for quick riches that produces a swindler also makes that swindler the easiest mark for other swindlers. The most transparent fraud can be successful because the victim usually thinks that he or she is actually cheating someone else.

When greed takes over, caution departs, a basis for the adage that you can't con an honest man. It also helps to explain how, years later, some of America's most expert political fixers and careful Congressmen could become drawn into Abscam.

Weinberg, dabbling in a variety of small scams on his return east, woke up one morning with the recollection that he had once talked to a man in California who told him that he had an exclusive contract for gold with an Indian tribe someplace in Mexico. There was a strong European market for gold and Weinberg decided that all he needed to make his fortune was his own name on the contract for Indian gold.

He flew to California, tracked down the contract holder, who was himself a member of the quick-buck set, and for $5,000 arranged to have the man introduce him personally to the heads of the Yaqui Indian tribe. The pair traveled to Mexico and met the Indians at their remote mountain stronghold south of the Arizona border. Handling English for the Indians was a beautiful black woman from Harlem who had jumped the border to escape arrest in New York on murder charges.

She explained that the Indians had hidden mines in the mountains and were willing to exchange the gold for rifles so that they could continue their war with the Mexican government. Weinberg agreed to provide the guns and the Indians produced a neatly typed contract giving him exclusive rights to deal with them for gold.

Returning to New York with the contract and samples of the gold, Weinberg shopped for a partner who could provide money for the guns. He was hungry to move quickly and to a man with that kind of hunger, Peter Norman Dawes looked like Christmas dinner. An adventurer from a wealthy family in Canada, Dawes was a bluff, hearty man with a huge handlebar mustache and a pervading desire to look and act like an Englishman.

Weinberg easily persuaded him to back the gold scheme. Dawes arranged to purchase the rifles and have them flown over the border to the Indians by private plane. The gold would be loaded onto the plane and flown to the Canal Zone for further refining and shipment to Europe. They ordered the plane to circle overhead until they arrived by jeep at the Yaqui stronghold and signaled the pilot to land.

SCENE

A jeep, clouds of dust in its wake, jolts down a rutted trail in the Mexican wilderness. Driving one-handed is a tall man in an immaculate bush jacket and pith helmet. In his left hand is a swagger stick that he raps smartly against the door. Seated next to him, looking slightly carsick in his Broadway version of a business suit, is Mel Weinberg. An Indian, accompanied by a black woman, steps onto the trail and motions the jeep to a halt. The woman explains that other Indians even now are coming from the mines with the gold. Peter Norman Dawes gets out of the jeep and gestures with his swagger stick to a plane circling overhead. The plane lands. As it rolls to a stop, there is a burst of gunfire and Indians charge the jeep. Dawes dives in, U-turns, and roars back up the trail. The Indians, still shooting, jump into a truck and chase the jeep. Dawes unholsters a huge revolver and orders Weinberg to shoot at the pursuing truck. Bullets are ricocheting off the jeep. Weinberg, his eyes closed and slumped as low as he can get, points the gun backward over the top of his seat and fires until it is empty. It gets dark but Dawes won't turn on the headlights. Several times the careening jeep nearly plunges off the curving mountain paths and soon the two men are lost. Hours later the trail widens and they see a sign. They have lucked back into Arizona. Weinberg straightens up in his seat and moans, "I shoulda known. I shoulda known by that contract. Where the hell would them Indians get a fuckin' typewriter?"

What happened to the pilot and plane carrying the guns, Weinberg never found out. Dawes left Arizona in search of new adventure. But Weinberg, already out $7,000 of his own money in advance expenses, schemed ways of turning the Indian ripoff to his own advantage.

He visited a Mexican border town to have a commercial firm type fifty copies of his Yaqui gold contract. He then went to a Mexican government office, where an official notarized his signature on all fifty copies. As is the custom in many Latin countries, the official attested to

Weinberg's signature with a government seal and ribbon on each copy. It was a device he would use often in the future. Although government seals and ribbons are only meant to verify the signature, they appear to verify the entire contract.

Slowly working his way cross-country back to New York, Weinberg sold nearly thirty copies of the contract to various marks who each paid him $1,000 after he solemnly assured them that the contract they were buying was the only one in existence and was—"look at the official seal here"—backed by the full force of the Mexican government.

If the quest for the Yaqui gold was one of the most exotic of Weinberg's schemes, he applied no less ingenuity to his efforts to resurrect the firm of M. Weinberg and Sons, Glaziers. But it was related activities rather than an honest day's work that caused the business to prosper. Weinberg's nighttime visits with the slingshot resumed because he had in his possession the complete list of stores insured by Cosmopolitan Insurance Company, purloined from the desk of a secretary with whom he was sleeping. Orders for glass at emergency rates for immediate replacement were placed as a matter of daily routine by Cosmopolitan, shortly after Weinberg and Sons opened at 8:00 A.M. His father, possessing notions of integrity that his son lacked, remained unaware of Weinberg's misdeeds.

On one occasion, Weinberg drove his truck out to Long Island at night to make an emergency glass installation for a customer. As he drove through the city of Long Beach, he noticed a recently built shopping center that had not yet opened for business. One of the stores, which still lacked doors, had a large glass display window. Weinberg pulled his truck in front of the store, walked in and set to work removing the window from the frame so that he could steal it.

As Weinberg lifted the huge piece of glass from the window frame a police car pulled up. A policeman got out, flashed his light on Weinberg and asked what he was doing.

"What's it look like I'm doin'?" countered Weinberg. "I put the wrong glass in here today and my Jew bastard boss told me to come back here on my own time without a helper to take it out. I got a wife and kids waitin' at home to have dinner and I gotta wrestle this thing to the truck by myself just because I made a little mistake."

The policeman was sympathetic. He told Weinberg that he had his own problems with Jews and cold-hearted superiors and he helped Weinberg carry the glass out to the truck and fit it into the carrying rack.

Another trick that Weinberg learned in the glass business was how to swindle his customers by subtle appeals to their ethnic pride. In the trade there is a type of product known as demiglass. This glass, polished only on one side, costs less than half the price of regular glass. But demiglass has a wavy look slightly distorting the view through it. Wherever he could, Weinberg substituted demiglass for the real thing and pocketed the difference.

To help with the scam, Weinberg had collected piles of small stickers that read: "Made in Ireland." Others said Israel, Spain, Germany, England, and Italy. He would note the nationality of his customer, paste the appropriate sticker on the sheet of demiglass and install it in his customer's storefront.

Invariably the customer would look at the newly installed window and complain about the wavy look. If, for example, his customer was Jewish, Weinberg would scratch his head thoughtfully and reply, "Gee, that's funny. This is supposed to be the best glass there is. See the sticker here? This glass is imported from Israel." The appeal to ethnicity was sure-fire. Never once, Weinberg recalled, was he asked to replace the demiglass he had installed.

On another occasion, Weinberg thought that he had pulled off a major financial coup when he bought 6,000 pieces of polished wire glass from the owner of an old Manhattan office building that was being demolished. He had heard that the wire glass (glass with circular or octagonal wire loops inside it) was selling for fifty cents a piece. He had paid the building owner less than a dime a piece for the wire glass. The glass was delivered to his shop, where it overflowed into another shop next door that he was forced to rent as a warehouse. But when he tried to sell it, he learned that the bottom had dropped out of the wire-glass market.

There he was, possessor of tons of polished wire glass that nobody wanted to buy. He picked up the phone and called one of Manhattan's largest glass dealers, a man who had scornfully refused to buy his wire glass the day before. Speaking in a disguised voice Weinberg identified himself as Sammy Lyons. "I need to pick up seven thousand pieces of polished wire glass tomorrow. Do you have it?"

Rockie, the glass mogul, blithely lied that he had all the wire glass Mr. Lyons would need, but said that it was in very scarce supply and would cost at least a dollar a piece. Rockie and "Mr. Lyons" bargained and the price was finally settled at eighty cents a piece for 6,000 pieces, all that Rockie said he had on hand. Weinberg in his pose as Lyons insisted that the glass be ready for pickup at Rockie's firm the next day by noon. Rockie asked where he might be able to reach Lyons by phone. Weinberg replied that he couldn't be reached because he was moving from one job to the other, but said he would arrive with his trucks to pick up the glass and pay in cash the next day.

Weinburg hung up and waited next to his phone. A few minutes later it rang.

It was Rockie. He announced that he had had a change of heart and hated to see anyone in Weinberg's predicament. He didn't need the glass but had plenty of storage space. He offered twenty cents a piece if Weinberg would deliver it.

Weinberg responded that he had two other prospective customers for the glass and bargained a now frantic Rockie up to fifty cents a piece for the 6,000 pieces. Rockie also agreed to pick up the glass in his own trucks that afternoon and pay cash. The mythical Mr. Lyons, of course, never showed up to buy the glass from Rockie. But Weinberg was $2,000 richer.

The steady flow of business resulting from Weinberg's window-breaking routine and the quick cash from his scams filled him with a sense of success. And he regarded this success as proof that the world was a jungle, most people were dishonest, and the only way to survive was to strike first.

In time the Cosmopolitan Insurance Company got onto Weinberg's glass sabotaging as well as his swindling. The result was that he was blacklisted by the entire insurance industry, and the telephone ceased to ring at Weinberg and Sons with early morning emergency orders.

However, after a succession of bleak days, one morning the telephone did ring.

It was an official of Manhattan Casualty, another insurance firm that provided plate-glass coverage to New York City storekeepers. He wanted to meet privately. At the meeting, he said that Cosmopolitan had warned him all about Weinberg's swindle.

"You're just the kind of man I need," said the official. "Kick back $700 a month to me and I'll give your firm all the plate-glass work from our insurance company."

Weinberg suspected a trap. It was too direct, too easy. But he was a desperate man. He was into horses, bar tabs and expensive women. The shylocks were turning nasty. He needed a new source of cash quickly. He agreed and arranged to pay off the official at a Queens diner at the end of the month.

Over the next several weeks, as business once again flowed into the shop, still suspecting a trap, Weinberg cheated cautiously. When the time for the payoff came, he arrived late and circled the diner, looking for a police stakeout in the parking lot. Spotting the official's car, he opened the door and slipped the envelope behind the sun visor. Then he entered the diner, carefully scanned the other customers and sat down next to the official. He told him where he had hidden the money. The official went out to the parking lot, returned with the envelope, took out the money, and counted it in front of Weinberg.

"When he did that," Weinberg recalls, "I knew I had a live one."

He was right. Within days, Weinberg had a list of Manhattan's customers, and metal bolts once again were smashing through different windows around town, and M. Weinberg & Sons was working twenty-four-hour shifts. With an inside man at the insurance company, Weinberg discarded caution and spent most of his time scheming new ways to swindle the company and its customers. Money cascaded into his eagerly spread hands.

The insurance company official, concerned at showing too much cash, asked Weinberg to invest his share of the money. Eventually the pair owned twenty-six dry-cleaning stores in Queens, staffed by pretty English girls, operating under the name of Ditmars Cleaners; a construction company used to build the cleaning stores; a cigarette vending machine company on the west coast of Florida and three more glass shops, all of which subcontracted for M. Weinberg & Sons. Another silent partner in Weinberg's growing business empire was a policeman on the staff of New York District Attorney Frank Hogan. The policeman was Weinberg's inside man in law enforcement.

Weinberg also invested with nine other people in a huge hamburger emporium in central Queens. Several of his other partners were relatives of James (Jimmy Nap) Napolitano, then a rising young mobster who is today a captain (*caporegime*) in one of the New York Cosa Nostra crime families. Later, when the hoodlum's relatives decided to shove Weinberg out of the hamburger business and take over his share, he characteristically walked away without protest. Even today, he is careful not to offend the mob.

"The mob plays for keeps," Weinberg explained. "Smart con men stay on the good side of those fellas. If they want you to step away from something, you step away. Tomorrow's always another day; you keep on livin', and you can always go to them for a favor."

Weinberg, as always, spent money as quickly as it came in. He was at the Copa nearly every night; he drank too much J&B Scotch and bought too much for the rest of the boys at the bar; he stuffed hundred-dollar tips into the pockets of delighted headwaiters; he made huge bets on horses and football games; and he showered jewelry and expensive dresses on a rapid succession of girlfriends.

By 1960 Weinberg had done such a thorough job of swindling the insurance company that it suddenly went out of business. This time, he was in real financial trouble. Only a steady flow of money from the insurance company had kept his various businesses solvent and operating. He had not only blown all of the profits, but also was deeply in debt to bookmakers and loansharks. He shivered on the other end of the phone as he pictured his carefully manicured fingers crushed by a pipe-wielding loanshark. Or worse.

Then he thought of his older cousin Hymie. Universally despised by the rest of the family, Hymie was greedy, crafty, miserly, mean and totally transparent. He was also rich, twice Weinberg's age, and eager to buy Weinberg's prosperous glass business. He called Hymie and made a deal. Hymie would buy the business from Weinberg, giving him enough to slake the sharks. Hymie would supervise, but Weinberg would actually operate the business and eventually be given a partnership by Hymie for his work.

The catalyst was Marie, a pert, blond bookkeeper whom Weinberg's cousin hired to keep track of the business. Naturally suspicious, Hymie was sure that Weinberg would cheat him. He hired Marie to watch Weinberg. He took her into his confidence. He told her that he intended to dump Weinberg as soon as he had learned the business himself and had bled Weinberg for all of his contacts. But Weinberg was dating Marie and she told him about his cousin's plan. Weinberg was furious. He determined to strike first.

Thus began a series of events that launched Weinberg on his most complicated, bizarre and enduring quest for revenge.

Without his cousin Hymie's knowledge, Weinberg opened a rival glazier's shop in Queens under the name of Ditmars Glass. He arranged for Marie to quit his cousin's firm and go to work for Ditmars. He put his father in charge of Ditmars and kept it stocked with glass smuggled every night out of Hymie's shop. Since Weinberg was the work foreman of Hymie's glass firm, he detailed some of his cousin's work crews part of each day to install glass for Ditmars. It was a no-lose situation. Through Ditmars, he was selling Hymie's glass and using his crews to install it. His cousin had all the expense. But the customers were sending their checks to Ditmars. Weinberg reaped the profits.

Weinberg was careful to leave his cousin just enough business to stay on the edge of solvency. If Hymie went broke, he knew, he would lose his own supply of free glass and workers. Things went well for nearly two years. Weinberg set up Marie in an apartment, beginning a wife-mistress syndrome that has continued ever since.

Hymie finally became suspicious and trailed one of his glass trucks to Ditmars Glass in Astoria. Confronting Marie in the shop, he threatened to go to the District Attorney. He left in a rage.

Minutes later, Weinberg called Marie from outside, asking for his phone messages. Quickly, she told him of his cousin's visit and threat. Weinberg cradled the pay phone, thought for a minute, and then dialed Hymie's shop. The new bookkeeper, a male, answered. Weinberg identified himself as Sidney Glasser from the union and asked to speak to Mel Weinberg.

"Due in any minute."

"Tell him the minute he comes in to call Sidney Glasser at the union," ordered Weinberg. He hung up, got into his car and drove to Italian East Harlem where a family of four brothers, all minor-league hoodlums, ran a combination garage and mob chop-shop. They were old friends of Weinberg's.

The youngest brother, Junior, was in the garage. Weinberg hurriedly explained both his problem and proposed solution. Junior agreed to arrive at Hymie's shop in a half-hour, his 38-caliber revolver loaded with blanks, and act out Weinberg's plan. Weinberg raced out of the garage, hopped into his car and gunned down Second Avenue to Hymie's glass shop.

His cousin was sitting behind his desk, a sour smile on his face, when Weinberg walked into the second-floor office. "Sit down," he snapped. "I want to discuss something with you."

"Just a minute," replied Weinberg, turning to the bookkeeper who was preparing to depart, to ask if there were any messages.

When the bookkeeper responded that Sidney Glasser of the union had called and that it was urgent, Weinberg waited for him to leave and then went into his act. It was such a dazzling and convincing display of virtuoso theatrics that the scene proved to be Hymie's undoing. Such charades would, years later, become indispensable to Abscam's success, and they would be regarded as Weinberg's special touch. Indeed the difference between good theater and bad is often the narrowest of margins as the incredible Abscam charades witnessed by millions of television viewers would indicate.

In this particular instance Weinberg, in Hymie's presence, dialed from memory a nonworking number and feigned an agitated conversation with the union boss on the other end of the line. Replacing the receiver, he turned with alarm to his cousin. Ditmars Glass, he explained, was not his but the mob's. Hymie's earlier threat invoking the District Attorney had invited a swift and certain reprisal: a contract had been put out on Hymie, and the "torpedo" was on his way over even as they spoke. A terrified cousin pleaded pitifully for intercession from Weinberg, but another "call" to the union boss ended with Weinberg speaking into a dead line. He had hung up, Weinberg explained.

At that precise moment, both men heard heavy footsteps on the stairway. Junior, the East Harlem minihood, had arrived on cue and was moving his 280-pound bulk slowly toward the office. The door burst open to reveal a hulking armed man intent on murder. Weinberg quickly drew his own pistol and fired at Junior, who staggered and crashed with a muffled cry to the floor.

Hymie, terrified of future mob reprisals and convinced by Weinberg that even the police belonged to the mob, helped Weinberg move the "body" to the trunk of Weinberg's Cadillac. For $5,000, he told Hymie, he had friends who would make the body disappear. "Can't we do it cheaper?" Hymie asked. But Weinberg insisted. Fetching the money, Hymie then watched in relief as Weinberg sped off. Several blocks away he let Junior, unhurt by Weinberg's blanks, out of the trunk and gave him $2,500 for his part. Then Weinberg returned to his cousin's shop to find Hymie in the office, door locked and lights out.

Convincing Hymie that when the hood failed to check in there would be more torpedoes forthcoming, Weinberg offered to arrange protection for his cousin for $150 a week, which Hymie would pass along through Weinberg every Friday.

Pocketing the first $150 from his cousin, Weinberg assured him that the unseen bodyguard would be covering Hymie as soon as he left the office for home. Meanwhile, promised Weinberg, he would negotiate with the mob to get the contract recalled. But, he warned his cousin, he was to stay away from Ditmars Glass.

On the fourth Friday, Hymie complained to Weinberg that he never saw his bodyguard. How could he really know that the bodyguard was protecting him? "For $150 a week, you don't see the bodyguard," explained Weinberg. "But if you want to pay $300 a week, he'll sleep with ya." Hymie instantly decided that the unseen bodyguard was doing a good job. Two months later, Weinberg announced to his grateful cousin that he had finally gotten the mob to call off the contract.

The Hymie swindle invited an interesting coup de grace. Rummaging through his cousin's desk drawer several months later, Weinberg discovered records proving that he had been cheating on his income taxes for years. He made copies of the records and returned them to the drawer. The following week, Hymie got an anonymous letter accompanied by one of the incriminating records. The writer threatened to inform tax agents unless Hymie paid $45,000 in blackmail.

Responding to his cousin's plea for help, Weinberg had his cousin meet two people who were his secret partners in the swindle, a New York

City detective and a young lawyer who had dipped into a client's funds and desperately needed money. They both advised Hymie to pay the $45,000, assuring him they would get back the remaining records and destroy them. Hymie gave Weinberg the money to pay off the black-mailer and Weinberg split it with his two associates.

SCENE

It is a gray, threatening day in mid-winter, 1979. Mel Weinberg is shiv-ering despite a heavy overcoat and cashmere scarf. He stands alone before his father's grave at Long Island's windswept Pinelawn Cemetery. His father has been dead for a year, but he still misses the old man intensely. Never once had his father praised him, but neither had he ever con-demned him. Looking around, Weinberg notices the grave of his cousin Hymie's wife. On the grave is a blue metal decal showing that the plot owner has paid for perpetual care. Weinberg removes the decal and places it on his father's grave. "From me, to you, Pop," says Weinberg.

During the 1960s Weinberg made heavy money from the glass business and his various scams, including an elaborate swindle of a doctor who charged exorbitant fees to perform abortions in Harlem which were, of course, illegal. With Big Harry, the detective from the local precinct who had aided him in the Hymie swindle, Weinberg confronted the doctor at his Riverdale home flashing police badges. They were armed as well with the knowledge (disclosed by a relative of Weinberg's who happened to be the physician's accountant) that the doctor had at least $50,000 in his safe from his cash-only abortions. Weinberg intimated to the doctor that a bribe might save him from prosecution.

When the pair left with only $3,500 in a paper sack, his angry rel-ative confronted Weinberg later to report that the doctor had told him about the shakedown—but that the two cops had made away with the entire $50,000. The relative who had gotten a one-third cut from the $3,500 demanded the rest of his money. Weinberg argued that the doctor had lied and produced Big Harry to back up his story. The relative wasn't sure he was convinced.

Weinberg may have been successful in his schemes, but his personal life was a mess. When he wasn't out at night breaking windows or pulling swindles, he was usually at the apartment he maintained for Marie or drinking with an assortment of hustlers and hoodlums. He would arrive home in Plainview, if at all, just before dawn and leave red-eyed for work a few hours later.

Unsurprisingly, Mary, stuck in the suburbs with three children, became increasingly suspicious. Confronting her husband she asked him if he had a girlfriend and Weinberg, in a rare moment of candor, admitted it. Mary, hitherto a model wife, had had enough. She divorced him and a short time afterward Weinberg married Marie, whom he had grown to appreciate as a well-read, intelligent, attractive and highly organized young woman. But, within five years, he was also maintaining Diane, a new mistress, in a Bayside, Queens, apartment. "Every man needs two women," he explains. "One for a loving home and the other for a happy love life."

TAPE ONE

Weinberg: I've always had two women. I know it's a challenge, but I'll tell you something. It ain't really a drain, because if you take a broad out to a hotel room to get laid, today you can't even afford it. So you figure, if you get a broad six times a week, in the long run it's cheaper to get an apartment and set them up and you got a steady thing. . . . Marie, I get along with. I love her. But she's the kind, you get up in the middle of the night to take a leak, when you come back, she's already made the bed. I spend a few days with Marie and a few days with the other one [Diane]. They live twenty-five miles apart and they don't know each other . . .

I bitch and say who needs this? . . . but I do. I go crazy without two women. . . .

Marie was my secretary when I married her. My first wife, Mary, didn't find out I was going out with my secretary. I confessed to her. I came off the plane from a trip and my wife says she wants a divorce. It was, you know, typical woman's bullshit, what they say to you when they're pissed. I said great, glad to hear it. We went home and she says, Mel, is there another woman? I told her, yes, and she hit me in the head with a lamp. She tried to kill me. One thing I learned. If your wife catches you in bed with a broad, you say: What broad? There's no broad here. You just keep denying it.

3

NAME OF THE GAME

A con man has a big suitcase. Nine hundred deals he puts on the table. He figures, if you take only one, he's got something going.

—MEL WEINBERG

It was 1970. In Washington, D.C., President Richard M. Nixon and members of his staff already were rationalizing the type of integrity gap that would make Watergate possible; Congressman Adam Clayton Powell of New York, having betrayed his responsibility to black America, was sulking on Bimini, and many of Powell's Congressional peers, including some who had judged him, were tiptoeing into Koreagate.

These heady events, however, were remote from the real world of Mel Weinberg. As Marie reminded him all too frequently, money was pouring in, but gushing out. The glass business, now that the insurance contracts were evaporated, was a so-so money-maker. The dry-cleaning stores were a gold mine and his occasional swindles were good for a steady supply of walk-around money.

But he was paying his first wife $1,500 a month alimony and child support; he was an easy touch for old buddies; some of his employees were cheating him; he was betting huge sums on losing football teams;

and his free-wheeling life-style was prohibitively expensive. So he did what he could to economize. He rented his stores and delivery trucks for extra cash to a hijacking gang and he began using hot credit cards when he went out at night.

The hot credit cards, obtained by Weinberg from his underworld friends, rarely caused problems. "I'd go to joints owned by wise guys [mobsters]," said Weinberg. "As soon as I started drinkin', I'd tell the bartenders that I had a hot card and I'd tell them to put $30 or $40 on the card for themselves. They loved me." The cards, obtained by the underworld from muggers and burglars, were discarded every few weeks and replaced with freshly stolen ones.

So much hijacked merchandise was stored in Weinberg's dry-cleaning stores, he recalls, that the shops looked like flea markets. Cases of razor blades, perfume and cigarettes would be stacked against the walls and piled nearly as high as the ceilings. Stolen suits, dresses and coats hung from piperacks. The stores became so cluttered that it was difficult for the clerks to conduct their regular dry-cleaning business.

Despite Weinberg's unique approach to economy, loansharks gradually began taking over the cleaning stores in settlement of his gambling debts, and once again, he was on a downhill slide. Then, at a cocktail party sponsored in New York by the British government, Weinberg met Diane.

His wife Marie, who came from the same Depression-impoverished middle-class background as Weinberg, was dedicated to self-improvement. Blessed with a natural sense of order, she provided Weinberg with a warm, loving home in stark contrast to his hectic outside life. She was an affectionate mother to their adopted son and catered to Weinberg's slightest whim; his only measure of stability. But Diane added a new dimension to Weinberg's life.

Diane had a blow-torch effect on Weinberg's brassy approach to gender relationships. His attitude melted and puddled leaving him awed, reverential and nearly tongue-tied. Both Diane and Marie were pretty, bright, and engaging; but the similarity ended there. Born and raised in

England, Diane spoke in a carefully modulated BBC accent and approached life with a continental sophistication. In contrast to Marie, Diane was subtle and slightly mysterious, with an air of hauteur. Moreover, Diane was quintessentially feminine.

This, at least, was both women as Weinberg perceived them.

Diane personified for Weinberg a type of refinement that still leaves him struggling ten years later for the right superlatives. He sensed in her echoes of the gentility he had seen on his visits to the big houses down the avenue in his Bronx childhood. He had caught glimpses of the same qualities in the continental polish of Peter Norman Dawes, his partner in the Yaqui gold fiasco.

Instinctively, Weinberg knew that he was reacting to one of those abstract qualities that most eluded him: good taste. As far as Weinberg was concerned, good taste was people who didn't say "shit" at the dinner table. Beyond that he found it impossible to define and imitate. Characteristically, Weinberg decided that if he couldn't be it, he'd own it. And he convinced Diane to become his mistress.

She took him to England to meet her parents and he was deeply impressed with British ways. There was a solidity about things English, he decided, and he reasoned that if it struck him that way, it would have an even more profound effect on the less cynical. From that moment, the London address, the leather memo book with the discreet gilt signature of Harrods on the cover and a string of mythical British bank references became integral parts of Weinberg's scam kit. Already he was aware that anything that inspires confidence, no matter how subtle, helps the professional swindler.

It was also while he was in England that Weinberg met a man whose name he has forgotten, but who would have a marked influence on his life. His new acquaintance had the impeccable manners of an English gentleman. But he was actually a con man who specialized in front-end schemes. This type of swindle, with occasional elaborations, was to become Weinberg's stock-in-trade.

The front-end scheme operates on the premise that there are always people, usually businessmen, desperate for money. Some need money to invest in a stock tip or a once-in-a-lifetime commodity venture. Others are sure that their own businesses can successfully expand with more capitalization. Still others have heavy business losses and need money to stay afloat. All share two basic problems: they need money urgently and they cannot get loans from legitimate banks.

Swindlers like Weinberg have a name for these people. They call them desperate men, DM for short. The front-end scammer poses as a businessman with links to banks that usually exist only on paper. The swindler, naturally, can produce the names of these banks and assures the DM that he has a successful record of getting loans from them for his clients.

There is usually a legally chartered bank in some country that is connected to the swindler's office by Telex. The bank may be and usually is without funds and consists of nothing more than one clerk, a telephone, a Telex and a batch of legal-looking stationery. A Telex is sent by the "bank" to the swindler's office, informing the DM that the bank will favorably consider his loan if it is properly processed.

The swindler offers to process the loan application for fees ranging anywhere from $2,000 to $50,000, depending on the size of the loan, the solvency of the mark and the mark's state of desperation. The processing fee must be paid in advance by the mark to the swindler and this is why it is variously known as the advanced-fee or front-end scam.

Once the processing fee is paid to the swindler, he plays a stalling game with the mark, using any convenient financial or political problem that catches his eye in the *New York Times* or the *Wall Street Journal* as a reason for the bank's slowness in granting the loan. Meanwhile, the swindler encourages the mark to tell his friends about this generous overseas bank, thus stimulating new loan applications for the swindler.

There finally comes a point when the mark cannot be stalled any longer. When this point is reached, the mark receives an official letter from the bank, informing him that because of a problem with the world money market, or a drop in the price of gold, or an unexpected commodity run, or even perhaps a war in Ethiopia, the bank cannot honor his loan application, which otherwise exhibits impeccable credentials.

But if the mark has some money, there is another possible course. Though the DM has been turned down by the bank for the loan, he is quickly reassured by the swindler that for another fee arrangements can be made for the bank to provide the mark with certificates of deposit.

These certificates, known as CDs, are a normal function of the legitimate banking world. If a businessman has, for example, $500,000 on deposit with Chase Manhattan in New York, Chase can issue him a certificate of deposit for any amount up to the $500,000, which he can use as security for a loan from another bank against the funds on deposit in Chase.

The swindler tells his victim that even though the mark has no funds on deposit in the overseas bank that has just rejected his loan application, that bank will provide him with certificates showing that he does have large sums on deposit. The mark is told that he can use these certificates as security for loans from his own local banks. The fee for the certificates, the mark is told, is anywhere from 5 to 15 percent of the face value of the certificate of deposit.

This is not always a bad deal for the mark. American banks make money by loaning money and they are covered extensively by insurance against various types of fraud. It has been Weinberg's experience that most of the worthless CDs he has sold to marks have been honored for loans by legitimate banks in the U.S. These banks usually Telex the bogus overseas bank that issued the CDs. A swindler at the other end of the Telex promptly confirms that the money represented by the certificate actually is on deposit with the phony bank.

The swindler who runs a front-end scam is, of course, a crook. So are the operators of the usually fundless overseas banks who play along with the swindler. In underworld parlance, these banks are known as "offshore banks." The swindler kicks back anywhere from 5 to 15 percent of his take to the operators of the offshore bank. And most of the time, the mark doesn't even know he has been taken.

Such a front-end scam struck Weinberg as a scheme of sheer beauty. Properly executed, it promised huge returns for little investment and almost no risk. And so at age forty-five, his hair thinning and eyes weakening, Mel Weinberg became a full-time swindler.

He reasoned that he had the aptitude, the experience, the audacity, the nerve and the contacts to become one of the best. And he was right. Within ten years he would make and spend nearly $3 million. Moreover, he would engineer the greatest scandal ever to involve the Congress of the United States.

Early in 1970 a new international banking and investment firm was listed as a corporation in the files of the Secretary of the State of New York. A carefully understated business card described the new firm as Swiss Bank Associates with offices in New York, London and Zurich. Actually, the only office of Swiss Bank Associates was at the Bayside, Queens, apartment where Weinberg kept Diane.

Weinberg had put considerable thought into the name of his new company. He had read enough to know that Swiss banks carried with them the image of solidity. A London address was chosen for the same reason, and the reference to Zurich is self-evident. And New York was not merely the financial capital of America, it was also where he hung his hat and paid his phone bill. The fact that SBA, the initials of Swiss Bank Associates, were also the initials of the Federal agency that backs loans to small businessmen, Weinberg maintains, was coincidence.

There was also a pragmatic reason for the addresses in London and Zurich. Weinberg had learned from other con men that the Hotel Zurich and the Hilton Hotel in London shared a unique custom. Neither hotel would tell a caller that the person he was calling was not registered at the hotel. Both hotels would simply accept messages for an unregistered guest on the assumption that the guest would arrive later. The caller was left with the impression that his party was registered at the hotel, a valuable aid to confidence men who thrive on the impression that they are flitting through Europe from one big business deal to another.

Until this phase of his life, Weinberg, not given to introspection, had fashioned his scams instinctively with little thought as to why some worked and some didn't. Now that he was into swindling full-time, he gave the subject more thought, dissecting previous scams into basic elements, searching for the common denominators of success.

He decided that all successful swindles are carefully contrived illusions largely based on the truth, that each must offer hope no matter how desperate the circumstances of the mark, and that the most credible swindler plays his part so intensely that he almost comes to believe his own pitch is true.

TAPE TWO

Weinberg: Truth is important. I learned from an old con man, never lie when you don't have to lie. The more truth in your story, the more convincing it is. Most scams are ninety percent truth and ten percent lie. You have to try to put yourself into the position and then believe it so much that you feel that you're tellin' the truth. I believe that before you sell a deal, you have to live the deal. You have to believe in it, because, if you don't believe in it, you can't sell it . . . Now as to hope. That's another important thing. A guy is in a jam and he comes to me for money. Under my breath I might say "fuck you," but I don't say that. Because when a guy is in a jam and lookin' for money it's my philosophy to give hope. If you say you can't do nothin', you're killin' his hope. Everybody has to have hope. That's why most people don't turn us in to the cops. They keep hopin' we're for real.

Weinberg went to work methodically building his scam. His first move was to insulate his wife. He bought a sprawling, fourteen-room house in Central Islip, Long Island, sixty miles outside the city, encouraging Marie to furnish it tastefully, before she moved in. He established his business phone and answering service in Diane's Bayside apartment, and let it be known to the fast-buck grapevine that he had lucked into connections with several European banks, while distributing his business cards. The action began almost at once.

What started as a trickle of front-end-scam customers soon grew into a torrent, constantly fed by the refinements that Weinberg added to the illusion he was creating. He traveled to meetings with his desperate men clients in chauffeured Cadillacs, Lincolns and an occasional Rolls-Royce. As an added inducement he swathed Diane in furs, Cartier jewelry and designer gowns, and introduced her to customers as the daughter of a prominent English banking family.

To be sure, Diane had the elegance that Weinberg lacked. She did not display her costumes, they displayed her. She moved with the well-bred assurance of old wealth, attractive but reserved, the type of beautiful woman who immediately triggers images of winters at St. Moritz, West End theater opening nights in London and yacht cruises along the Côte d'Azur. Traveling in her own chauffeured limousine, trailing the scent of delicate perfume, casually deferring business propositions to Weinberg, Diane was his ultimate weapon.

"When you're building a scam, you gotta pay attention to detail," explained Weinberg. "You gotta make people believe. They wanna believe, because they need the money and you're their only hope. So you arrange for them to see and hear things that give them more of an excuse to believe. Diane has so much class, she looked so rich—legit money rich—that the DMs would think, this guy's gotta be real; why else would a broad like this be hangin' around him? . . . The chauffeured cars, the phony telephone calls from London and Zurich while you're talkin' to a client, all of these are part of the illusion. You don't have to come on that strong; sometimes it helps to play hard to get. You let the client high-pressure himself with what he sees and hears. It's like, you know, that psychology stuff."

Gravel-voiced, slightly sinister-looking, garment-district trendy, Weinberg himself played a vital part in the illusion. He cast the subtle impression that if he wasn't a mobster, he was at least on good speaking terms with the wise guys. To the average DM, the thought of the mob's infinite riches is almost as attractive as the friendly European bank which, he reasons, may be owned by the mob anyway. Instead of scaring customers away, Weinberg's Runyonesque image was an added lure.

More than once during his career as a swindler Weinberg used this image to direct advantage. And in later years, it played a vital part in convincing the Abscam influence brokers that he was a safe man with whom to deal. After all, a crook like this couldn't be a government agent, could he?

Weinberg's deceptive image had proved an expensive experience for a Bayside doctor who wanted to kill his wife. Weinberg was busy on the phone in Diane's apartment one day shortly after he had formed Swiss Bank Associates. Suddenly, he felt a spasm of pain in his chest. Calmly finishing his phone conversation, he asked Diane to check the Yellow Pages for the closest doctor.

Diane gave him a name and address and over her protests he drove alone to the doctor's office. By the time he was on the examining table, he was feeling better and chatting with the doctor as he worked. One subject led to another and as Weinberg tells it:

"A guy like me, as soon as I speak to you, you know I'm a wise guy. I'm talkin' to this doctor and we're talkin' about bets and betting. He asked me do I take action. I tell him, yeah, I can get action handled. Right away, he'd like a favor done. He says he'd like to have his wife killed. So I looked at him and says, yeah, I could arrange it, and this guy gives me $10,000 advance right on the spot. He was the most anxious bastard I ever met."

Secure in the knowledge that the doctor couldn't complain to law enforcement about how he had been swindled, Weinberg pocketed the money, went home with a prescription and never bothered to call him back. But he warned Diane: "If I ever get a heart attack, don't take me back to that fuck. He'll kill me."

Weinberg's front-end swindle boomed as his list of contacts expanded and one deal fed on another. Soon he was traveling around the country, wheeling, dealing and talking big finance. He made all-expense-paid trips to Europe, Australia and the Orient at the request of businessmen eager for the loans that Weinberg offered from his string of ersatz European banks.

Sometimes he worked his swindles with other con men while other times he worked alone. Soon, so many deals were in operation that Weinberg took on an assistant, a pudgy, sometimes bumbling salesman who used the name Lou Host. If the prospective client was paying all expenses, Weinberg sometimes would bring along his sister Sylvia and her husband, introducing Sylvia as his traveling secretary and her husband as his staff engineer.

One such trip was to Texas, where a Long Island lawyer wanted to show Weinberg various properties he planned to expand with a Weinberg-processed European bank loan. The lawyer introduced Weinberg to a number of prominent Texas businessmen whom he promptly fleeced. During the Texas tour, Weinberg was so convincing that he was given the use of the Governor's plane and presented by the Lieutenant Governor with a certificate proclaiming that he was an honorary citizen of the Lone Star State. Weinberg's photo of the presentation is one of his proudest possessions.

Time and again while he was running Swiss Bank Associates, Weinberg's ability to come up with a quick answer when he was in trouble saved him from possible disaster. On one such occasion, Weinberg was running a successful scam on the owners of Botony Clothes in Baltimore. Before the clothiers realized that they had been swindled, they had recommended Weinberg to a California businessman who was also seeking loan money.

The businessman sent Weinberg a first-class ticket to fly out to the coast and discuss the prospective deal, known in the con business as a package. The businessman met Weinberg at the Los Angeles Airport; and as they drove toward the city, he scowled at Weinberg and said, "I just checked with Botony Clothes and they say that you ripped them off for $50,000." He was right and Weinberg almost choked on his cigar.

"But, I didn't blink," Weinberg recalls proudly. "Right away, I said, 'Stop this car. I wanna get out right here. I don't wanna do business with anyone who accuses me of something like that. Let's forget the whole deal!' This stops him for a minute. He says, 'You only have a one-way ticket; how do you think you're going to get back east?' I shout, 'I don't need your ticket. I got plenty right here.' Then I pull out a big roll of bills. Now he's shook and he starts to apologize. I explain that Botony and I have a disagreement and it's in the courts. Right away he calms down and he feels sorry for accusing me. After that he was a cinch. I nicked him for ten grand."

Quick presence of mind, Weinberg believes, is absolutely essential to the successful swindler. If events take an unexpected turn, says Weinberg, "You gotta think fast. You can't hesitate at all. Talk fast and bluff like hell."

Gradually, Swiss Bank Associates assumed a smooth routine. A wide variety of customers flowed into Weinberg's net—all of them seeking substantial loans from his mythical European banks. Some were substantial businessmen riding a down-slope and desperately trying to save their name-brand companies. Many were lawyers, looking for quick money to get a piece of one of their clients' deals or trying to replace money that they had stolen from escrow accounts. Some clients were swindlers themselves, hoping to fleece Weinberg's bank contacts.

And then, there were the inventors. Weinberg remembers one who proudly displayed his patent for miniwindshield wipers that were supposed to keep car headlights clean. Another, a ranking army officer, wanted money to produce a magnet hoist that would be suspended from helicopters and used to move skyscrapers from one city to another.

As long as clients had $2,500 to $3,000 to put up for appraisals and loan processing, Weinberg took their money and assured them that his banks would come through. The appraisals would be done by Lou Host, who would make a cursory visit to a client's firm or home, take a quick Polaroid shot, examine tax records and write up a short report. He did as many as five a day in the New York area.

The appraisals were part of the con. Host's businesslike appearance was reassuring to clients who had just surrendered their front money. The appraisal made the scam look reputable and Weinberg could assure any investigator of the law that it was part of his own legitimate cost that he had passed on to the client. Host, of course, was not an appraiser.

Advance-fee swindles, now classified as white-collar crime, were only vaguely discerned by law enforcement in the early 1970s and a complaining victim was usually referred by police to civil court. Always one to hedge his bets, Weinberg quickly established a legitimate contact with a New York City FBI agent and tipped him whenever he got information on the movement of stolen securities. He regarded the FBI contact as a form of insurance.

Weinberg was also careful about using the U.S. mail. Although most local and Federal authorities paid little attention to white-collar crime, postal inspectors were another matter. Weinberg frequently had to send his clients letters of commitment, promises by his offshore banks to produce the loan money when the client met certain other financial obligations. Such letters are accepted by many legitimate banks as security against advance loans that they themselves may give to the client. Since Weinberg's letters of commitment were fraudulent, sending them through the mails was a Federal offense.

His solution was ingenious. He would send the letters to out-of-town clients by commercial airliner, explaining that he knew speed was important and that the U.S. mails were too slow. The clients were always impressed.

Weinberg learned from fellow swindlers a number of ways to dodge state and Federal laws, although he generally tended to laugh off their advice on legal matters. "Con men listen to everybody who tells ya when you're breakin' the law and when you're not breakin' the law. But ninety percent of the guys who tell ya that you're not breakin' the law don't know what the hell they're talkin' about. The law's a funny thing."

Early on, Weinberg decided that it was safer to swindle smaller amounts from a large volume of clients than it was to go for a few big scores every year. This is why he limited his front-end fees to sums in the $3,000 to $5,000 range. "People are less suspicious if you go for a reasonable fee instead of a huge chunk," he explained. "And a guy who only loses a small amount either never catches on to the fact that he was scammed or figures it isn't worth the bother of goin' to the law. Even if he does blow the whistle, the cops figure it ain't enough money to get bothered about."

Weinberg realized that volume was the answer, and he was right. During the five years that he operated Swiss Bank Associates, he netted $250,000 a year and never had any problems with law enforcement agencies. He was able to net this amount despite Lou Host's cut of the profits, heavy outlay to entertain clients, first-class business travel throughout the world, the expense of clothing and bejeweling Diane and the high cost of chauffeured cars.

There was another secret to Weinberg's high profit margins. He never paid taxes. "I work too hard for my money to hand it over to the government," he explained. He had never filed a personal income tax return. Since he had no business office (he used the apartment only for phone calls) and kept all of his records in his head, there was no way for the government to know that he even existed. "The best place for a con to operate is out of his hat," says Weinberg. "Records can only get ya in trouble."

His entire stock-in-trade was a stack of letterheads, business cards and the apartment telephone. He would meet prospective clients and discuss business at clubs, restaurants or their own offices. When he needed a Telex, he would borrow the use of one in somebody else's business office. Even his first-class travel was usually paid for by eager clients.

Occasionally, Weinberg would go for a bigger score if he was dealing with a large corporate client or he saw a way to get more money without increasing his risks. At one point, he took a large U.S. oil company for more than $50,000 and huge expenses. On that scam, Weinberg and Host soared over the country for a month on one of the company's Lear jets under the pretext of appraising the firm's property. Never failing to seize an opportunity, he arranged to have other potential customers meet him at various airports. They were universally impressed to see Weinberg and his aide casually disembarking from what they believed was his own private jet.

Weinberg learned something else as his business grew. The swindling business, just like the garment business and the publishing business and other legitimate businesses, has seasonal cycles. "The heaviest months in the con business," he explained, "are September, October and November. I don't know why, but more people are trying to make a fast buck in the fall of the year." The deadest seasons for swindlers, he said, are January to March and July and August. "Who could believe there's a scam season?" he asked in mock disbelief.

Like the shark that instinctively chews its way through the seas, Weinberg had no pity on his victims although he liked some of his marks personally. "If the people comin' to me for loans were honest," he said, "they wouldn't be comin' to me in the first place. Most of them had been turned down by their own banks because they had no security or were bad risks. So then they'd come to me bragging about how much their plants were worth and how honest they were. I'd make believe I believed them, so when they thought they were puttin' somethin' over me, I just ripped them off instead."

Weinberg's rationalization is universal to con men. They view their victims as amateur swindlers or people who are avidly trying to get something of great value for little or no cost. The vast majority of people, they feel, are also dishonest. They point, for example, to the fact that most supposedly honest people will eagerly buy merchandise that they are sure is stolen as long as they can get it at bargain prices without risk to themselves.

As a result, the swindlers' credo is: Get them before they can get you.

As his career track expanded, Weinberg met an increasing number of fellow swindlers. Methodically he entered the name of each new acquaintance, along with his specialty, phone numbers and business covers on index cards which he filed for later reference. These acquaintances spanned five continents, all of them representing a worldwide network of assistants that Weinberg could use for his scams. They could provide him with business covers and on-the-scene representatives in all the major cities of the world. They operated offshore banks, legitimate banks, real estate firms, brokerage houses and mortgage companies. And they were willing to assume a variety of poses from nobility to safari directors. Their fee for services rendered was a fixed cut of the particular scam in which they were involved.

Weinberg was happy with the arrangement and, for a similar cut, he provided his fellow scammers with reciprocal services from New York. Crucial to his education over this period was his discovery that swindlers did not conform to any particular mold. Some were white-haired, distinguished gentlemen who lived in country manor houses and operated from some of London's most impeccable business addresses. Others, like Weinberg, were flashy American businessmen who dazzled prospects with the smell of big money and the aura of business success. Still others were deadly mob gunmen, scamming on the side.

TAPE THREE

Weinberg: They knock each other like mad, con men do. There's a lotta homosexuals in con men. I would say that nearly half of them that I met in my life were homosexuals. Why? I don't know. And as far as broads go, not most con men seem to have too good a sex life. Because, you gotta remember one thing. When a con man is connin' somebody, he's under tremendous pressure. Number one, he sells you. After he sells you, number two, he's gotta worry about you comin' up with the bread for the final payoff. Three, he's under a big strain that this is the setup where he's gonna get caught. That's the kinda pressure he's under. So when they make a killin' most con men, I'd say ninety percent of them, go on a splurge. They go buy some new clothes; they go on a vacation. I just can't explain the kinda pressure they're under. The schemin' to get the idea goin', the worry that you're gonna run to the cops. It's like you get to walkin' around the hotel checkin' to see if anyone's lookin' at you. If somebody looks, right away you think he's a fed. I guess it's because of the strain that most con men seldom have a sex life. Maybe, after it all comes down, you make your bread, you tie up with some broad and you take off for a week or two, have a ball. But then you gotta start workin' again because you just pissed your money away on vacation and you gotta get back to work because the overhead is tremendous. How else do you think you're gonna keep payin' your bills? Take the telephone alone. Ninety percent of your con is done on the telephone. Your phone bills run anywhere from $500 to $2,000 a month. You lose your telephone and you're out of the con business.

Some fellow swindlers with whom Weinberg was associated during the SBA years are standouts in his memory. All had assumed names. People like Judy Johnson, the hard-as-nails Texas con girl; Raphael, king of the Puerto Rican con men, who took Cartier on New York's Fifth Avenue for its most expensive watch plus the watch's cash equivalent; the Dragon Lady, a wrinkled Filipino woman in New York who scammed a huge annual living from Oriental businessmen; and, perhaps the most memorable, the Maharaja of Tahonga alias Dr. Haas.

Weinberg first met the Maharaja while he was running an advance-fee scam on a California firm known as Moped of America. Impressed with Weinberg's business hustle and European bank contacts, a company official showed him three checks totaling $2.8 million. The checks, all made out to Moped, were drawn on the Maharaja's account at the Overseas Investment Bank in Switzerland. All of the checks had bounced.

The official complained that the Maharaja, who originally came from India and now lived in Bangkok, Thailand, had agreed to loan Moped the $2.8 million from his own Swiss account in return for an advance fee of $100,000. The official said that the slightly built Maharaja had particularly impressed him because he had been able to call the Indian consulate and an official of the consulate had arrived a short time later in a car with diplomatic plates and had treated the Maharaja like visiting royalty.

The official was upset, naturally, when the checks returned from Europe forty-five days later marked no account. He had sent one of his vice-presidents to Bangkok to question the Maharaja, who seemed equally upset.

According to the Maharaja, the official explained, the money to cover the Moped loan was supposed to have come from the sale of a large diamond owned by the Maharaja known as the Red Cross Diamond. The Maharaja had ordered the bank to sell the diamond and deposit the proceeds into his account. Only after he got home to Thailand, he said, did he learn that the Swiss government through bureaucratic bumbling had impounded the jewel for nonpayment of taxes. If Moped would issue him a first-class plane ticket to Zurich, the Maharaja would then be in a position to sell the diamond on consignment, once having straightened out the tax difficulty.

The company official, like most scam victims, while desperately wanting to believe the Maharaja, was concerned enough to ask Weinberg and his assistant to go to Switzerland to ensure that the Maharaja performed as promised. In return the official promised Weinberg either a cut of the money from the diamond, or part of the $100,000 advance paid the Maharaja, which Weinberg was to recover if the diamond sale evaporated. He also gave Weinberg a hefty cash advance to cover his expenses.

The next day Weinberg and Lou Host took a Swissair flight to Zurich, where they checked into the Hotel Zurich, and waited to hear from the Maharaja. A fastidious person and especially finicky about personal cleanliness, Weinberg noticed with distaste that night that Host's underwear was dingy and that his assistant wore a Daniel Boone hat to bed every night to keep his thinning hair in place. "Of all the people in the world, I draw this schmuck for a roomie," he muttered.

When the Maharaja knocked on Weinberg's hotel room door early the next morning, the door was answered by Host still in his dirty underwear and Daniel Boone hat. The Maharaja stood openmouthed at the door. An apologetic Weinberg ordered Host into the bathroom to dress and invited the Maharaja in. For the next hour the Maharaja sought to impress Weinberg with his huge wealth and vast financial connections. Weinberg, sniffing a scam, forcibly took the Maharaja's passport and ordered Host to guard him in the room until the story could be checked out. The Maharaja, most likely suspecting that Weinberg was a mobster, didn't resist.

Quickly Weinberg learned that the Maharaja didn't own the Red Cross Diamond, had no cash or credit in Switzerland, was a professional swindler and had left the $100,000 that he had scammed from Moped with his wife in Bangkok. Weinberg had the Maharaja wire his wife to send the money to London. Then, with the Maharaja as an involuntary prisoner, evidenced by Weinberg's possession of his passport, he and Host flew to London where they all checked into adjoining rooms at a Holiday Inn.

Days passed but there was no sign of the money from Bangkok. The Maharaja suggested a variety of excuses ranging from political unrest to monsoons, but Weinberg scoffed, warning that he would spend the rest of his life in the Holiday Inn if the money wasn't forthcoming. Tiring of the wait, Weinberg flew back to New York, leaving Host with the passport and instructions not to release the Maharaja until the money arrived.

Several days later Weinberg took a transatlantic call from Host. "Mel," said Host, "we got trouble."

"Whaddya mean?" Weinberg asked.

"The Maharaja seems to be having a heart attack," Host explained. "He's really pissing and moaning. The doctor's here and we gotta send the Maharaja to a private clinic. The clinic wants $500 to take him in. Send me the money."

"Clinic?" Weinberg exploded. "That fuckin' Maharaja is a god-damned swindler. Put his ass in a welfare hospital!"

"But, Mel," asked Host, "how can we ask a real Maharaja to go to a welfare hospital?"

When he had finished sputtering, Weinberg ordered Host to put the Maharaja into a public hospital and to hold onto the passport.

The next day, Host called again. There was another problem, he explained. The hospital demanded the Maharaja's passport when he was admitted and Host had given it to the nurse. The hospital had routinely given the passport back to the Maharaja after he was bedded down and sometime during the night the Maharaja had dressed and left the hospital.

"Who'd think a guy that near death would wander out of the hospital," asked Host.

"Can I tell you one thing, Lou?" Weinberg asked in a very quiet voice.

"Sure, Mel," answered Host. "What is it?"

"You're the world's number one schmuck!" Weinberg screamed, slamming down the phone.

TAPE FOUR

Marie: Mel is a very thoughtful, considerate husband. He has to go out of town often on business, but, like today, he's already called twice today. He always remembers birthdays and anniversaries with flowers and presents. He's a wonderful father. He's got a very good brain, not educated, but what you'd call street-smart. He likes challenges; sometimes when I listen to him, I can almost hear the wheels turning. He's got a very good sense of humor, too. He likes to find your weakness and tease a lot. You know, I don't think I've ever seen him do a malicious thing.

If he's at a party, he's talking to everyone, making sure that everyone is mixing. . . . He's an impossible eater. When he eats, he does it so fast that I'm always telling him to slow down. I wouldn't say he's a big eater, but he's always having a little of something. He can't pass a hot-dog stand without getting the urge. I guess chicken soup with mandles is his favorite dish; he makes it himself for us. But I think he'd rather have a sandwich than anything else. He just loves Jewish deli, you know, corned beef, pastrami, the rest of it. He's terrible for having big sandwiches before bed . . . I guess watching TV is his favorite pastime, he'll watch anything, but don't sit there watching it with him. He'll drive you crazy. He's switching the channel every couple of minutes. . . . He says he doesn't snore, but he does.

Sometimes he's so loud he keeps us all awake . . . and what a driver! He knows how to drive very well, but when he's driving, he has this habit of turning to face you when he's talking to you. I'm always telling him to please watch the road before we crash. . . . He's out of town often on business, but we are always in touch and he shows that he cares. He's awful with machinery, he gets too impatient. When we lived on Long Island, I remember he got impatient with the barbecue grill because it wasn't burning fast enough. He just ignored the warnings and squirted lighting fluid over the hot coals. It backfired and singed off his eyebrows. . . . But, like I said. He's a good husband and a good father and he's a nice man.

4

A Class Touch

SWINDLER: thief, cheat, impostor, con man, pretender, char-
latan, mountebank, conjuror, prestidigitator, trickster, rogue,
rascal, ringer, knave, bunko man, sharper, deceiver, diddler, pecu-
lator, counterfeiter —*Dictionary of Synonyms and Antonyms.*

Con guys have a tendency to stick together. There's a lot of
money in the game. You make a damned good living and you
don't work very hard. So I went into it and I made a damned
good living and I didn't work very hard. —MEL WEINBERG

New York State Route 110 starts on the edges of Long Island Sound in the
hamlet of Huntington and slashes south across the width of Long Island,
past shopping malls, sod farms and gleaming new office buildings, ending
abruptly just short of the Great South Bay and the Atlantic Ocean.

An hour's drive to the west of the crowded, four-lane highway is
Manhattan; seventy miles to the east are the Hamptons, summer playpen
for the world's jet-setters, blue-bloods and authors suffering from tired
blood. Long Island, like Los Angeles of yesteryear, has been described as
three million people in search of a downtown. In the early 1970s, while
government officials and $50,000-a-year planners pondered innards and
raised wet fingers to the wind, the people of Long Island quietly decided
on their own that Route 110 was downtown.

The decision made, Route 110, also known as Broad Hollow Road, exploded in a feverish burst of construction. White-collar businesses filled the glass-sided office buildings, professional organizations and colleges hung out their shingles; the island's newspaper moved there. Then came an avalanche of doctors, lawyers, salesmen, engineers, merchants and, of course, swindlers.

In an expensively paneled suite on the third floor of one such office building at 275 Broad Hollow Road sat Mel Weinberg. It was noontime, time for lunch, and as the pace of business activity temporarily slackened, Weinberg leaned back in his lushly upholstered executive chair, sucked expansively on his cigar, and contemplated his good fortune.

Through the partly opened door of his office he could hear the clatter of the Telex machines in the outer office and the fast-paced gossip of the leggy receptionist and the rest of the office staff. The windows behind him were framed in custom-made drapes, accenting the colors of the decorator furniture and the deep, plush carpeting.

Across the way, he could see the huge, double doors of the conference room. In his mind's eye, he proudly pictured the room's interior. A sixteen-foot conference table of polished wood, ringed with chairs of the softest leather, side tables, a silver water carafe. One wall was completely covered with a map of the world; on the opposite wall, a huge set of cattle horns sent to him from Texas by an admiring mark still unaware that Weinberg had scammed him years before.

Down the carpeted corridor, out through the staff room and reception room, were the main doors to his office suite. They bore the same legend as the embossed business cards nestled in his kid leather credential case:

LONDON INVESTORS
275 Broad Hollow Road
Melville, L.I., N.Y.
New York   London   Zurich

It was early in 1976 and London Investors, little less than a year old, was the realization of Weinberg's most ambitious dream: a gigantic front-end scam with a permanent office and more than 500 franchised agents sending in marks from all over the world. Wreathed in cigar smoke, he closed his eyes and stuck imaginary red pins into a mental map of the world. He had agents in every state of the United States, veteran "Arab" con man Yassir Habib at the Hotel Zurich in Switzerland, others in Paris, and others in London, Vancouver, Hong Kong, Rome, Sydney, Beirut. He stopped counting. He couldn't remember, much less pronounce the names.

Weinberg had made his decision to be the biggest, nearly a year ago. The offices rented for $1,200 a month and the furniture had cost him more than $70,000. But he had made it all back in the first month.

He was startled from his thoughts by the machine-gun chatter of his assistant Lou Host in the smaller office next door. Host was on the phone talking to a mark. Weinberg thought about lunch. It didn't pay to eat with the help.

His natural inclination was to have a quick frankfurter, but to a person in Weinberg's vocation smart restaurants were prime hunting grounds, places to meet new marks and spread the word that he had easy money for the taking. There were few potential clients to be found among the munchers at the local hot-dog stand.

He might head north on 110 and meet his lawyer, Vince Cuti, for lunch at Orlando's in Huntington. The place bulged with politicians, judges and contractors who routinely clinked glasses with fellow patrons from the underworld and its fringes. Men like Anthony (Tony Ducks) Corallo, Joe Trocchio and John Del Mastro. Besides, he reflected, he was treated like an important man there and he still felt an inner glow when he opened the menu and saw Herring with Sour Cream Weinberg listed among the appetizers.

Checking his watch, he dialed his bookmaker and bet on several horse races. Then he shrugged into his cashmere coat, copped an appreciative look at the receptionist's swelling cleavage, descended in the elevator and made his way out the door to his reserved parking spot. Climbing into the new Lincoln, he turned on the stereo and eased his way into the stream of traffic.

The bubble music gave way to news and the announcer held forth about a recent conference in Helsinki and Jimmy Carter's statement on human rights. It was, suggested the newscaster, a warning to friendly despots like the Shah of Iran and President Somoza of Nicaragua.

"Who gives a shit?" Weinberg sighed as he switched the station to country western.

London Investors was begun in typical Weinberg style—with somebody else's money. He had dazzled a Texas businessman with his important European bank connections and convinced him to advance three checks for $5,000 so that they could go into the investment business together. He paid a deposit and advance rental on the office suite with one of the checks and used the others for deposits on telephones, Telex machines and furniture. There was a momentary snag just before the grand opening, when the furniture company called to report that the checks had bounced and that it was holding the furniture.

Frantic, Weinberg called Texas and convinced his reluctant partner to make good the checks. Meanwhile, customers were arriving at the office and staring suspiciously at the empty rooms and telephones strewn about the floor. Undaunted and punctuating his conversation with threats of a multimillion-dollar lawsuit against the furniture company, Weinberg sat his customers down on packing boxes and talked investments.

Within the first week Weinberg had grossed $28,000. His silent partner from Texas finally made the checks good, but after a few months Weinberg bought him out and was in business for himself. And by the end of the first year, he had netted and spent nearly $500,000.

London Investors was Swiss Bank Associates reborn, but this time with more flair. Like SBA, London Investors specialized in front-end swindles and bogus certificates of deposit. But the entire operation was on a far grander and more sophisticated scale than its predecessor. It was, as Weinberg later boasted, "The biggest, sweetest con game ever born and a helluva money-maker."

The centerpiece of the swindle was the office suite on Route 110. It presented a reassuring scene to a prospective borrower. While Telexes chattered busily, the phones were constantly ringing and the staff were courteous and accommodating. Mr. Weinberg and his assistant, while a bit uncouth, were most friendly and solicitous. And they dealt with banks in London, Paris, Geneva and even Monte Carlo. The entire setting exuded an aura of success and money, precisely the illusion Weinberg sought.

What his clients didn't know about, of course, was the bugged Lincoln Continental limousine, Weinberg's worldwide net of commission agents and his secret list of more than eighty offshore banks, all operated by hustlers or fellow swindlers. Most important, they didn't know that Weinberg was a totally dedicated crook.

As soon as he set up shop on Long Island, Weinberg called every swindler in his card file and offered a flat $500 for each mark steered to London Investors for a loan, promising more if the plucking was better. The word spread, and soon many legitimate attorneys and mortgage brokers were also sending him clients, completely oblivious to Weinberg's true nature. "I was very democratic," laughed Weinberg. "No matter who sent 'em, I scammed 'em."

A typical London Investors swindle proceeded as follows:

Weinberg would receive a letter or phone call from one of his steerers, reporting that a client was being sent to London Investors to arrange a loan. The steerer would give Weinberg basic background information on the mark's assets and needs.

Weinberg would send his chauffeur-driven Lincoln to the airport or the mark's office to bring him back to London Investors. Once the DM got into the Lincoln, he was as good as scammed. Weinberg boasts of a fail-safe technique he developed. "Anybody who sat in that limousine was at least $3,500 sure money in my pocket," he said.

First, there was the chauffeur, a retired New York cop named Steve. Weinberg paid Steve by the trip, but anticipating that curious customers would try to pump the driver, he paid Steve a bonus of $3 a plug for each time he praised Weinberg's loan-getting ability during the course of the ride to the office.

Steve's commercials could be counted accurately because the limousine was bugged with an electronic device that recorded every word spoken in the car. Once on the premises, while the mark was being charmed by the receptionist in the outer office, Steve would bring the tape into Weinberg's inner sanctum for a careful debriefing. Only then was the visitor escorted into Weinberg's office.

On the wall behind his desk hung a huge picture of President Lyndon Johnson affectionately inscribed to Weinberg by a Texas swindler who himself was warmly shaking hands with the former Chief Executive. Displayed on the walls were other pictures of leading movie stars and show-business personalities, all of them supplied by another professional acquaintance and autographed with glowing testimonials to Weinberg.

"My supplier was a good forger," he observes.

The visitor, gazing about appreciatively, would sit opposite Weinberg's executive desk and explain why he needed a loan from one of Weinberg's client European banks, disclosing what he had in the way of security, and how much money he would need. Weinberg would carefully examine the mark's package, questioning him with the thoroughness of a legitimate bank loan officer.

After considerable mulling, Weinberg would have a member of his staff Telex the bare bones of the proposal to one of the many impressively titled offshore banks on his list. After a decent time interval, the bank would Telex that it would consider the loan application favorably pending Weinberg's appraisal of the security and proper presentation of the full proposal. Only at this point would Weinberg temper his client's barely masked jubilation with the suggestion that the presentation would cost $3,500 in advance.

Eager to get the money quickly, the visitor was nearly inevitably hooked on the spot. For the skeptics, however, Weinberg had other resources at his disposal.

TAPE FIVE

Weinberg: First off, you have to understand that this mark is comin' in to sell himself, to get money. I haven't offered him anything yet . . . now I sit there and I tell him that maybe I can do something for him. This comes as a shock to him. Then I hit him with the bottom line: I want money. Now, some of these guys begin to think that maybe I'm not for real. He asks for a reference. Right away I'd tell him that some of the banks we represent are Swiss banks and we're bound by the Swiss bankin' code; we can't do that. What the fuck does he know from Swiss bankin' codes? . . . Then, I'd make like I was thinkin' for a minute and I'd lean forward real confidential and tell him that I wasn't supposed to do this, but there was one guy he could check with. I'd give him the name of Mr. Haney. He's a real person, very rich, he owns ski resorts all over the world. I'd tell the mark that I was giving him the name of Mr. Haney as a personal favor. But I'd warn him to be real careful, you know, gentle, when he talked to Haney about me and any business Haney done with London, because he's very busy and very rich and important.

Now, I would give the mark a phone number for Haney. It was the number of a phone that I kept in my desk drawer. Sooner or later the phone would ring and it would be the mark askin' for Mr. Haney. I had like a muffler over the mouthpiece so the mark couldn't recognize my voice. He'd say he's dealing with London for a loan and he'd ask me for a reference. Let's say the mark's name was Tannenbaum. I'd say: "Mr. Tannenbaum, I'm Mr. Haney. I've dealt with London for the past five years. They haven't done all my deals, but of all the people I finance with, if they do it, I know that I have a knowledgeable deal. I recommend them very highly." They almost always bit after talkin' to Haney.

If the suspicious clients should come in pairs or small groups as business partners, and Weinberg was asking for $10,000 or $15,000 in advance money for phony certificates of deposit, he had another ploy: the bugged conference room. This room was used when partners would blanch at Weinberg's mention of a fee and quickly look at each other. Quick to sense such hesitation, Weinberg would invite them into the conference room to discuss it privately between themselves.

While the partners discussed the deal in imagined privacy, Weinberg, notebook in hand, would listen to every word in the comfort of his own office through another bugging device. Most often, the partners were reluctant to buy the certificates because they didn't have enough ready cash to pay Weinberg's advance commission. Their bugged conference would usually reveal how much cash they actually had. If it was enough to suit Weinberg, on their return to his office, he would shave his commission to a sum just slightly less than the actual cash that he knew they had available.

"I always left the marks with a little somethin'; I was never greedy," he said magnanimously.

Once a mark had paid his advance fee to process the loan, Weinberg went into the classic swindler's maneuver known as the stall. Simply explained, this entails keeping the mark convinced for as long a period of time as possible that he is going to get his loan. The technique is the same as that used by a salt-water fisherman trolling for tuna and other fish that swim in schools. When the fish bites on one of his several hooks, he doesn't reel it in right away. He delays, sure in the knowledge that other fish, attracted by the first one, will swallow his other hooks.

So it is with swindles. An expectant mark tells his friends about his good fortune and they become other marks. Weinberg, a master at the stall, explained that the theory was to "always give the guy a ray of hope."

He said, "Deep in his heart, the guy listens to your excuses and he knows you're givin' him a buncha bullshit . . . but you're givin' him a little hope and that night he can sleep and say to himself maybe he will get the money; he wants to have hope . . . People would call me and pressure me, when's the money comin'? I'd always say it's on the way, we had some problems, but we straightened them out. . . . The con man always gives them an answer; he never denies you anything. He tells you what you want to hear. I give them an answer, even though it's a lie."

Eventually, if Weinberg should decide that a mark couldn't afford an extra fee for CDs, he would have his confederate at the offshore bank send a letter of regret turning down the loan application. Weinberg would commiserate with the mark and the scam was complete.

(Several years later, Weinberg's ability to stall delivery of promised loans from bogus Arab sheikhs to members of the United States Congress without arousing their suspicions allowed Federal authorities to keep the Abscam investigation going for months beyond its original cutoff date.)

Business boomed and Weinberg, often accompanied by Lady Diane, was jetting twice a year to Europe and making frequent trips to Canada, Mexico, Australia and the Orient. Wherever his commission agents discovered potential marks, either Weinberg or his helper Lou Host went to fleece them. The huge volume of business soon forced Weinberg to break his cardinal rule against keeping files. He knew that they might one day be used as evidence against him, but there was no other way to keep track of his activities.

The files of London Investors reveal that Weinberg was dealing with Red Chinese counterfeiters, leaders of the Red Brigade in Italy, Korean generals, South American politicians, American mobsters and a world-wide gaggle of businessmen.

Some were associates, though most were marks.

SCENE

Mel Weinberg, wearing a coolie hat, stands in the back of a pickup truck jammed with similarly attired Chinese laborers as it climbs out of Macao into Red China. Red guards chat with the driver at the border and casually walk around the truck peering contemptuously at its human cargo. Weinberg groans inwardly and wonders, "Why the fuck did I ever get into this?" The soldiers wave the truck on and it slowly chugs through the countryside, dropping off its passengers. Weinberg is finally standing alone as the truck wheezes to a stop behind a remote farmhouse. He dismounts and his guide takes him inside to reveal a secret factory where workers are stamping out counterfeit U.S. gold coins in various denominations, all of them marked with dates in the early 1900s. Thinking only of the value of gold (the market was still low), Weinberg shrugs off the offer of a truckload and pays a small amount for a few coins to bring home as souvenirs. Arriving back in Hong Kong, he makes a casual call to an American coin dealer and learns the coins are valuable collectors' items because of their rare dates. Frantically, he calls Macao, trying to locate his guide. He has disappeared. "What a schmuck I am," groans Weinberg. "I coulda retired on a truckload."

SCENE

Weinberg is sitting in an Italian cave that overlooks the sea. The cave is floored with thick rugs. Weinberg sits at an exquisitely set dining table with Lady Diane and a crippled man with braces on both legs. An impeccably attired waiter, sniffing at Weinberg's request for pizza, serves entrées of veal scallopini à la Marsala. Farther down the cave, a pianist plays Italian love songs. The cave belongs to Anthony, the crippled man, whom Weinberg calls Squeaky. He is the son of a wealthy Italian contractor and is a leading fund-raiser for the terrorist Red Brigade. Anthony's legs were ruined in an accident at a secret Rome bomb factory operated by the brigade. Weinberg keeps him supplied, for $5,000 each, with blank certificates of deposit from offshore banks, which Anthony uses to raise much more money for the brigade. Anthony's translator is Mario, his omnipresent bodyguard. Weinberg gazes around approvingly, lifts a wineglass to his host and says, "Hey, Squeaky. Bein' a commie bomb-thrower ain't such a bad line of work."

The packages that Weinberg handled at London were as varied as the people. Weinberg scammed one mark while pretending to interest the Mexican government in plans to build a Disneyland in Tampico. On another occasion he sent Host to Korea to talk to several Korean generals who wanted a loan to build a sumptuous whorehouse just outside of Seoul.

It was one of the few deals on which Weinberg didn't make money. After Host arrived in Korea to prospect the package, Weinberg didn't hear from him for two months. When his helper finally called, Weinberg ordered him back to New York. "The bum spent two months on his back sampling the merchandise instead of makin' money," Weinberg complained.

The highlight of his career with London Investors, according to Weinberg, was his fleecing tour of South America in 1976. Within a month's time in South America he had netted $200,000, having nearly been jailed in Bolivia, and being "laid so often I was walking bow-legged."

Key to the South American scam was a wiry little Bolivian hustler named Mariano Pacheco, who lived in Brazil and was a Latin American counterpart of Mel Weinberg. Early in 1976, Pacheco walked into Weinberg's Melville, Long Island, office and told him that he wanted to be his exclusive agent in South and Central America. He had, he said, a string of other commission agents, known in the trade as five percenters, located in nearly every country south of Mexico. Overjoyed, Weinberg equipped Pacheco with a letter of authorization, business cards, a stack of letterheads and sent him back home.

Pacheco churned so many customers that London was overwhelmed with inquiries from prospective marks in Latin America. Spanish names became familiar on the Telex: Carlos Walter Higzy Rivero of La Paz; Calso Castedo and Maestanza Angarill of Santa Cruz, Interior Minister Jorge Espan Smith of Bolivia, Ivan Mesias Lehu of Santiago, and others from Brazil, Paraguay and Nicaragua.

Pacheco asked Weinberg to come to Latin America and close front-end deals with more than sixty prospects that he had lined up, and sent three round-trip first-class air tickets for Weinberg, Lou Host and a friend of Weinberg's who had been invited to join the tour. Pacheco wrote Weinberg that the Bolivian prospects were so eager to see him that they had financed the entire trip. Weinberg was just as eager to go. In less than a month Pacheco had sent him $60,000 in advance fees. South America, obviously, was the land of bilk and money.

Weinberg dropped Host off in Brazil and went on with his other friend to meet Pacheco in Bolivia. After landing in Santa Cruz, Weinberg and his companion were taken by limousine to the Holiday Inn, only to notice that it was surrounded by soldiers. "Probably another one of them fuckin' revolutions," Weinberg snorted to his pal as they entered the lobby to register. He signed the registry card with a flourish and handed it to the clerk, who peered at it and nodded to an army officer posted nearby.

The officer tapped Weinberg on the shoulder and told him in very precise English that he and his friend were to go to their rooms and remain there.

"Why?" asked Weinberg with a smile.

"Because, for now, you are my prisoners," snapped the officer. "You are a suspected swindler."

There is a Yiddish expression which, roughly translated, says, "On a thief's head, the hat burns." A prominent New York labor racketeer defined it this way: "I get a subpoena to appear before the grand jury and I'm sitting on a wooden bench outside the grand jury room waiting to get called in. I know I'm not an honest man. I'm not asking myself why I'm here. I'm asking myself, which one have they got me for?"

Despite his Jewish background, Weinberg's knowledge of Yiddish is limited to words like *schmaltz* and *schmuck,* expressions common to all New Yorkers. But the mythical hat burned on his head that night as he sat alone in his room at the Santa Cruz Holiday Inn. He knew he was a swindler, but he hadn't yet swindled anyone in Bolivia. Where had he slipped up? Did they shoot decent hard-working swindlers in South America?

He got the answers early the next morning when he was led into one of the hotel conference rooms. Approximately thirty glowering businessmen, all Bolivians, sat expectantly in their chairs. A high-ranking government official, who was running the meeting, motioned Weinberg to a chair near the head of the table. Looking around, Weinberg noticed Pacheco, his head bowed, sitting nearby.

The government official got to the point quickly. "Mr. Weinberg. These other gentlemen here and I were most eager to do business with you. When Mr. Pacheco came to each of us privately and asked us to advance money for your plane fare and that of your assistants, each of us willingly did so. But, you must understand, Bolivia is a small nation. We have all talked to each other. We have discovered that each and every one of us has given the money to Mr. Pacheco for your tickets. Surely, you and your assistants do not need ninety round-trip tickets?"

Weinberg did some fast mental calculations. Each of the first-class tickets with intermediate stops was worth about $2,000. That totaled $180,000 for ninety tickets, minus $6,000 for Weinberg's, his friend's and Host's tickets. That left Pacheco with $174,000. That sonuvabitch Pacheco hadn't only swindled the Bolivians, he had swindled Mel

Weinberg. Didn't the schmuck realize that these guys were gonna talk to each other?

He glared over at Pacheco, who wouldn't meet his eyes. Then he went into an act that can only be described as pure Weinberg. He rose from his chair, quickly assuming the expression of shocked hurt befitting an honest banker who has just uncovered a thieving cashier. "Gentlemen," he said, "no one is more amazed and angered to learn of this than I. I trusted this man to be my representative and he has destroyed my reputation and my business." He scowled at Pacheco. "Look at him. He won't even look at me. Pacheco! What did you do with this money?"

He posed the question confidently, knowing that he himself hadn't gotten the money. Pacheco squirmed in his chair. Weinberg read his thoughts. Pacheco undoubtedly suspected that Weinberg was an American mobster. He knew that he had scammed Weinberg and now shuddered at the thought of his body, air-conditioned by underworld bullets and lying at the bottom of the ocean in a cement sports jacket. Deciding he was better off in the hands of his own countrymen, he confessed he had scammed the money.

Weinberg had relied on what he calls the "hope factor" when he fingered Pacheco. He knew that the government officials and businessmen were far more angry over the fact that they might not get huge loans because he was a fraud than they were about losing $6,000 each. Now he could see the hope return to their eyes. This man Weinberg has been betrayed just like we have, their eyes seemed to say. He is for real, and if he is for real, so are those huge loans that we have been promised from his European banks.

They clustered around him, apologizing for their unfounded suspicions. A few of the more emotional ones hugged him in an *abrazo*. He was most understanding and kind. It was almost impossible, he agreed, to get good help nowadays. A week later he left Bolivia with nearly $50,000 that he had scammed from government ministers and other businessmen in Santa Cruz and La Paz. "Honesty pays," he chortled.

To this day, Weinberg doesn't know what happened to Pacheco. "He's probably workin' off the dough he owes pickin' coffee beans on some goddamned plantation," he mused.

The rest of South America was a triumphal tour. In Paraguay Weinberg was the guest of a wealthy rancher who needed a $70 million loan for an irrigation project. Host, a pudgy New Yorker with horn-rimmed glasses, was fascinated with the gaucho life-style at the ranch. He started wearing a cowboy hat with his business suit and became a constant target for Weinberg's barbed humor.

Weinberg scammed the rancher for $100,000 in advance fees. He took another $40,000 out of São Paulo, $20,000 from Rio and another $20,000 from a Santiago businessman who needed a loan to run the Coca-Cola franchise in Chile. Now Weinberg faced the problem of getting more than $200,000 past U.S. Customs when he landed in Miami. He solved the problem quickly.

"I put all the money in my back pockets and I walked up to the customs guy at the Miami airport," he recalls. "He asked me if I had anything to declare. I said I had nothin' except for a coupla ceramic pots that I was carryin' in my hands. I'd picked them up in Bolivia so I would look like a tourist."

"He asked me if I had anything else," said Weinberg. "I said, no, no. I had my raincoat over my arm. I handed it to him. Then I took off my suit jacket and handed him the suit jacket. I'm literally throwin' my clothes at him. He backs up and says, 'Okay, okay, I believe you, I believe you.' That's how I walked into the country with $200,000 in my pockets."

Once back at the London Investors office in Melville, packages poured in from all over the world. Clients sat in the reception room and stared open-mouthed as Host and other staffers rushed back and forth answering phones, shouting orders and fighting for space at the Telex. They burbled contracts for tallow to Korea, shucked clams from Chile to Ghana, telephone equipment from New York to Rome. They talked easily about letters of commitment, standby loan guarantees, cash flows, depreciation and relative productivity.

It was still a learning time for Weinberg. He began to scan the financial pages of the *New York Times* and the *Wall Street Journal*, to follow the local news in *Newsday* and to absorb minidoses of world events from TV. He became adept at the language of finance and began to fashion his stalls from such current events as a printers' strike in London or a revolution in Lebanon.

He kept spending more, however, to maintain the illusion. Tristar Cars, Ltd., a car rental firm at Heathrow Airport outside London, was typical of the firms exposed to heavy doses of Weinberg's fast-buck philosophy. In a 1976 Telex message to London Investors in Melville, Tristar wrote:

"Your Mr. Weinberg is using credit facilities for chauffeur cars at the rate of 50 pounds per day and the present balance is 150 pounds and expected to reach 500 this week. As your company is not known to us, we should appreciate your advice of any special invoicing instructions and bank details for credit instructions." Host Telexed back a glowing reference for Weinberg and the firm.

Interestingly, Weinberg kept his own counsel and masked the true nature of his dealings even at London Investors. He saw no point in telling Lady Diane or even Lou Host that he was a swindler. "The less anyone knows, the better, even those closest to you," advises Weinberg. He was sure that Host knew, although there were moments when he had doubts. "Lou could be awful dumb at times," he said. "After all, it's not much of a jump from bein' a thievin' businessman to bein' an out-and-out-crook."

The peripatetic con man was almost constantly on the move, darting cross-country to various cities where his commission agents opened branch offices for London Investors. On these trips he used Lady Diane sparingly, reserving her for only the most important clients. "She was the salad dressing, the schmaltz," he explained. Unaware of the details of his business, in a sense she was also a victim of his illusion.

It was during one such trip to his Las Vegas branch office with Lady Diane that Weinberg was introduced to singer Wayne Newton. Newton, at the time, was in between fortunes and sought a loan to build a new ranch on land that he owned in Nevada. Weinberg was only too happy to take the package. But he only nicked Newton for $850. Soon Newton, Weinberg and Lady Diane became a threesome, though before long it was a twosome. Weinberg was too busy to notice the light in Lady Diane's eyes.

One afternoon, while Weinberg and Lady Diane were staying at the swank Balboa Club in Newport Beach, California, he saw Newton leaving her room. "I'm goin' back to New York, babe," Weinberg told her. "Either come with me or stay for him." Lady Diane accompanied Weinberg on his flight back to New York.

Although Weinberg had no way of knowing it at the time, three events took place while he was operating London Investors that would later play a vital part in the formation and execution of the FBI's Abscam investigation. The first was a casual brush with Meyer Lansky, the dyspeptic old crook who functions as a sort of House of Rothschild to organized crime. The second was a chance meeting in the first-class section of a Pan American 747 with a wealthy Arab businessman. And the third was a routine front-end swindle of a Pittsburgh real estate man named Lee Schlag.

It was Weinberg's casual relationship with the FBI as a tipster that indirectly put him on the other end of a telephone call from Lansky. Like many of the events in Weinberg's colorful life, the incident had a complex beginning. It started when Weinberg was asked by a fellow swindler from Huntington, Long Island, if he knew anyone interested in buying a stolen $100,000 U.S. Treasury note. Weinberg tipped his FBI contact, Special Agent Bill Roselli, who told him to play along with the deal.

One event followed another and several months later Weinberg found himself on the Caribbean island of St. Martin. He had taken Lady Diane with him for the sun and they stayed at the St. Martin Isle Casino and

Hotel, which was owned by an aging, wealthy American named Allen Goberman.

Goberman was afflicted with the naïve idea that anyone with enough money could own a casino without taking in the mob as a partner. He was being stolen blind and was deeply in debt. He was also smitten by Lady Diane and rushed her with flowers, gifts and unswerving attention.

Lady Diane was cordial but reserved, a posture that merely increased Goberman's wheezing ardor. Weinberg was in his usual pose as Lady Diane's business adviser so Goberman approached him for advice on how to thaw her reserve. "She really likes you, Allen," Weinberg confided. "But she thinks you're only after her money." Appalled that Lady Diane had him pegged as a fortune hunter, Goberman decided upon a spectacular demonstration of selflessness. He gave Lady Diane the hotel and casino, and she in turn passed the gift to Weinberg.

Weinberg beelined to the books and quickly discovered that Goberman's gift was not as magnanimous as it appeared. The operation was deeply in debt. Still, he thought, it was nice to own a hotel and casino and it might make a great prop for a swindle until the creditors snapped it away.

A few days later Weinberg got a telephone call from Miami. The caller identified himself as Meyer Lansky and mentioned enough about some of Weinberg's underworld friends to convince him that he was indeed talking to the withered mob financial wizard. Weinberg was advised by Lansky that he and his associates now owned the hotel and that Weinberg would be seeing a visitor from Las Vegas in a few days. Two days later an obvious hoodlum entered Weinberg's hotel office.

"Are you Weinberg, the owner?" he asked.

"Yeah," Weinberg gulped.

"Lemme see da stock certificates," ordered the hood.

Weinberg, his hands shaking, pushed them over the desk. The hoodlum ripped them up and threw them on the floor.

"Now you ain't the owner no more," he said.

Such was Weinberg's first brush with the legendary Meyer Lansky.

Weinberg's hasty retreat from St. Martin typifies his attitude toward the heavy hitters in organized crime. He has deep respect for them. "Con men don't carry guns," he explained. "We ain't out to hurt anybody, just to take some money. But when you talk about organized crime, you're talkin' about people who'd as soon whack you out as look at you. I don't play in that league. If they need a favor from me, they got it. I always want them to have good thoughts about me."

The second Abscam-related event came when Weinberg and Lady Diane were homeward bound from Europe in the first-class section of a Pan American jetliner. They ascended to the lounge for dinner and were seated at a table with an elderly, sophisticated Arab who introduced himself as Kambir Abdul Rahman of Beirut and Nice. He was a delightful, obviously wealthy old gentleman and Weinberg warmed to him at once.

He was staying at the Plaza in New York and Weinberg insisted that he and Lady Diane drive him to his hotel in their chauffeured limousine. During the ride, the Arab told Weinberg that his wife had given him an order to bring home American towels. Weinberg, a true expert on where to buy the best, insisted that the Arab allow his chauffeur to pick him up at the hotel the next morning and take him to Fortunoff's on Long Island, whose selection of towels was both varied and reasonable. It was done.

A few days later Weinberg and Lady Diane accompanied the Arab back to Kennedy Airport in their limousine. Trailing behind were two more limousines hired by Weinberg to carry the Arab's newly bought towels.

Weinberg's impulsive generosity toward his new Arab friend was not unusual. He is a proud crook and his craft is swindling, but he is capable of warm personal relationships, occasional honest dealings and even a rough form of loyalty toward people that he decides are "stand-up guys."

Just one year later Weinberg and the FBI chose the name Kambir Abdul Rahman for one of the two mythical Arab sheikhs that they used in Abscam.

The single event that finally made Abscam possible, however, did not occur until 1977. It was then that the law finally caught up with Mel Weinberg.

For years Weinberg had never been particularly concerned about the law. Advance-fee schemes were deemed civil cases and when marks complained, they were usually referred by law enforcement to the Better Business Bureau. But times were changing. The post-Watergate FBI had dropped its preoccupation with stolen cars and bank robberies and had begun to concentrate on organized and white-collar crime. Weinberg was too busy making money to read the handwriting on the wall of London Investors.

The first hint came from the office of the New York State Attorney General in July 1976. A deputy Attorney General wrote Weinberg at London Investors demanding to know exactly what Weinberg had done to earn the advanced fee he had scammed from an irate New Jersey real estate broker. Surmising that the Attorney General's office was staffed by political hacks who wanted to do as little work as possible, Weinberg wrote a long, devious answer. The matter was dropped.

The earlier Schlag case, on the other hand, carried a hint of trouble almost from its start. It began routinely enough when a steerer directed Schlag to Weinberg for a loan. The Pittsburgh real estate man needed $1.9 million to buy a Pennsylvania dairy firm. Weinberg checked out the package and wrote Schlag in August of 1975, telling him that the advance fee for appraisal and processing the loan would be $3,564. He advised Schlag that after the loan package was sent to Europe there would be a thirty- to forty-five-day waiting period before the bank made a decision.

Schlag sent the check on September 10, 1975, stating that he understood from Weinberg's letter that he would have a firm loan commitment from the bank within fifteen days. Weinberg promptly replied that the original waiting period still stood. At the end of September, he asked Schlag for a financial statement and other information. Two weeks later, Schlag asked for a copy of the proposal Weinberg had sent to the offshore bank in London.

It was unusual for a mark to ask for a copy of the loan proposal. Weinberg simply ignored Schlag's letter. But, by November 21, Schlag started to threaten. He complained he still hadn't gotten a copy of the proposal and expressed the hope that the loan would come through immediately. If it didn't, he added, "I will find it necessary to establish a firm and complete investigation as to the reasons for this refusal." But Schlag was still hoping. He concluded with the wish that "we may always be the best of friends now and in the future."

Weinberg had been giving Schlag the standard stall treatment, but Schlag was not reacting like a standard mark. Weinberg decided to throw a scare into Schlag and then quickly hold out another carrot. On December 9, 1975, he wrote Schlag indignantly that the whole process had been delayed because his investigation had revealed that Schlag had given him a false financial statement and his staff had to rework the entire loan application before sending it to Europe. He said that if Schlag kept up his harassment, he would drop the entire application and sue Schlag for the extra expense to London Investors caused by his "falsification of a financial statement."

The letter to Schlag reflected Weinberg's firm belief that Schlag's eagerness for the loan would overcome his suspicions and the threat to sue him would shut him up. The carrot came the next day in another letter to Schlag by Weinberg. In this letter he merely apologized for the delay, blaming some unnamed errors in the application "that had to be rectified." He said that the package was now in front of the bank's board of directors and "we should have an answer shortly." Early in January 1976 he again wrote Schlag telling him: "You will also have a definite yes or no answer regarding the approval of your loan no later than February 15, 1976."

But Schlag had already turned the matter over to his lawyers. And when the bank letter came declining Schlag's loan, they turned the case over to the Pittsburgh office of the FBI. Later that year, after seizing the files of London Investors, FBI agents emerged with more of Weinberg's current scam. A Federal grand jury in Pittsburgh indicted him in February 1977 for wire fraud, mail fraud and conspiracy.

Worse still, Weinberg learned, the Federal government had an arrest warrant out for Lady Diane. He moved Diane to an apartment complex in a large southern city that was used by organized crime as a hideaway. Favors done for the wise guys were favors returned.

Diane, totally unaware of what was happening, grudgingly accepted Weinberg's excuse that she was being kept temporarily in seclusion for business reasons. But time was running out. His lawyer, Vince Cuti, had powerful political connections but they didn't extend to the Federal government. Weinberg's wife stood by him loyally through these months, mothering his bruised ego and optimistically assuring him that everything would turn out all right. But it was almost impossible to make a living with the government looking over his shoulder and he sensed that each day the FBI was getting closer and closer to finding Diane.

For the first time in his life, Weinberg knew that there was no way out. Nobody could be bought. No political connection could fix things. Nobody could be conned. He had no place to hide.

Late in the summer of 1977, Weinberg called some of his old contacts in the FBI. He would surrender Lady Diane. She had never known, he explained, that he was using her as part of a swindle. Weinberg then did something he had never done before. He begged. "When I give Lady Diane to you," he pleaded, "treat her like a lady."

He called Diane and asked her to meet him in Florida. He told her what he really was and what had happened to the two of them. She was shocked, angry and, when she realized the full import of what he was telling her, terrified. She began sobbing. Weinberg gently took her into his arms and softly said, "Don't cry, babe. I'll make everything all right."

On October 7, 1977, Mel Weinberg stood before a Federal judge in Pittsburgh and pleaded guilty. He was sentenced to three years in prison. He had agreed to the plea arrangement after Federal prosecutors had privately agreed to drop all charges against Lady Diane.

TAPE SIX

Weinberg: The way I got caught was, I gotta explain. They wanted me the worst way. I was getting too big. I was hurting a lotta people and I stepped on a couple of politicians in Pittsburgh. So Pittsburgh came after me. It was hard for them to prove, because I never really gave a commitment by mail. If I wanted to give a person a commitment letter, I'd send it by plane. That way you don't violate the law on mail fraud. Eastern Airlines has a plane that delivers and it would cost you $37 from Florida to New York or even the West Coast. That's the way I sent it. When we used to get our certificates of deposit that got printed up for us in Puerto Rico or overseas, we always had them sent by plane. . . . But my thing was to get the girl off, because I did her wrong. You can only be so much of a heel in this world. So my deal was that all charges were dropped against her and I would cop a plea. They grabbed it because they knew that if I fought 'em in court I'd beat 'em. You gotta remember that half the people that brought in these loans was lawyers. . . . The feds have cracked down quite a bit on swindlers; guys in the business now have to be more careful. But the feds will never knock us out of the box. I know one con man right now, he's in jail for pullin' a sting.

He's runnin' a swindle right from the jail. He's sellin' bullet-proof cars to the Arabs and he's got guys on the outside backin' him up. He's got $300,000 on deposit with his attorney right now. That's what I mean. No matter what the government does, as long as there's a sucker, there'll be a sting man.

5

An Artful Deal

I have always depended on my mouth to keep me out of trouble. I'm not an extra tough guy. I can handle myself, but I found out with a mouth you can do more.   —MEL WEINBERG

Gusting rain pelted the windows of the midtown Manhattan building housing the offices of the Federal Bureau of Investigation. It was mid-spring, 1977, nearly six months before Mel Weinberg would admit to fraud in a Pittsburgh Federal court, and supervising agent John Good sat hunched in deep concentration over his desk.

A sandy-haired man with blue eyes that always seemed tired, Good was part of a new breed that was slowly, inexorably, assuming control of the FBI. During the long reign of J. Edgar Hoover, power within the Bureau was almost exclusively a WASP perquisite. Masonic rings, tautly knotted ties and unswerving devotion to the Bureau way as articulated by the Director were essential to ambitious young agents.

Times, however, were changing. Now it was the turn of the big-city ethnics, particularly the Irish. They were the upwardly mobile sons of bricklayers, policemen, politicians, firemen and mail carriers and were largely the product of such Jesuit colleges as Fordham, St. Peter's, Fairfield, Boston College, Holy Cross. Honed in the discipline of Aristotelian logic, imbued with a sense of morality, possessed of both flexibility and imagination, they filled the Bureau's new ranks.

Good was one of them. He was a native of the Bronx, lace-curtain Irish, a graduate of Fordham, the son of a retired FBI agent: in fact, one of six children, five of whom had worked for the Bureau. He was careful, methodical, totally dedicated to his work. But he disliked and frequently ignored the dress code, spent more time on the street than in the office, and was prone to use new approaches to old problems. This latter trait occasionally ran contrary to "the book," the standard FBI way of doing things.

He was, however, married to the Bureau. After sixteen years on the job, he still found it exciting and rewarding. Hours didn't count and his creative, energetic approach had churned an impressive wake as he apprenticed his way through FBI offices in Springfield, Illinois; Monterey, California; and El Paso, Texas. Now, after handling a series of special squads in the New York office, he was assistant to the supervising agent. Totally result-oriented, Good fit the classic corporate definition of a bottom-line man.

It had been a long day and Good sighed when he looked at the stack of paperwork teetering on the lip of his IN basket. He hated paperwork and openly envied the brick agents who spent most of their time in the field. He glanced through the glass wall that marked off his small office from the sea of desks beyond. Most of the desks were deserted. He checked his watch. The stainless-steel Pulsar read 9:00 P.M. No wonder the office was empty. Where the hell had the hours gone?

He pulled a memo from the top of the stack. It was interoffice from Pittsburgh, routinely sent to Good because it involved charges against someone from the New York area. The Bureau had been concentrating on white-collar crime and Good was looking for informants, people involved in white-collar crime who could help make some criminal cases. He studied the heading on the memo he held in his hand: SUBJECT: MELVIN WEINBERG.

He read on. Arrested on Long Island on a warrant issued from Pittsburgh, a swindler specializing in advance-fee scams, has cooperated with FBI in the past, willing to plead guilty and cooperate to protect his girlfriend.

Good thoughtfully tapped his pencil against the memo. Before being chained to a desk by his own ambition, he had been expert on the selection and development of informants. It was a tricky business. Some promised miracles if only the FBI would give them a break. But they gave as little as possible. Others used their informant status as a license to commit new crimes. More than one good agent had blown his career because he had become too friendly with an informant to keep the relationship in clear perspective.

The files revealed, however, that Weinberg had always produced in the past. He was obviously up to his neck in white-collar crime and had extensive contacts throughout the world. His base of operations was New York and Long Island. Why not give it a shot? Good scrawled a notation on the memo ordering Myron Fuller, one of his agents, to travel to Pittsburgh for an interview with Weinberg.

Abscam was born at that precise moment.

What would later become the most sordid scandal in Congressional history and the FBI's most redeeming investigation was conceived as a scrawled note. The idea was still formless, a toss of the dice, targetless. The decision was so mundane that Good tossed the memo into his OUT basket and dismissed it from his mind.

Wounded Congressmen and obfuscating defense lawyers would later thunder that Abscam had been created to ensnare members of the legislative branch. They would ascribe a potpouri of motives to the sinister plot. Some would charge that it was an attempt by the executive branch to regain the dominance over Congress lost in the debacle of the Nixon presidency. Others would say that it was a right-wing smear of liberal Congressmen.

The record reflects, however, that Abscam began as a simple exercise in catching crooks. The fact that it netted a U.S. Senator and seven Congressmen during the last six months of its two-year existence is merely validation of the widely held premise that if you set out to catch crooks, you will often catch Congressmen.

Good looked at the remaining pile of paperwork and decided to hell with it. Tomorrow was another day. He tugged at the hated necktie, shrugged on his sports jacket, bid goodnight to the duty agent, and walked out to the elevator. He still had a seventy-five-minute drive along the dark, rain-slicked Long Island Expressway to his home in East Islip. His wife and children would probably be in bed. He'd make a sandwich, catch the eleven o'clock news and crash-dive. He was really bushed.

A few days later Agent Fuller called Good from Pittsburgh to report that Weinberg was anxious to deal. He wanted nothing for himself, just legal absolution for a woman he called Lady Diane. As matters stood, the case against her wasn't very strong. Good, for his part, wasn't taking any chances.

"Tell Weinberg we'll do what we can for her, if he delivers," he told Fuller. "But let him know that we don't produce unless he delivers first. This guy's a professional swindler and the Bureau isn't going to wind up as one of his marks."

Fuller called back later. Weinberg would cooperate.

Free on bail, Weinberg returned to Long Island. Good assigned Fuller and Agent Jack McCarthy of the Bureau's Suffolk County office to handle him on a day-to-day basis. Good gave them a general target at which to point Weinberg. The Bureau, he said, was interested in any kind of white-collar fraud. He ticked off some of the possibilities: stolen art, forged or stolen securities, gold certificates and certificates of deposit, advanced-fee scams, counterfeit money, bankruptcy bust-outs. It was a long list but certainly familiar terrain to Weinberg.

The assignment of McCarthy and Fuller to Weinberg had mixed results. Both men were solid, experienced agents and their work with Weinberg over the next year would result in major fraud arrests and provide a solid foundation for the later phases of Abscam. But there are very few people in this world who can control Mel Weinberg and make him like it. He tolerated Fuller but quickly grew to dislike McCarthy. It was largely a matter of personality and style.

A pleasant, gray-haired man, McCarthy exuded the Calvinistic attitudes peculiar to some Irish Catholics. He had spent a lifetime fighting crooks, compromises and corruption. No matter what Weinberg professed, he was still a crook as far as McCarthy was concerned and had to be watched carefully. Both McCarthy and Fuller, who was less rigid, were book men. There was the FBI way and the wrong way. They were careful, conservative, cautious. Neither would have made it as a swindler in the outside world.

Weinberg, by contrast, was a highly volatile informant, disliking orders and preferring to work alone. His expensive and flamboyant style was anathema to his supervisors. Further, McCarthy and Fuller quickly saw that he was shifty and quick-witted, that his stock-in-trade was the lie, the stall, the convincing half-truth. They recognized that he was egotistical, thrived on admiration, despised rules, scorned conventional morality and regarded crookdom as a proud and much maligned profession.

Weinberg for his part also saw nothing incompatible about working for the FBI and making a quick buck on the side.

The two agents and Weinberg launched the project with a talk alongside the swimming pool at Weinberg's Central Islip home in the early summer of 1977. They finally decided to have Weinberg focus most of his attention on two local swindlers with whom he had worked in the past.

The selected targets were Fred Pro, a New York front-end scammer who had once owned his own offshore bank, and Joe Trocchio, a veteran hoodlum with ties to organized crime who occasionally provided muscle for Pro's operation. Trocchio, the more important and dangerous of the two, was awaiting trial in neighboring Nassau County on charges of peddling $150,000 in stolen Swiss travelers checks. Four potential witnesses in the case had already been murdered.

Weinberg regarded Pro as just another swindler, but he was worried about working on Trocchio. "He has heavy friends, the kinda people I don't like to cross," Weinberg explained. But the two agents were insistent. "I figured if I hadda do it to get Diane off the hook, I'd just have to do it," said Weinberg. "When you're workin' for the government, they don't take a pounda flesh, they take a ton."

Each of the agents had his own idea about how Weinberg should begin, but the cocky swindler was determined to do it his own way. He would pretend to go back into the advanced-fee business using the European bank ruse. But he proposed adding a new gimmick.

"I been readin' the papers about all this OPEC shit," said Weinberg. "Everybody thinks all Arabs are loaded with dough. Just before I got locked up, I started tellin' marks that I had a coupla Arab guys with dough to invest. People were bustin' down my door to give me packages. I'm gonna push that with these guys." The agents agreed and the Arab aspect was added to the emerging Abscam scenario.

When the two agents left for home after that first meeting, Weinberg remained at the pool, puffing on his cigar and thinking. McCarthy and Fuller obviously didn't trust him. He could understand their caution, but it rankled. Although both agents were polite and interested, he could sense their disdain. He felt like a bug under a microscope. He could handle that. He could easily control the relationship by convincing the agents that his ideas were their ideas.

But, if they didn't trust him now, why should they trust any future information that he might give them? And, if this were the case, how would he ever protect Diane? He ambled into the house and rummaged through boxes until he found an old Norelco tape recorder with a telephone attachment. He was resolved to tape every key conversation in the investigation. Only in this way, he was convinced, would he be able to prove that he was telling the truth.

This decision, conceived in equal parts by distrust and desperation, was the genesis of the constant tape-recording that became Abscam's trademark.

A few days later, Weinberg had his sting going strong and his Norelco working overtime. One of his first moves was to reach Trocchio, the sixty-three-year-old tough guy. Both men talked about their impending trials. Both hoped that they would get probation and both agreed that now, more than ever, they needed to make plenty of money quickly. Weinberg then set the hook.

> *Trocchio:* And I would like you to meet with them [business acquaintances]. Maybe we could do somethin' and meet easily.
> *Weinberg:* Yeah. We could do somethin'. Uhh, in fact, I got somethin' very good cookin' right now.
> *Trocchio:* Oh yeah?
> *Weinberg:* Yeah, I got, uhh, remember that friend of mine, that Arab I was dealing with?
> *Trocchio:* Yeah.
> *Weinberg:* Ha, well, he sent some people into town, 'cause he heard I was in trouble and may need some bread.
> *Trocchio:* Uhhmm.
> *Weinberg:* Uhh, for investments.
> *Trocchio:* Hm, hey, I got two deals. I got one deal, uh . . . which I'll tell you that'll make your head spin around. . . .

One of Trocchio's deals involved a Long Island firm known as Brookhaven Mortgages. The firm had its offices in the same building on Route 110 that had housed Weinberg's London Investors, now defunct. Trocchio told Weinberg that he and Fred Pro were using forged securities to buy into the firm. Then they would use Brookhaven to wash money for two of New York's largest crime families. Eventually they would loot its assets.

Weinberg told Fuller and McCarthy about Trocchio's plans for Brookhaven. He backed it up with the tapes. They were impressed. Within a few days Weinberg introduced Fuller to Trocchio and Fred Pro as one of his business associates. After that, the FBI was able to monitor step by step the attempted takeover of Brookhaven. Trocchio meanwhile offered to supply Weinberg with counterfeit $50 bills and certified checks drawn on a large New York bank. Weinberg asked for samples and Trocchio directed him to come to his house in rural Manorville, Long Island, that night.

SCENE

It is a dark, moonless night. Weinberg cruises his Lincoln slowly down a country road. He stops in front of a large house, flanked by a junkyard. A man stands in front of the house: Joe Trocchio. The two men talk softly. "The samples are in an envelope," says Trocchio. "The envelope is fastened to the inside wall of the rabbit hutch behind the house. Go back and get it." Weinberg walks to the rear of the house, thinking that Trocchio is clever enough not actually to handle the counterfeit samples just in case Weinberg is part of a police sting. He finds the hutch, opens the wire gate and reaches in for the envelope. Something chomps down on his hand and he shouts in surprise and pain. Peering into the hutch, he sees a very large rabbit. "You sonuvabitchin' bastard," he growls as he boots the rabbit out of the hutch. The rabbit hops away and Weinberg pockets the envelope. He goes out front to Trocchio and complains, "Ya schmuck. Ya didn't tell me ya had a fuckin' guard-rabbit back there." Trocchio runs off in frantic pursuit of what he describes as his prize rabbit. "Prize, my ass," Weinberg mutters as he drives away.

Though Weinberg professes to like animals, there are only two types that he really has use for: those that are edible or respectful or both. He likes tail-wagging dogs, tolerates farm stock, ignores birds, and has no use for the rest of the animal kingdom.

"Everybody wants to save tigers and alligators," he complains. "Those bastards eat ya, if you give 'em the chance. Who wants them? As far as I'm concerned, if you can't eat it, kill it."

It was another kind of killing, however, that Trocchio discussed with Weinberg several days later. His pal Fred Pro, he said, was outraged and embarrassed. Pro the swindler had been swindled by a supposed mark from Cleveland named Lucio. Pro wanted a mob hit man to murder Lucio and get his money back. He had asked Trocchio to make the arrangements, but Trocchio had no connections in the Midwest.

Patiently, Weinberg extracted the details from Trocchio. Pro, who ran his front-end scam from a plush Manhattan office, had arranged to take a loan from Lucio and his group on some properties that Pro supposedly owned. His ownership papers were actually forgeries. He agreed to pay the Lucio group $30,000 in advance fees for a loan of several million on the imaginary properties.

When the time came to pay Lucio's fees, however, the only money Pro had on hand was an out-of-town check for $110,000 that he had just gotten on another deal. It would take up to ten days for his bank to clear the check and give him the cash. Lucio's lawyer said that he could get it cleared at his own bank in forty-eight hours. He said he would deduct Lucio's $30,000 and deliver the $80,000 balance in cash to Pro's office. Pro agreed. But Lucio and his friends banked the check in Cleveland and kept all the money.

Pro wasn't only angry over being swindled, said Trocchio. Lucio was telling everyone in Cleveland how he had scammed Pro and word was drifting back to New York. Lucio had no respect. Could Weinberg have him whacked out? Weinberg pondered a moment and said that he knew a Midwest contract killer named Jim Pagett, J.P. for short. Weinberg volunteered to contact Pagett.

Disguising his voice, Weinberg called back Trocchio and identified himself as Jim Pagett. He said that the price of the hit would be $10,000—$5,000 in advance and the balance when Lucio was killed. Trocchio agreed to send the money to J.P. through Weinberg.

TAPE SEVEN

Weinberg: I go to Trocchio's house to collect the money and the bum only gives me $2,500 in advance instead of the $5,000. He gives a drawin' of the hotel this guy owns, what his car looks like, where he eats, where he hangs out. Everything a killer needs. I took the $2,500 and call back Trocchio a week later and tell him J.P. won't do nothin' till he gets the other $2,500. Trocchio gets pissed and says, "I'll send out a hit on him." I said go ahead. Then I called Fred Pro and told him I was J.P. I said, "Pro, you didn't keep your promise, you promised five grand in advance and five grand afterward. I only got $2,500." Pro swore up and down that he'd given Trocchio $10,000 for me. Trocchio was cheatin' Pro and holdin' out on me. That's the kinda people these are. There's no honesty anymore.

McCarthy and Fuller were concerned that Trocchio might later turn to another hit man. They arranged for the FBI's Cleveland office to tell Lucio he was a murder target and that Pro was behind the plot. Lucio immediately called Pro and told him that the Federal government had warned him about the contract on his life. Pro called Trocchio in a panic and Trocchio asked Weinberg to meet him again at his house.

When Weinberg arrived, Trocchio confided, "Mel, we gotta leak. The FBI told Lucio there's a contract on him. Can we trust J.P.?"

"Absolutely," lied Weinberg. "J.P.'s a mob hitter. He'd never talk to the feds. Maybe there's a tap on Pro's phone or yours. Maybe they found out that way."

Weinberg persuaded Trocchio that his tap theory was true. Trocchio was plainly worried. "Tell J.P. he doesn't have to kill him, okay?" said Trocchio. "We still want our money back, but it's okay if J.P. just breaks his legs a little."

Weeks passed. Trocchio asked Weinberg whether J.P. had made any progress. Weinberg shook his head. "He's pissed," he said. "He said you guys held out on his money. He wants nothin' more to do with ya. I ain't gonna push him either. I'm not gettin' anything outta this and he'd whack me out in a minute if he gets mad at me." Trocchio shrugged his acceptance of the inevitable and dropped the subject.

Trocchio's loyalty to Fred Pro was short-lived. Less than a week after he and Weinberg had their final discussion about J.P., Trocchio called with another proposition. Pro was doing so well with his front-end scams, Trocchio complained, that he was acting like a big shot. Trocchio wanted Weinberg to send a muscle man to Pro's office and "slap him around a little bit." The hood was to tell Pro that he had been sent by Trocchio. Trocchio said he would walk in the day after and take over Pro's operation, splitting it with Weinberg.

McCarthy and Fuller checked with John Good. What part, they asked, should the Bureau play in this? Good assigned Ernie Haridopolos, a tall, broad-shouldered FBI agent, to act as Weinberg's professional slugger. After several meetings with Weinberg and Trocchio, Haridopolos visited Pro's New York office.

Weinberg had urged the FBI to go along with Trocchio's scheme and let Haridopolos work over Pro. "He's a sissy," Weinberg advised. "One shot to the gut and he'll turn in everyone he knows." But word came back down the chain of command that Good wanted no rough stuff. Haridopolos was to lean on Pro very lightly.

The agent told Pro when he arrived at his office that he had come to take over the business for Trocchio. Pro, awed by the agent's size, but reassured by his polite approach, said that he wouldn't allow Haridopolos to take over the business, but he could work for Pro. While the agent pretended to consider the offer, Pro showed him where he kept all of his secret office records. Haridopolos declined the job offer and left.

A week later, FBI agents, armed with search warrants, raided Pro's office. Unerringly, they went to the hiding places where he kept his packages. The swindler was stunned by the Bureau's efficiency, totally unaware that Haridopolos, the friendly thug, had given the agents a detailed map of where they should look. Within three months, Weinberg had given the Bureau solid cases against both Trocchio and Pro.

As fishermen know, once a net is cast, there is no controlling the quantity or quality of what it traps. Weinberg, once back in action, served up a veritable smorgasbord of potential fraud cases for the FBI. Good, by now, had been given his own FBI command, the twenty-three-agent Suffolk office. He had already launched some of his best agents on a successful investigation of the country's billion-dollar sewer scandal. But he wanted to keep the pressure on white-collar crime. Through McCarthy, Good relayed a request to Weinberg. Would he follow through on the cases that he was churning up?

Weinberg agreed to work if the FBI paid his expenses. Good faced an immediate problem. If the Federal government indicted Pro and Trocchio, it would have to surface Weinberg as a witness. This would blow Weinberg's cover and kill any chance he might have of developing the other cases. Tom Puccio, Director of the Eastern District Federal Strike Force, agreed to hold off indictments until the other cases were completed. Neither he nor Good could know that these were the first of a long series of indictments that would have to be stalled as Abscam widened and probed the innards of crime and corruption.

Abscam had no name at this point. Good put Weinberg on a limited expense account. The Bureau had allocated $32,000 to conduct the white-collar crime sting. The FBI supervisor figured that if he kept expenses down, he could get at least eight months out of the project.

Bureau cost accountants had not reckoned on Mel Weinberg, however. He had spent as much as $32,000 in a single week when London Investors was in its prime. He had done it all for the illusion. He had spent without a moment's thought or hesitation; no vouchers or receipts required. He saw no reason why he should operate any differently as an agent of the richest, most powerful nation in the world. Eventually he prevailed. Two years later the government's bill for Abscam would total well over $500,000. But that was later.

Weinberg complained to McCarthy that he was sick of operating out of his house. Besides, he said, it was dangerous for Marie and their son. If the government wanted him to act like a big swindler, he would need a big office, expensive furniture, secretaries, and at least one Telex. He said that he was embarrassed using his own tape recorder and buying his own tapes. He was also putting too much mileage on his Lincoln. It was time, he complained, for the government to pony up.

McCarthy relayed Weinberg's demands to Good. "This guy's got to be out of his mind," Good moaned. "He wants to spend $30,000 just for office furniture. We can't justify that kind of outlay." Good, however, got in a supply of tapes and secondhand recorders. Weinberg promptly complained that the recorders were old and faulty. He had a point. "In the beginning this investigation didn't have a very high priority," Good concedes. "We were using junk."

Confronting Weinberg, McCarthy told him that Good was exploring possibilities for an office. He ordered Weinberg to keep working with the available equipment, vetoed his other spending ideas, and told him to hold down his expenses. Weinberg was totally unfamiliar with the Federal budgeting process. He decided that McCarthy was cheapskating the project to win favor with his bosses. He fixed on the idea and his resentment against McCarthy grew stronger. McCarthy's personal frugality served to confirm Weinberg's impression.

Nevertheless, Weinberg kept working. During the years that he had operated as a bona fide swindler, Weinberg had derived enormous satisfaction at outwitting his marks. He found it even more rewarding to beat his fellow swindlers. "It was sorta like the Super Bowl of scam," he explained. "I was playin' against the best and I was winnin'."

Although Weinberg dangled his bogus Arab investors at potential targets, he continued to use the mythical European bank contacts that had been his stock-in-trade with Swiss Bank Associates and London Investors. Lady Diane, still his mistress, was no longer part of the scam. But it still worked.

Weinberg's home phone rang constantly. A blind stock swindler from Manhattan was offering forged bank certificates. A New York–Miami group had an offshore bank on Antigua and was willing to supply millions in certificates of deposit for 8 percent of their face value. Weinberg fielded them all. In some instances, where targets could be nailed and indicted and tried without surfacing Weinberg, the FBI made arrests. The other cases were quietly shelved for later action.

Weinberg knew that when Abscam ended and he took the stand as a witness, his days as a con man would be over. He would never be trusted again by his underworld contacts, the operators of offshore banks, or the steerers who were vital to any economy-sized swindle. This was, he knew, his own last hurrah. So he used every device, ruse and illusion he had learned over the years to fashion the sting into a lasting monument.

One of these devices was careful attention to detail, the casual conversation gambits, for instance, that lent an aura of reality to the good swindle. In fact, Weinberg had no real ties with European banks. But two early tape conversations with a suspected swindler show how he could create the illusion that he was in constant contact with those banks.

First Day Tape:

Weinberg: Uh, we're gonna have to make that Monday or Tuesday. I'm sorry to disappoint ya . . . Let me explain to ya why . . . Uh, because right now the books are ready to close over there [in Europe]. You know there's a five-hour [time] difference . . .

Swindler: Okay.

Tape Several Days Later:

Weinberg: Uh, I heard from Europe again this morning.

Swindler: Yeah?

Weinberg: Fuckin' guys, they wake you up in the morning, these cocksuckers . . .

Swindler: Yeah, huh.

Weinberg: Well, you know, its a six-hour difference.

Swindler: I know.

Weinberg: And these fucks call ya . . . nine A.M. their time . . . You know what time that is here?

Swindler: Yeah.

In stressing the time difference between Europe and Long Island, Weinberg was using a conversational device to strengthen the illusion that he was in contact with the European banks. The conversational snatches are also a classic example of the stall. Weinberg was promising the swindler funds from Europe that he never intended to deliver and he was using the time difference as an excuse for the delay.

Late in 1977, FBI Agent Tom McShane contacted Weinberg with an urgent problem. He explained that a rotund thief named Dominic Caserele was trying to peddle stolen paintings valued at more than a million dollars. The paintings had been snatched several years before by hoodlums tied to organized crime. Caserele and his accomplices had then stolen the paintings from the original thieves.

The problem, McShane explained, was that Caserele was too cautious to be approached by the FBI. The Bureau needed someone whom Caserele would trust so that the FBI could flush out the paintings and arrest the entire gang.

Weinberg called Caserele and introduced himself as the agent for a rich Texan who wanted to buy stolen art with no questions asked. Weinberg said that he didn't expect Caserele to trust a stranger on a delicate matter like this. He suggested that Caserele call mobster Anthony (Tony Ducks) Corallo, an old glass-clinking associate of Weinberg's at Orlando's Restaurant in Huntington.

"Don't tell Ducks what it's all about," Weinberg warned Caserele. "Just ask him what he knows about me and whether I can be trusted. He'll vouch for me. If you're satisfied, call me back and we'll talk some more."

Weinberg was following standard underworld protocol when he gave Caserele the name of Tony Ducks as a reference. It is the usual way in which members of the underworld, meeting for the first time, establish that neither is an undercover law enforcement agent. The practice is called vouching.

Weinberg sat and waited. A week later Caserele called back. He arranged to meet Weinberg at a bar in upstate Ellenville, New York. Weinberg got to the appointment early and learned to his delight that he knew the bartender, a bookmaker who used to work in the city, and the bartender's waitress girlfriend. When Caserele finally arrived, suspicious that the meeting was a trap set by either the mob or the law, the bartender and waitress enthusiastically vouched for Weinberg.

Weeks dragged by as Caserele and Weinberg exchanged phone calls and haggled price. Caserele and his friends wanted a million for the art. Weinberg set a maximum of $750,000 and refused to budge. Since the FBI never intended to pay over any money, the price was academic. But Weinberg argued that he would create suspicion if he didn't try to get the stolen paintings at the cheapest price possible.

Caserele finally agreed to Weinberg's terms and said that his group was ready to deal. "They wanted to make the switch, paintings for cash, in a downtown hotel," Weinberg recalls. "I said no way. I'm not walkin' into no hotel with $750,000 . . . I'm not going anywhere where's there's only one door out. If anything goes wrong, I get killed. I'm not stupid." Weinberg was serious. Even with FBI protection, he was afraid he could get involved in a hotel-room firefight with no way out. His hesitation further eased Caserele's doubts. If Weinberg had been an undercover cop, he wouldn't balk at the hotel-room meeting.

Weinberg made Caserele a counterproposal. He would meet Caserele at a New York City area airport and fly him in Weinberg's private plane to any other airport which Caserele would designate after they were in the air. That way, Weinberg explained, neither he nor the art expert he was bringing with him would know in advance the location of the stolen paintings. Once they landed, Weinberg said, his art expert would authenticate the paintings and the exchange would take place.

The idea of an airport exchange had not been mentioned to the FBI by Weinberg before he proposed it to Caserele. Unsurprisingly, it came as a shock to McShane and then to Good when McShane told him about it. The logistical problems posed by such a complicated exchange were enormous. When McShane mentioned this to Weinberg, the ebullient swindler dismissed the complaint with an airy wave of his cigar and chortled: "You guys are paid to handle details."

For the entire next week Good switched his attention from the high-priority sewer probe to plans for the unusual exchange. The FBI rented a four-passenger plane to be flown by a Bureau pilot. The passengers would be McShane, who was to play the art expert, Weinberg and Caserele, or anyone he might designate. Two smaller planes were rented as chase planes and staffed with FBI pilots and agents. Good groaned as he calculated the cost of Weinberg's air flotilla.

Caserele told Weinberg that the exchange would be at an undisclosed upstate airport on a Friday night early in February 1978. He ordered Weinberg to fly first to Stewart air base in upstate Newburgh, New York, to pick him up. Then he would direct Weinberg's pilot to the final rendezvous once Weinberg's plane was again in the air.

The FBI gave Weinberg a suitcase. Inside were bundles of simulated money. A few real bills were at the top and bottom of each bundle. Between them were bill-sized pieces of paper cut from phone books. Weinberg was warned not to let Caserele look at the bundles too closely after they picked him up for the final flight from Stewart.

Weinberg's plane flew through the cold, moonlit night from La-

Guardia Airport to Stewart, landed and taxied to the small terminal. Weinberg peered expectantly out the window for Caserele. Then he saw him.

"He musta weighed 320 pounds and he was real short," said Weinberg. "He looked like a bowlin' ball. He comes waddlin' out to the plane and gets in. He plops into the seat and nearly breaks the plane. He's hangin' over the seat on both sides. I never thought we'd get back off the ground."

But fly they did. Once in the air, Caserele pulled out a roadmap and pointed to a small airport about fifty miles away. "Here's where we're goin'," he wheezed. "Now lemme see the dough." Weinberg unlocked the suitcase, gave him a brief look and snapped it shut again. "I wanna count it," argued Caserele. "Not till we land," snapped Weinberg. "If you shift in your seat, you'll tip the plane over."

The pilot agreed with Weinberg. A novice at flying in small planes, Caserele gulped, blanched and nervously tried to balance himself in the center of his seat. The pilot broke the tense silence, asking if he could radio the designated airport for landing instructions. Caserele, trying to keep as still as possible, gave him a sick nod. The pilot's call to the airport was heard by the two chase planes flying behind.

While the pilot of Weinberg's plane purposely wasted time flying in wide circles over the Hudson River Valley, the two chase planes flew directly to an airport near the community of Peekskill and landed. The planes parked near the taxiway and the agents disembarked and pretended to busy themselves checking the wheels and tying the planes down. Weinberg's plane landed and the fat man pulled out a hand radio and spoke to his accomplice, who was waiting by the side of a van several hundred feet away.

"We're here," said Caserele.

"Do they have the money?" his accomplice radioed back.

"Yeah, but they won't let me count it," complained Caserele.

"Screw it," said the other man. "We don't have time. Send the art guy down here to look at the merchandise and stick to that money like glue."

McShane walked toward the van and Caserele stood next to Weinberg on the runway. As soon as McShane signaled, the FBI agents planned to rush both Caserele and his associate. Earlier, they had warned Weinberg to get as far away as possible from Caserele in case there was gunfire when the agents made their rush.

Now Weinberg tried unobtrusively to move sideways, putting distance between the hefty Caserele and himself. But the fat man stayed glued to him.

In desperation Weinberg whirled on Caserele and shouted, "Will you get the fuck away from me. You got body odor so bad I can't stand it!"

But the bulk wouldn't budge. "Up yours, mac," he snarled. "I stay with the bread."

Weinberg again shifted sideways. His unwanted companion shifted with him, moving even closer. From the corner of his eye, Weinberg saw McShane signal from the side of the van. The art was authentic. The FBI agents started their rush. Weinberg, frantic, threw himself to the ground and covered his head with his arms, his eyes screwed shut.

Seconds later he heard a rustling sound and the click of what sounded like handcuffs snapping shut. He looked up into the faces of several grinning FBI agents. Other agents were already thirty feet away escorting their prisoners to a waiting car.

Weinberg got to his feet, collecting his dignity as he slapped puffs of runway dust from his overcoat.

"Fuck you too," he growled at the agents as he turned and trudged toward the car.

"Hey, Weinberg," called one of the agents. "Where did you get the idea for the airplane exchange?"

"Watchin' TV," answered Weinberg. He was telling the truth.

Weinberg had more than one reason to feel relieved. Good had kept his promise. No charges had been filed against Diane. And a Pittsburgh judge had suspended his own three-year jail sentence and placed him on probation.

While he waited for McShane to finish the paperwork on the arrests in the office of the local United States Commissioner, Weinberg got more good news. The insurance company that had issued policies on the stolen paintings was giving him a $10,000 reward for their recovery and the Bureau promised a bonus.

Maybe, Weinberg mused, he could make a living as a government crook.

TAPE EIGHT

Weinberg (On vouching): If someone you meet is movin' with the wise guys and you wanna get close to him, you gotta come up with a name that he knows. Like, you ask him if he's from Brooklyn. If he says he's from Brooklyn, give him the name of some wise guy from Brooklyn like Sonny Franzese and tell him that Sonny is a friend of yours. That's called vouchin'. He figures if you're a friend of Sonny's you must be okay and you must be pretty heavy. Right away, he's your good friend; he can't do enough for you. . . . In New York almost every wise guy you meet says he used to work for Sonny. Sonny's gotta lotta respect. If all of those wise guys really did work for Sonny, he woulda had an army. But most vouchin' is pure bullshit. No way these big guys in the mob can remember all the people they've met over the years. But they don't wanna say they don't know someone. That might make them look stupid and no wise guy wants to look stupid. So vouchin' usually works whether you know a big mob guy or not. . . .

Weinberg (On watching TV): It's nervous work bein' a con man. You spend a lotta time sittin' in your hotel room just waitin'. Most of the time you're waitin' for the mark to bring the money. When you hear a knock on the door, you don't know what to expect. Maybe it's the mark with some friends and they've come to beat the shit outta you. When you hear the knock, you never know for sure. It's a very nervous time. I used to sit there waitin' and bitin' my fingernails. After a while, I learned to turn on the TV. I don't care what I'm watchin', anything will do, sports, news, soaps, westerns, commercials. I don't give a shit. I find it soothing. It relaxes me. Now, whenever I got nothing to do, I turn on the TV and just stare at it. It's a habit. I know a lotta con men are the same way. Sometimes, just watchin' TV you learn somethin' that can help with a con, so it's not a complete waste of time. I really enjoy "60 Minutes"; don't ask me why. Otherwise, I'll watch anything.

6

THE HONEY POT

It was without a compeer among swindles. It was perfect, it was
rounded, symmetrical, complete, colossal.   —MARK TWAIN

When they asked me to go to work for the government, they
built it up and made it sound great. After a week of workin' I
figured they were even bigger bullshit artists than me.

—MEL WEINBERG

Mel Weinberg sat alone in a booth at the Blue Dawn diner. He was on
his second cigar and his third cup of coffee and the waitress was throwing
him dirty looks. He checked his watch again, tapped the case with his
finger and held it to his ear. It was still ticking. No question about it. FBI
Agent Jack McCarthy was a half-hour late.

Bored and irritated, he looked out the window at busy Veterans Memorial Highway. Cars and trucks bound for various Long Island communities whizzed by in both directions. The biting March wind kicked
up swirls of dust and tiny pieces of grit tattooed the steamy windowpane.
He took a sip of coffee. It was cold. If he asked for another cup, they'd
probably charge him rent. He concentrated instead on skimming a copy

of *Newsday* abandoned by an earlier customer. He opened the bulky newspaper and ran his eye over the upfront stories.

Former Italian Premier Aldo Moro had been kidnapped, apparently by the Red Brigade. A Suffolk grand jury had indicted two officials of a local hospital for ripping off $1.8 million in insurance payments. Two other events were packaged on the next page. Investigators charged that South Korean President Park Chung Hee had helped plan his government's attempts to influence the U.S. Congress, and a former Federal judge was being asked to look into corruption charges against Pennsylvania Congressman Daniel Flood.

He wondered if his old buddy Squeaky from the Red Brigade was involved in the Moro snatch. Probably. Squeaky was involved in all the big jobs. He nodded his head appreciatively at news of the hospital swindle. Very pretty. It was too bad they had been caught. As for the hints of Congressional corruption, so what? There was no point in running for office if you couldn't make a bundle afterward. Besides, the Congressmen would beat the rap. They always did.

Weinberg looked up from the paper as McCarthy, red-faced from the wind and exertion, slid into the booth and apologized for being late. There had been a major break in the sewer probe, he said, and he had just left the office and raced down Veterans to the diner. Weinberg was curious about the sewer case. Some of the contractors involved were friends from Orlando's Restaurant. He asked a few questions, but McCarthy gave him carefully guarded answers.

McCarthy's professional caution triggered the volatile mixture of impatience and resentment that had been working inside Weinberg for weeks. He let it all out. He had been promised an office, good equipment and expenses as part of the deal to follow up on leads that he had developed. He complained that he had no office, forcing him to meet hoodlums at his nearby home. This, he said, posed a potential danger to his family. He grumbled that most of the equipment was faulty and that the only expense money he ever saw was an occasional $50 bill that he pried from McCarthy.

Softly responding to Weinberg's angry words, McCarthy reminded him that he had just gotten a $10,000 reward for his part in recovering the stolen paintings. Weinberg snapped back that he was already spending some of the reward money on the government cases. He was still using his own tape recorder and tapes, he was making most of his phone calls from his home and he was still racking up the mileage on his own car. Besides, he asked, how was he supposed to support his family?

Weinberg was also bothered by things he didn't mention to McCarthy. His father had died the month before, February 21, 1978, a sad event that focused his own sense of mortality. His blood pressure was bubbling, according to his doctor. He was paying Eastern Airlines a small fortune for his frequent flights back and forth from Florida, where he was keeping Diane in a trailer. Most of all, though, he was frustrated because he couldn't work with his accustomed style and flair.

McCarthy promised to talk to John Good. He said he knew that Good had submitted plans to the Bureau for a much more ambitious program, using Weinberg as the fulcrum. If the Bureau approved Good's proposal, McCarthy hinted, Weinberg might be put on salary plus better expenses. He warned, however, that the okay from Washington, if it ever came, might still take several months.

It was the kind of hope that Weinberg had once used to stall his own marks and he knew it. But he also knew that right now it was the only direction open to him. He seized the hope and embraced it.

"There's two things you gotta do, if you want to do this right," he told McCarthy. "Number one, you gotta beat them at their own game. The con game is one round robin. Each con man knows the next guy. They're in touch with each other. When you have a sucker on the line, you gotta keep calling him night and day. Never let him off the hook, because as soon as you forget to call, he'll go somewhere else and the other guy'll

grab him. Number two, you gotta set up a class sting. You gotta hire offices, limos, classy secretaries, something a little different like that. A
plane would be great."

A few days later, McCarthy called Weinberg. There was no news yet
from Washington, but Good wanted to get a running head start on the
project. He had talked a friendly real estate owner into loaning him space
just vacated by a bank on the ground floor of the Hauppauge building
where the FBI had offices. Weinberg chuckled at the irony of the location, but he was elated.

He remembers saying: "We're on our way."

Well, almost on our way, Weinberg thought the next day as he surveyed the huge room that had once housed the bank. He had just learned
that there was no furniture, no phones, and no money for them in the
budget. He drove to the Huntington office of his lawyer, Vince Cuti, who
had stored some of Weinberg's furniture from London Investors after his
arrest. Telling Cuti that he was back in the investment business, Weinberg
brought the few remaining pieces of furniture back to his new office.

There was only his desk, which he placed in the middle of the room,
and three chairs, which he arranged around the desk. It looked like a
small oasis of furniture in a vast desert of empty space. From home, he
brought his cordless telephone and put it on the desk. The room still
looked empty. Weinberg wasn't discouraged. He remembered the first
days of London Investors. No furniture, telephones on the floor, but
customers fought their way in.

Weinberg, McCarthy and Myron Fuller huddled around the desk to
devise a theme for the sting. OPEC and oil still dominated the headlines
and Weinberg's hint of ties with Arab investors over the past few months
had brought the hustlers swarming. Weinberg suggested the idea of
naming a specific Arab and then agreed when the two agents proposed
the idea back to him. He decided to use the name of the aging Arab millionaire he had befriended a year or so before on the flight back from
Paris with Lady Diane.

The original theme, quickly approved by Good, fleshed out over the following few months. Weinberg supplied most of the ideas, although Fuller, McCarthy and Good all added touches before the sting was full-blown.

The emphasis sometimes changed, but the basic version of the sting had Weinberg acting as the American agent of his old pal, millionaire Arab businessman Kambir Abdul Rahman (the spelling of Kambir was changed slightly several times). According to the scenario, Abdul, who supposedly resided in one of the Arab Emirates, when he wasn't living in Switzerland, Beirut or Cannes, was related to Arab royalty.

Some targets of the scam were told that Abdul's money could not be loaned out at interest because of Islamic laws against usury. As a result, these marks were told, Abdul needed an unlimited supply of bogus certificates of deposit from offshore banks or forged certificates from legitimate banks. These certificates would be given by Abdul to his Moslem banks and he would then be able to withdraw cash equal to the face amount of the certificates and quietly invest the cash at interest elsewhere.

Other targets were merely told that Abdul wanted to invest as much of his millions in the U.S. as possible because he felt it was only a matter of time before he would have to flee the wrath of his ripped-off citizenry. This version was used more often as the scam progressed and Weinberg promoted his friend Abdul to the ruling rank of Emir.

For still others, the story was that Abdul was a lavish patron of the arts, both classic and pornographic, and was not averse to purchasing paintings, jewelry and other items that were hotter than his native desert. At times he was also described as a connoisseur of sex films so tawdry that *Behind the Green Door* in comparison would look like a Walt Disney production.

Although he was blissfully unaware of what was going on, Weinberg's Arab pal had been cleverly fashioned into a scam for all seasons. He offered opportunity to forgers, swindlers, thieves, influence peddlers, smugglers, pornographers and corrupt public officials and politicians.

It was only natural that Abdul would have a corporation to handle these various activities. It was created by Weinberg and called Abdul Enterprises, Ltd. Everyone had a title and all except Weinberg used aliases.* McCarthy was chairman of the nonexistent board. Weinberg was president. Fuller was financial director. Tom McShane, the FBI agent who had posed as Weinberg's art expert in the airport arrests, was art consultant. And Agent Ernie Haridopolos, the friendly thug who had leaned on swindler Fred Pro, was executive vice-president.

Once the corporation was formed, Fuller fabricated a letter from a U.S. Ambassador under a State Department letterhead giving a background to Abdul and naming the various FBI agents, under their aliases, as members of Abdul's staff. Fuller then constructed a ruse which time and again in the months to come made the difference between success and failure for Abscam. He called a friend at Chase Manhattan.

The friend he called was listed as a high-ranking official at the bank's international department in New York. His name was Michael Elzay. The bank official agreed to tell anyone who might call that Kambir Abdul Rahman had millions on deposit with the bank. Fuller correctly guessed that future Abscam targets might be suspicious of the scam and demand proof of Abdul and his money. The letter on State Department stationery would prove that Abdul existed and Chase Manhattan would verify his wealth.

Weinberg was given the direct-line number for Elzay. If doubting marks asked for a financial reference, Fuller told Weinberg to give them Elzay's name and phone number. Fuller's meticulous planning proved vital to Abscam. The banker was called over the next eighteen months by agents for Congressmen, mobsters and even other banks. Always, he confirmed that Abdul was a multimillion-dollar customer.

The bank was technically telling the truth about Abdul's hefty coffers.

---

* To avoid confusion in the recounting of the Abscam stings, the real names of the agents will be used.

Before enlisting Elzay's aid, Fuller had taken Weinberg's advice and persuaded the Bureau to deposit $1 million to the account. The money was part of the FBI's annual Congressional appropriation. Elzay, an expert on the Mideast, was the bank officer in charge of the account. When Abscam surfaced publicly, the money was returned to the government.

Abscam jurors and newspaper editorialists would later wonder how supposedly intelligent people like Congressmen and lawyers could have fallen for Abscam. Seen on flickering TV screens, the scam seemed too obvious. But, like all great swindles, Abscam was an illusion built on careful attention to details, subtle presell and the targets' own greed.

Many of those ensnared by Abscam were initially suspicious. Influence-peddler Howard Criden, for instance, was constantly questioning Weinberg about Abdul and his organization. But even his questions were fewer after he called Chase Manhattan. If Abscam was real, the marks believed they would get rich. They wanted Abdul to be real and the bank fed their hopes.

What the swindle now needed was some kind of style, a way in which the various performers could act to enhance the carefully contrived plot. The style was provided by Weinberg. Weinberg was widely known in the business as a crook and swindler. If he pretended to be anything else, he would raise immediate suspicion.

Faced with this known quantity, he constructed a role that allowed him to be both a crook and a semi-legitimate businessman. He created the impression that he was hugely paid by Abdul and didn't want to do anything so outrageously crooked or disloyal that he would lose his cushy job. On the other hand, he let it be known, he was a crook at heart and wasn't averse to jacking up the price of something that he was purchasing for Abdul and splitting the difference privately with either the seller or the agent who set up the deal. The Arab, he said, would never notice an odd million here or there.

The Abscam tapes are laced with quotes from Weinberg playing this role.

In one conversation with middleman Criden, he acted the careful steward to his Arab employer when Criden pressured him to buy a bank.

He told Criden: "Ya know, when these guys come and give ya something one, two, three, I'm leery of them. Okay? I don't mind something as long as we can check it out. I don't want them to think that we're idiots. Ya know, nobody gives up $3 million tomorrow."

But on another occasion, he winked knowingly at Criden and told him: "I have nothing to hide. I'm an open book. If I can make a buck, I make a buck."

Another time, Weinberg warned Camden Mayor Angelo Errichetti: "You just can't go [to his Arab employer] and say . . . I need your twenty million, thirty million."

But he also told Errichetti: "Ya know . . . let him explain to you what he wants to do. Ya know, if there's a way of doing it dishonestly. I'll know how."

And, when he was giving a $50,000 bribe to Congressman Michael (Ozzie) Myers of Philadelphia, Weinberg said, "We got like the goose that lays the golden egg; we all like to make a buck."

Such a role, however, has built-in problems. Any swindler tossing millions to politicians and fellow crooks would normally ask them for cash or other side gifts. It is also standard etiquette in these circles to make such goodwill presents to anyone who can move sizable amounts of money your way.

As an agent of the United States Government, it would be improper for Weinberg to solicit or take such gifts. But in his role as Mel Weinberg, Abdul's light-fingered representative, he would create deep suspicion if he didn't. At the ensuing trials defense lawyers insisted that he had asked for and gotten gifts. Weinberg, a picture of wounded innocence, maintained that he did not.

Abdul Enterprises now had an impressive string of corporate officers, a cavernous if unfurnished office, a glowing bank reference, and a unique style of doing business. Everyone was anxious to see if it worked. They decided on a dress rehearsal with a real target. But only the strength of the plot and a skillful mop-up by Weinberg saved the trial run from complete disaster.

The target was Ron Sabloski, a New York businessman and hustler with whom Weinberg had dealt in the past. Weinberg proposed renting a suite in New York's posh Plaza Hotel and producing an FBI agent who could play Abdul. Weinberg would bait Sabloski to the meeting with news that Abdul had millions, spent freely, and wanted to add to his vast art collection. Sabloski would be asked to bring samples.

Weinberg reached Sabloski and issued an enticing invitation. He reported back that Sabloski would be delighted to meet Abdul. He said that he could almost hear Sabloski's teeth snap on the bait before he hung up the phone. Everyone involved in Abscam except Good wanted to be in on the act. The final result was overkill.

The cast included McCarthy, Fuller, McShane, FBI Agents Edward Woods and Margo Denedy, as Abdul's pilot and personal secretary respectively, and Abdul himself, played by FBI Agent Mike Denehy. Pulled from the New York FBI office at the last minute, Denehy warned that he spoke no Arabic and had no idea how Arabs were supposed to act. He was assured that Sabloski didn't either. No sweat.

Then came the bad news. The Bureau would only allow $250 for the Plaza sting. Weinberg fumed. Didn't they know the price of a luxurious Plaza suite? It would cost more than $250 just to stock the bar and serve Plaza hors d'oeuvres. "What kinda asshole dreamed up a limit like that?" But the Bureau was firm. No more money.

Sighing in defeat, Weinberg called the Plaza and ordered the hotel's cheapest suite, two small rooms. The agents volunteered to bring in half-filled bottles of liquor from home to put on the bar in the suite. On the appointed day, as an FBI electronics specialist taped a recorder to the underside of the suite's coffee table, Weinberg and the agents, all carrying booze in brown bags, crowded into the small sitting room.

One of the agents carried a large box containing an Arab's burnoose and robes for Denehy. The Arab gear had been rented from a theatrical agency for $37. Denehy self-consciously tried on the robes. They didn't fit. He put on the Arab headdress. It fit, but it was badly wrinkled from the box. There was no time to get back to the West Side for a replacement. Denehy, it was decided, would wear the wrinkled Arab headdress over his business suit. The robes were put back in the box and shoved under the bed in the other room.

Denehy argued that he would have to give some greeting in Arabic to Sabloski, even if he said nothing else. A phone call was made and the Bureau produced an adviser who told Denehy that he should greet Sabloski with the traditional Arab words of welcome: *Asalam alaikum*.

Weinberg looked at the room-service price list and gulped. He left and returned a short time later with a paper sack bulging with delicatessen products, known in New York vernacular as "deli." He would have preferred a food display of salmon fumé, champignons à la Grecque, and assorted canapés accompanied by several bottles of icy-cold Dom Pérignon champagne. After all, wasn't Abdul supposed to be a very, very rich Arab?

Instead, he piled paper plates with mounds of kosher corned beef, pastrami, tongue, potato salad and coleslaw. If he couldn't have the best, he might as well have his own favorite food, he thought. The incongruity of an Arab serving kosher cuisine did occur to Weinberg for a moment. But he reasoned that if Arabs hated Jews, they should love Jewish food because it had killed more Jews than all the pogroms in Russia.

The phone rang. Sabloski had arrived in the lobby. The agents raced for chairs and poured themselves drinks to create the impression of a social gathering. Denehy, who paced back and forth in his wrinkled burnoose repeating his Arabic greeting over and over, was shuttled into the bedroom and the door was closed behind him. He was only to emerge, he was told, when he heard Weinberg flush the toilet in the adjoining bathroom.

Weinberg returned to the room several minutes later with Sabloski and seated him in the only vacant chair after introducing him to the various "officials" of Abdul. The room was so small and crowded, people narrowly avoided bumping into each other as they rose to shake hands.

Weinberg did a double take. The chair that the agents had left for Sabloski stood by itself in the center of the room. Weinberg remembers musing: "They must think they're in an old-time police station, puttin' him in the middle of the room like this. What the fuck are they gonna do now, grill him?" He felt the urgent call of nature, something that occasionally happens when he is upset, and he walked into the bathroom. When he finished, he unthinkingly flushed the toilet.

The bedroom door slowly opened as Denehy prepared to make a grand entrance in response to the prearranged signal. An alert agent, spotting the unfolding debacle, jumped up and shoved the door shut in Denehy's face before he could emerge. A dull thunk sounded from the door's other side.

Sabloski showed his paintings to McShane. Because they were slightly warm, he hinted, Abdul would be able to get the paintings at a much reduced price. As Sabloski talked, the tape recorder under the coffee table took down the conversation. Finally the time came when the agents felt it was appropriate for Denehy to make his appearance.

One of them knocked on the door and Denehy stepped out grandly. As he moved toward Sabloski, preparing to give his Arab greeting, Sabloski rose and said, "Emir, *Asalam alaikum*." Though a superb FBI agent, Denehy was no actor. Sabloski so stunned him by the theft of his greeting that all he could reply was "Ohhmmph." One of the agents quickly gave up his chair and guided Denehy into it. He sat there staring at Sabloski with a dazed expression.

Sabloski then explained to his English-speaking hosts that he had once done business in Moslem countries and was generally familiar with Arab customs. He could tell that Abdul was an Emir (Arab chieftain) by the markings on his burnoose. That is why, he said, he rose when the Emir entered the room and only sat after the Emir had been seated. He apologized, though, for knowing almost no Arabic. That, his relieved hosts assured him, was completely understandable. Weinberg, in momentary shock, was thinking, Of all the marks in the world, I have to pick this schmuck.

But McShane picked up the cue when he heard that Sabloski knew no Arabic. Explaining that Abdul understood English but spoke it poorly, McShane displayed Sabloski's pictures for Abdul. "Do you like this one or that one, Emir?" McShane would ask. Each time Denehy would answer "Ohhmmph." McShane would nod knowingly, point to the picture, and say, "He likes that one."

Each time Denehy shifted in his seat, or stood to get a better view of a picture, Sabloski rose and the rest of the agents and Weinberg also rose. When Denehy sat, they sat. Traffic to the bathroom was exceptionally heavy as one agent after the other, unable to suppress laughter, rushed across the room and sought safety behind the bathroom door.

Suddenly, for no apparent reason, the tape recorder broke loose and thunked to the floor under the table. An agent deftly kicked the recorder under the couch before Sabloski noticed it, but the mishap triggered another run of agents to the bathroom. Everyone, except for Sabloski, who looked mystified, and Weinberg, who looked sick, was red-faced trying to stifle giggles.

Denehy, deciding that there could be a disastrous slip-up if he stayed longer, rose from his chair imperiously, drawing the rest of his audience to its feet. Beckoning to Margo Denedy, an attractive, redheaded agent, he strode into the bedroom, waited for Denedy to follow, and closed the door.

"Where's the Emir going?" asked Sabloski.

"Ya gotta understand," lied Weinberg quickly. "The Emir can't fuck around with the ladies in his own country. You know, Ron, them Moslems are very strict. But the Emir loves to get laid. The minute he leaves his country, he's bangin' his secretary all the time. This is the fourth time today."

Sabloski grinned and winked. More to distract his attention than anything else, Weinberg invited Sabloski to have some food. For the first time, Sabloski focused his attention on the mounds of deli gracing the antique coffee table.

"The Emir likes this food?" he asked incredulously.

"Loves it; can't get enough of it," Weinberg replied blandly, silently cursing government parsimony. "He can't dare eat Jewish food in his own country. They'd cut off his head for bein' a traitor. But the minute he comes to New York where he can get vintage deli, that's all that he eats. He drinks booze too."

Weinberg had forgotten plastic knives and forks on his visit to the delicatessen. He scooped up a handful of coleslaw and ate it. The agents similarly attacked the potato salad. Weinberg passed the coleslaw to Sabloski. "Here, Ron," he said. "Dig in Arab style."

The next day Weinberg sat alone at his desk in the huge, bare Abdul office. He was, to put it mildly, depressed. He leaned back in his padded chair, chewing on his cigar, and waited for the phone to ring, as he knew it would.

Finally, the phone rang. It was Sabloski.

"Mel, I really don't understand what was going on at the Plaza yesterday," he complained. "The Emir and his staff acted like crazy people, giggling and falling over each other. Can we do business with people like this?"

Weinberg sighed in relief. Sabloski was still on the hook. He went into his spiel. "Ron, there's some things you gotta understand. When the Emir leaves his country, he drinks like crazy. He goes on binges. And you know how it is with royalty. You gotta do what they do; that's what they call protocol. Like yesterday. You stood up when he stood up. When the Emir drinks, he insists that his staff drinks with him. They do it 'cause they gotta do it. But none of them are really what you call drinkers. They can't hold it."

"Oh," said Sabloski. "Now I understand. Do you think the Emir will buy any of the pictures, Mel? We both can make money on the deal?"

Gottcha, Weinberg thought. He then went into his stall. Good had ordered Weinberg to delay delivery of any paintings. Arrests would have to be made if the paintings turned out to be stolen and Good did not want to expose Weinberg as a witness. Weinberg explained that McShane was researching the history of Sabloski's paintings and would report back to the Emir in about a week. Sabloski was satisfied and said he'd keep in touch.

"Sonuvabitch," exclaimed Weinberg as he hung up. "This mother really works."

Abdul the Emir was both promoted and retired as a result of the Plaza fiasco. After that date, he was always referred to as the Emir or Sheikh. But he also never made another public appearance in Abscam. Good decided that if Abscam ever again produced a live Arab, he would have to be played by an Arabic-speaking agent. The new Arab couldn't be called Abdul because of the danger that some potential target might compare notes with Sabloski. Thus was born another spend-crazy Arab Emir named after Weinberg's old swindling buddy from Switzerland's Hotel Zurich—Yassir Habib.

But Abdul never died. Over the following months Weinberg would tell targets that Abdul was variously back in his native land, in Egypt, in London, in Switzerland, in the south of France and, on occasion, jetting in and out of New York on overnight trips.

There were other lessons learned from the Sabloski dress rehearsal and they were gradually incorporated into the sting. The number of agents at later meetings with marks was kept to a minimum. Back-up recording devices were added. And, as millions of TV viewers later saw, targets were guided into chairs that seemed to be a casual part of the furniture arrangement instead of being plonked in the middle of the room. No matter how hard Weinberg tried, though, the government never quite went for the salmon fumé and chilled Dom Pérignon.

Grumbles Weinberg: "If we nailed Congressmen with hot pastrami, who knows how high we woulda gone with champagne and fancy hors d'oeuvres?"

Good's modest Abscam budget was approved by the Bureau late that spring and by July 1978 the pace quickened. Weinberg was hired at a salary of $1,000 a month plus his sparse expense account. Abdul Enterprises moved into a small, three-room suite of offices at 4250 Veterans Highway, Holbrook, near Long Island's MacArthur Airport and just a few miles down the road from the Suffolk FBI office.

The entire suite measured only 600 square feet. McCarthy moved into one of the two office rooms in his role as Abdul's board chairman. Weinberg took the other. The third room was a tiny area which Weinberg grandly labeled the conference room. The furniture was cheap, functional, institutional. Weinberg wanted to put on a better front. "If we're supposed to be throwin' around millions, how come we're sittin' on this kinda shit," he argued. He was told there was no money.

"It looked like a goddamned bookie parlor," Weinberg recalls. "I was ashamed to have our marks come visit."

There were, however, other trappings. From now on, said Good, a twin-engine private plane with an FBI pilot would be at MacArthur Airport for Abdul's use. And he agreed to pick up the monthly payments on a customized van, replete with bar, that Weinberg wanted to buy. The van, outfitted like a small, luxurious living room, was used both as a traveling Abdul office and to pick up potential targets at the nearby airport. Despite his complaints, Weinberg had to admit that things were slowly shaping up.

Added to Abdul's new business cards was the phone number of a branch office in northern New Jersey. Actually, the phone was in a trailer owned by Weinberg at a recreational complex near Great Gorge. Callers were asked to tape their messages which were routinely picked up by FBI agents. At first the New Jersey office was window dressing. Later, when Abscam's focus centered on the Garden State, the trailer became an important phone link.

Financial problems continued to nag Weinberg. His government salary of less than $250 a week was little more than cigar money for a man with his life-style and appetites. It certainly didn't pay for his monthly visits to Diane down in Florida, much less support two households. Although he was paid by the government, he got none of the regular government benefits.

He needed more money in a hurry. His opportunity came a few weeks later while on a visit to Diane near Palm Beach. A Nevada con man named Frank Kelly was flying into West Palm Beach Airport to deliver $60 million in bogus gold certificates. Weinberg had asked Kelly to deliver the certificates there in the hope that he could charge some of his Florida expenses against the Kelly case. But he needed FBI agents to cover him.

Weinberg called McCarthy, who referred him to the West Palm Beach office of the Bureau. One of the agents assigned was Gunnar Askeland, a Bureau specialist in fraud. Askeland was so impressed by Weinberg that he got in touch with supervising agent Bob Fitzpatrick in Miami. Fitzpatrick hired Weinberg for another $1,000 a month to help the FBI in Florida.

The Miami office of the FBI was starting its own white-collar sting. Between Abscam and Miami, Weinberg was now making $2,000 a month, spending more time in Florida with Diane and charging his round-trip plane tickets against expenses.

Weinberg's Florida ties were accepted as a mixed blessing by Good. Although there was a greater risk that he could be exposed as a government agent, Good believed Weinberg's complaints that he could no longer afford to work for the government. The Florida sting relieved Weinberg's financial pressure and allowed him to continue with Abscam. A sting man at risk, Good decided, was better than no sting man at all.

One of Weinberg's first Florida operations involved Sabloski's brother Perry, an erstwhile Shakespearean actor with a bashed-in profile and a phony English accent. Perry Sabloski and his partner, a former Texas official named Arthur C. Ellis, were ready to supply millions in bogus certificates of deposit in return for a percentage of the face value in cash.

At Askeland's instructions, Weinberg told them to deliver the CDs to the Ramada Inn in West Palm Beach.

The Ramada was chosen because it was comfortable, efficient, convenient to where Weinberg lived with Diane. As time went on, both the Florida sting and Abscam used the Ramada often as a place to meet swindlers and corrupt politicians. So many cases came down at the Ramada that both Weinberg and the agents began referring to the place as the Gottcha Hotel.

Weinberg's pitch to Perry Sabloski and Ellis, with variations, was the one made through most of Abscam.

The sheikh, he confided, wanted to get his money out of Moslem banks overseas and invest it in the United States. He could only do this, Weinberg explained, by giving the Moslem banks CDs representing money that he supposedly had deposited in the offshore banks that issued the deposit certificates. Then, said Weinberg, the Moslem banks would give the sheikh money equivalent to the face value of the CDs to take out of his country.

No one would ever know that the CDs were worthless pieces of paper, Weinberg assured the two targets. He said that the Moslem banks would only demand cash for the CDs on the sheikh's orders. Those orders, Weinberg promised, would never come. He said he would pay Sabloski and Ellis 7 percent of the face value of the CDs they produced. The sheikh, he said, would then invest the money at up to 17 percent in the U.S., quickly making back his original costs.

There was only one little hitch, continued Weinberg. The bogus CDs would have to be sent overseas to be checked by members of the sheikh's personal staff. If these people felt that the certificates looked legitimate enough to be accepted by the Moslem banks, they would send back money totaling 7 percent of the face value to be paid to the persons who had supplied the CDs. This process, he explained, took anywhere from sixty to ninety days.

What Weinberg described as a little hitch would turn into an endless wait. The idea was to get the CDs, evidence needed by the Federal government to prove a crime, without paying for them. As the months stretched out, the swindlers constantly nagged Weinberg on the phone.

But they were dealing with a master at the stall. Always assuring them that it was just a matter of time, Weinberg snatched instant excuses from daily newspaper stories: a plane crash, a strike or a revolution. He would also hint vaguely that if he were pestered too much, he would call overseas and have the CDs returned and the deal canceled. Since the marks knew that their CDs were worthless and expected to get millions for them from the sheikh, they were accommodating.

At the Ramada, however, Perry Sabloski insisted on a $500,000 advance against his 7 percent. Weinberg assured him that he would try to get Sabloski his advance as soon as possible. Grudgingly, Sabloski passed Weinberg the CDs, but he warned:

"You know, Mel, I know some right people. If you people try to pull a fast one, all I have to do is make a call and you're dead."

Weinberg knew he was bluffing. The proper term for important mobsters is "good people," and Weinberg knew that if Sabloski knew any "good people" he would also know what to call them.

So Weinberg replied: "Perry, I know those people a helluva lot better than you do and if anybody's gonna get pushed around here, it's gonna be you. If you don't trust me, I don't trust you. Take back your goddamned CDs."

Sabloski immediately backed down, once again proving Weinberg's thesis that the only way to handle people who push is to push back harder. Eighteen months later, when Abscam hit the headlines, Perry Sabloski was still calling Weinberg for his money and still accepting his excuse that it was temporarily frozen in a Teheran bank because of the trouble over the hostages in Iran.

Several weeks after the Ramada meeting, Gunnar Askeland called Weinberg from the West Palm Beach Bureau office with a problem. The problem's name was Joseph Meltzer, a nickel-and-dime con man that the

Bureau was using as an informant in the Florida sting. Askeland said that Meltzer was being threatened by a New York shylock named Black Sam to whom he owed $40,000. Moreover, Meltzer claimed that Black Sam also dealt in CDs. Since an informer with two broken legs would be hardly mobile, Askeland asked Weinberg if he and the New York Abscam group would assist in nabbing Black Sam on CD fraud charges.

The Miami office of the FBI had given Meltzer approximately $7,000 to set up a phony real estate firm for use as a cover in the sting operation. Meltzer's move was to buy an expensive new car to build the illusion that he was a successful wheeler-dealer in real estate. Black Sam had heard about Meltzer's flashy car and supposedly bustling real estate business. He wondered, naturally, why Meltzer, who claimed he was too broke to pay back the $40,000, could afford these sudden luxuries.

Black Sam was not the type who wondered about anything overly long. When in doubt, he leaned. And, at this particular time, he was leaning very hard on Meltzer.

McCarthy flew down from New York and he and Weinberg met with Black Sam in the Elvis Presley suite of a Sheraton hotel in the Fort Lauderdale area. Black Sam hinted that he could supply CDs, but the meeting was inconclusive and Weinberg left with the feeling that Meltzer deserved to have at least one of his legs broken. Even so, something would have to be done about Meltzer's credibility vis-à-vis Black Sam.

The Miami FBI office had asked the Abscam group to provide Meltzer with some kind of excuse for his newfound wealth. McCarthy gave him a letter to show to Black Sam which indicated that Meltzer had been commissioned by Abdul to buy certain property in Florida. The letter was extremely limited in scope. McCarthy gave Meltzer enough of a build-up at the meeting to explain his sudden cash. He assured Black Sam that Meltzer would make enough in the near future to repay the loan. Meltzer, Weinberg insists, never actually worked with Abscam and the letter was given solely to cover Meltzer's role in the Florida sting operation.

Weinberg's queasy feeling about Meltzer, whom he had met only that one time, was more than justified the next week when he got a call from Ron Sabloski in New York. Sabloski reported that Meltzer was telling people that he was working for Abdul Enterprises. Sabloski complained that he had far more contacts than Meltzer and should have been hired first by Abdul. Weinberg assured Sabloski that Meltzer was lying, hung up, and told both McCarthy and Askeland about the call.

Weinberg then had two phone conversations with Meltzer in which he warned him not to pretend that he was involved with Abdul. He told Meltzer that he would wind up in trouble if McCarthy, Abdul's board chairman, ever heard about it. Meltzer pleaded that he had only used the Abdul cover to do a favor for a friend and promised to watch his step in the future.

But unknown to either Weinberg or the FBI, Meltzer already had more Abdul letterheads which he had gotten from an unsuspecting agent. He moved to California, tailored a letter to identify himself as Abdul's West Coast agent, and began running a scam on businessmen for personal profit.

As Meltzer built his own swindle on the West Coast, several California businessmen apparently complained to the FBI. Their stories indicated that Meltzer had successfully pumped Florida FBI agents for enough information about Abscam to be dangerous. For example, when Western businessmen asked him for bank references for his firm, which he set up as a successor to Abdul Enterprises, he would refer them to Michael Elzay at Chase Manhattan. Elzay would apparently routinely confirm Abdul's account. The Bureau has refused to talk about any knowledge it may have had about Meltzer's swindle on the coast while Abscam was developing in the East.

If the Bureau did know, as has been claimed, it obviously was faced with a major dilemma. If Meltzer had been arrested for his swindle while Abscam was still alive, he could have exposed the entire operation just when it was reaching deeply into the United States Congress. The only alternative would have been to allow Meltzer to continue his swindle. This would have posed a sticky moral problem for the Bureau.

In the absence of comment from the FBI the only record is the bottom line. The businessmen did complain. The FBI did not move against Meltzer until Abscam became public knowledge more than a year later.

The hectic pace of Abscam made it easy for Weinberg to dismiss Meltzer from his mind, although the porky swindler later would re-emerge like a bad penny to testify as a defense witness at some of the Abscam trials.

Weinberg, for his part, was too busy with other things. He made repeated trips between New York and Florida, Marie and Diane. The phone rang ceaselessly with new packages to be considered and old targets to be stalled. He bounced from one motel-room meeting to another. So many deals were coming down that names and dates blurred in his mind.

Then came the most gut-grabbing, terror-filled moments of the entire Abscam investigation.

It began in September 1978, when Weinberg met an elderly mortgage hustler, Edward Linick of Columbus, Ohio, who was making a business swing through Florida. Linick eagerly swallowed the Abscam bait and a week later he was at Abdul's Long Island office trying to sell two Florida banks to Weinberg and McCarthy.

Weinberg sensed that Linick was a live one. He and McCarthy flew with Linick to Florida and pretended great interest in buying the banks. Then Weinberg set the hook. The money to buy the banks, he said, would have to come from Abdul's bank deposits in the Mideast. And to get the money out, he explained, he and McCarthy would have to send over phony CDs in the same amount.

Linick said he had a connection for the CDs and arranged for a meeting between his connection and Weinberg at the Ramada in West Palm Beach. His name, Linick said, was William Bell.

FBI files reflect that Bell, then fifty years old, was a tough soldier of fortune, an expert at firearms, the owner of the Eagle Manufacturing

Company that produced arms in Pompano Beach, Florida, and a man with covert CIA connections. He was on the suspect list of the Drug Enforcement Administration and had been arrested the year before in Raleigh, North Carolina, on a narcotics charge. He was also suspected of taking part in a plot to overthrow a South American government and assassinate its leader. The FBI report on Bell states that DEA efforts to check on this activity were "thwarted" by the CIA.

None of this was known to Weinberg and FBI Agent Askeland, posing as Weinberg's Abdul associate, as they checked into the Ramada Inn at West Palm Beach a week later for their initial meeting with Bell. "What the hell," Weinberg assured Askeland, "this guy's just another paper scammer and all those types are pussy cats."

Late that evening Bell came to their room. He was a hulking six-footer with a military crew cut. He came to the point quickly. Would the sheikh be interested in buying any machine guns? Weinberg didn't bat an eye. "Sure," he answered. "He needs lotsa them. If he can pay off the PLO in guns, they'll stay off his back. How many you got to sell?"

Bell responded that he owned a machine-gun manufacturing plant in Guatemala and could supply an unlimited number of machine guns and high velocity pistols equipped with silencers. Once again, Weinberg explained the need for CDs to make cash deals.

Bell said that he and some associates would fly to Long Island the following week to negotiate a price for the CDs with Weinberg. Then he left. Askeland departed a few minutes later and Weinberg got into his pajamas and reclined in bed to watch TV. Fifteen minutes passed. There was a knock on the door and Weinberg grumped out of bed and opened it.

Standing in the doorway was Bell. In his hand was a pistol and screwed to the end of it was a silencer. Weinberg moved slowly backward on jellied legs, his mouth dry. In terror he reached the bed and plopped down abruptly, watching Bell's slow advance saucer-eyed.

"All I'm thinkin' to myself is how did he find out," Weinberg recalled. "Then I start tryin' to say a prayer but I couldn't remember any. All I could say was, 'Oh shit, here it comes and here I go.'"

Bell moved to the bed and stood towering over Weinberg. Casually, he aimed the pistol down toward the huddled swindler and slowly squeezed the trigger.

Pffffftt.

Weinberg looked up at Bell. The gun obviously had fired but he was still alive. He looked down to his side. There was a bullet hole in the mattress about an inch from his still-quaking thigh.

"Isn't this gun terrific," Bell enthused. "Absolutely accurate and you can hardly hear a sound. And the best part of it, Mel, I can get you all you want."

Suddenly more enraged than scared, Weinberg screamed, "You crazy schmuck. You just shot a hole in my fuckin' mattress. I gotta sleep on this. What the shit did you do that for?"

Bell contritely responded that it was only a small hole and the bullet probably wouldn't have gone through the floor. Thankful for small favors and convinced that he was dealing with a crazy, Weinberg dutifully admired the gun and assured Bell that the sheikh would want an arsenal of them.

As Bell once again left for the night, Weinberg called after him.

Bell turned. "What can I do for you, Mel?"

"We'll buy the machine guns too," said Weinberg. "But you don't have to bring one in here and show me how it works."

The scene shifted to New York the following week. An FBI agent posing as an Abdul driver was sent to fetch Bell and his group from the airport while Weinberg, Fuller, McCarthy and FBI Agent Bruce Brady, also playing an Abdul factotum, waited in the Holbrook office. When Bell arrived he was accompanied by Linick; Donald Eacret, an attorney from Columbus, Ohio; and Jack Morris, a contractor from Myrtle Beach, South Carolina.

The agent who drove them from nearby MacArthur Airport took

Fuller aside, nodded toward Bell and whispered, "He's packing a gun." Fuller quietly spread the word. Weinberg remembers wondering what Bell might blow a hole through at Abdul's office to demonstrate his weapon and silently hoped that it wouldn't be him.

McCarthy retired to his own office while the rest of the group haggled over the price that Abdul would pay for $200 million in certificates of deposit from an offshore bank known as International Bank and Trust Company of the City of London, Ltd., Grand Turk Island, British West Indies. The bank, Bell explained, was owned by several friends of his.

The price for 300 CDs totaling $200 million was finally set at $17 million in cash. The transfer of the cash for the CDs was set to take place on October 4, 1978, at a private conference room in the United Airlines Red Carpet Lounge at New York's LaGuardia Airport. Bell, who prided himself on being a detail man, told the Abdul representatives that they would need five suitcases to hold the money.

The day before the transfer, McCarthy and Weinberg drove to Korvettes, a discount department store in Commack, Long Island, and bought five cheap suitcases for $114. McCarthy presented his Bank-Americard in payment but was told that his credit for the month was already at its limit.

The two men told the cashier to hold the bags aside and drove back to the local FBI office to get cash from Good. It was nearly closing time for the store and McCarthy drove furiously all the while complaining about wives who make credit-card purchases without bothering to tell their husbands. Weinberg, for once, remained tactfully silent.

On the night of October 3, Suffolk County FBI headquarters resembled a military command post. Good, who had taken personal charge of the operation, conferred in his office with John Jacobs, the forceful Assistant U.S. Attorney from Puccio's Strike Force assigned responsibility for the entire Abscam investigation. Jacobs's job was to monitor Abscam constantly, making sure that it avoided the pitfall of legal entrapment, and assuring that all of the cases were clear violations of the Federal law.

In another office, agents carefully wrapped real money around bundles of similar-sized wads of paper cut from phone books and stuffed the bundles into the five suitcases. Other agents tested and retested the walkie-talkies that would keep the arresting FBI agents in touch with the Abdul group inside the airport conference room while they met with Bell and the others.

It was a scene that would be played with increasing regularity as Abscam expanded. Because Abscam was a sting operation that would continue beyond Bell and his group, the airport caper presented Good with logistical problems. The entire Abscam project would be blown if Weinberg or the other agents posing as Abdul officials were exposed as government undercover agents. Nor could Weinberg or the agents appear as witnesses at any trial in the near future.

Good and Jacobs decided to use FBI agents from the nearby Queens office to make the actual arrests. They were to arrest McCarthy, Fuller and Weinberg along with Bell and his group. Following the arrests Weinberg would keep the deception alive by accusing one of Bell's contacts of being an informer and demanding that Bell's backers make good on the $17 million of Abdul's money that was to be seized in the raid.

Jacobs agreed to stall indictments for several months. By that time, he and Good felt that Abscam would have ended and they would be able to surface Weinberg and the two local FBI agents as witnesses. Neither of the two planners could know at that time that Abscam would last for another year.

The next day at the appointed hour Weinberg, Fuller and McCarthy arrived in the Red Carpet Lounge with the five suitcases. Fuller was equipped with a hidden transmitter that would carry the conversation to the arresting agents waiting nearby. Everyone was nervous because of Bell's propensity for guns. The raiders were told to break into the conference room as soon as they heard Fuller remark that all of the CDs looked okay.

Bell and his companions arrived and went into the private conference room where Weinberg, McCarthy and Fuller joined them. Weinberg asked to examine the CDs. He checked to see that each of the 300 certificates was signed. Then he left the room to get the first two of the five suitcases outside. He returned and set them down. Bell wanted to look inside but Weinberg said the cases were locked and he would only open them after he had all five in the room.

Portable transmitters, known in the trade as body-mikes, are the bane of all professional investigators. They always work when they are tested in the office but frequently flop in the field. They either don't transmit at all, cut in and out, or garble conversations with static or other outside interference. It was no different that day in the Red Carpet Lounge. Fuller pronounced the words that were supposed to bring the arresting agents crashing through the door, but nothing happened.

Weinberg looked at Fuller and McCarthy, shrugged and left to get the next two suitcases. Looking around frantically, he saw none of the agents. He hefted the suitcases and returned to the group. Once again Fuller said the magic words and once again nothing happened. Perspiring profusely, Weinberg fetched the last bag and brought it in.

"Open them," ordered Bell, his hands deep in his topcoat pockets.

Weinberg, trying to still his rising panic, carefully watched Bell's hands as he fumbled for the keys. He was still stalling when he heard a thud against the door. As it later developed, the raiders had decided to make their move, but they couldn't swarm through the door because it was stuck. Every eye in the conference room was riveted on the closed door. After several more thumps it sprang open and everyone was placed under arrest.

The agent responsible for frisking and arresting Weinberg pushed him against the wall so hard that he half-swallowed his cigar. "Police brutality," he screamed when he stopped choking. Weinberg, Fuller and

McCarthy were handcuffed and taken to court with the Bell group. All were then released on bail.

In the following days, Jacobs skillfully played his part in court and Weinberg performed on the telephone. In fact, Weinberg did his job a little too well. The Bell group was so convinced that Abdul was both blameless and real that it filed a suit in Brooklyn Federal Court demanding that the government return the $17 million contained in the five suitcases taken by the FBI.

In a brief filed with the court on December 4, 1978, by the Goldsboro, North Carolina, law firm of Braswell & Taylor, Esqs., the International Bank and Trust Company of the City of London, BWI branch, argued that the government's seizure of the money violated the bank's Fourth and Fifth Amendment rights and was otherwise "inequitable, contrary to law, and violative of the plaintiff's rights."

An assistant U.S. Attorney argued that the arrests were part of an ongoing probe by the government of Abdul Enterprises and the Bell group. Privately, Jacobs submitted an affidavit to Federal Judge Jacob Mishler advising him of the Abscam operation. And six months later, Puccio himself gave another confidential affidavit to Judge Mishler pleading for more time because Abscam was now deeply into political corruption in Atlantic City and the rest of New Jersey.

The original criminal charges were dropped pending later indictment, but Judge Mishler let the government keep the bundles of worthless paper, thus guarding Abscam from exposure. Because of this participation, Mishler later had to disqualify himself as the judge scheduled to sit on almost all of the Abscam cases.

Meanwhile, Abscam flourished. And so did the schools of little fish swimming close or into its nets in both New York and Florida. People like real estate promoter Herman Weiss of Miami, Florida lawyer Ben Cohen, Big George Cannon, Sonny Santini, and Virginia scammer and influence-peddler John Stowe. All but Stowe would play bit parts and then disappear from the stage.

All, however, are proof that Abscam started exactly as the government has claimed, a sting aimed at white-collar crime. What eventually made the difference was the tenacity of John Good and the awesome skill of Mel Weinberg.

Late that October, a man who catalyzed that difference into one of the nation's biggest scandals, walked into Abdul's Long Island office. His name was Bill Rosenberg.

TAPE NINE

Weinberg: The biggest thing a con man has goin' for him is knowin' how to stall, keepin' marks on the hook. Usually you wanna do this so you can either get more outta them or to keep 'em from goin' to the cops or doin' some other drastic thing. But there was another reason in Abscam. If the targets got convinced that we were swindlers, they'd tell other people and all of a sudden we'd have no customers. They hadda believe that we were real and tell other people that we were real. So we hadda come up with some money and the promise of a lot more to keep 'em on the hook. The government wouldn't come up with enough dough, so I had to make 'em believe that the promises were gonna come true, the big potta money was comin' in any day. That's what we call the stall. . . . People would call me and pressure me— when's the money comin'? I would always say it's on the way, we've had some problems, but we're gettin' it all straightened out. I always gave them an answer. You can't go oh, ah, oh. You gotta have a fast answer and you gotta give it to 'em even if it's a lie. That keeps 'em happy. So when the trouble in Iran started, I told them all our money was in Iran. The banks are closed. We got problems. The marks would say, "I know, I know. I read it in the papers. Do you think we'll get it straightened out?"

We would stall 'em for months on Iran. In fact, one mark even called the bank in Iran one day. He called me all excited and said that the banks are open over there. Our money should be comin' out. I said the banks are open for everyday business but the money is frozen over there. And he says: "Oh yes, that's probably the case." This mark [Perry Sabloski] would call up and call up and he got to be a pain in the ass he called so many times. But that's part of the game. You gotta talk to them and accept them. Every day I had calls from ten or twelve people we were dealin' with on CDs and stuff like that. It was my job to speak to them and give them a line of bullshit, it's comin', it's comin'. Thank God nobody ever got wise. We satisfied everybody including Big George. They all went along with it. In fact they wanted to give me more CDs. But the Bureau was getting a little tired of CDs and the people we were dealin' with. And I was waiting for which direction they wanted to go . . . I'm a wheeler-dealer and I gotta keep movin'!

7

BUZZING FLIES

I don't get into politics, because, uh, politics you can go nuts
with. They're all a buncha humps as far as I'm concerned.

—MEL WEINBERG

Mel Weinberg, chin propped in his hands, sat at his desk in the mi-
nuscule office of Abdul Enterprises in Holbrook and willed his mind to
go blank while he awaited the arrival of William Rosenberg. He stared
out the window and watched Allegheny's Washington flight break its
lingering hold on the runway and climb into the cold, blue sky over Mac-
Arthur Airport. Gleaming silver in the October sun, the plane did a lazy
half-circle and headed south over the Atlantic.

High up, so high that it looked like a black V painted on the sky, a
flock of geese, coming down the flyway from Canada, speared in futile
pursuit of the disappearing plane. Even the goddamned geese knew
where they were going, he thought. Everyone knows where they're going
except me.

No matter how much he tried to make his mind go blank, doubt
shouldered back in. He was risking his neck for nickels. He had been
working for the government for nearly a year and now he was supposed

to lick Jack McCarthy's hand because he had been raised to $1,500 a month. Two years ago he had been making $500,000 a year and he'd been his own boss. He didn't like McCarthy. The FBI agent was too square, too cheap, devoid of imagination, suspicious, trouble.

McCarthy, Weinberg decided, thought small. He might be a good FBI agent, but he was no sting man. Weinberg sighed as he thought back on the few times when McCarthy had to act out his part as Abdul's board chairman. Always he either overacted or sounded like he was reading from a prepared script. His face turned red when he lied. His wardrobe was strictly Bond's clearance sale, two pairs of pants and a reversible vest with every suit, take it and run for $99. Weinberg looked ruefully at his own $300 designer sports jacket. He shook his head. Only in the government, he mused. A board chairman dressed from the rack.

He sighed again. McCarthy and Fuller stood out like Boy Scouts at a whorehouse picnic on their occasional forays into the society of hustlers and wise guys. They didn't understand the language; they knew none of the hundreds of little mannerisms, gestures, figures of speech that identify one crook to another as surely as men sharks to lady sharks. And when someone offered either one of them a broad, the basic currency of well-met wise guys, they not only stuttered, they refused.

He'd done his best to educate them, but nothing helped. They were hopelessly straight-arrow. He still remembered with a shudder the recent disastrous trip to Las Vegas. A CD deal had led them into a group who were trying to sell the Aladdin Hotel. Herman Weiss, Miami associate of con man Joe Meltzer, acted as the go-between and invited the Abdul group out to Las Vegas for a talk with the owners and a look at the hotel casino.

The Bureau had been interested because it wanted to confirm information about hidden mob holdings in the Aladdin. What better way than discussing a sale with the owners? McCarthy announced that he and Fuller were going to Las Vegas. He told Weinberg that he was also welcome to make the trip if he paid his own expenses. Weinberg quietly refused, masking his outrage in silence. He even did his best to make the trip work. Part of one taped phone conversation with Weiss involved a discussion about how the owners should treat McCarthy and Fuller.

> *Weinberg:* You know . . . you don't have to come on strong. He's [the owner] not dealing with wise guys. He's dealing with two bankers that, uh, are not used to the Vegas life. They're not high rollers, you know. They're very conservative.
>
> *Weiss:* I'll speak to him.
>
> *Weinberg:* You know what I mean?
>
> *Weiss:* He'll [McCarthy] have everything that he wants. If he wants broads, he'll have broads. If he wants wine, whiskey, some entertainment, the casino, whatever he wants. I'll open the whole town for them.
>
> *Weinberg:* They're very conservative fellows. I don't think they've ever been to Las Vegas.
>
> (Weiss laughs)
>
> *Weinberg:* I don't think they were ever inside a gambling casino.
>
> *Weiss:* [inaudible] . . . walking around with their mouths open.
>
> *Weinberg:* Yeah. If they ask stupid questions, it's not that they mean to ask stupid questions.
>
> *Weiss:* They haven't been exposed to this. . . .
>
> *Weinberg:* They haven't been exposed to it. You know . . . they don't know what skimming is.

Prior to the trip, Weinberg had urged McCarthy to get some new suits so that he could cut a substantial figure as the chairman of a wealthy firm like Abdul. The day before he left, McCarthy came to the office in an obviously new but painfully evident bargain suit.

"What do you think, Mel?" McCarthy asked.

"Jack," Weinberg moaned, "that suit looks like it just came from Sears, Roebuck."

"What's wrong with that?" flared McCarthy.

Weinberg winced and changed the subject.

The Las Vegas trip, as he had predicted, produced nothing.

Now, as he sat at his desk and gazed at planes and geese, he still smoldered at the cheapness of the government, personified by McCarthy, in trying to make him pay his own expenses on the Las Vegas trip. What kind of an outfit was he working with? What was he doing with his life? What was in it for him? Why bother? Nobody seemed to appreciate what he was doing. They always looked at him with fish-eyes. Screw them!

In minutes he would be meeting William Rosenberg, a swindler with an armful of packages sent to Abdul by Weiss. It sounded like the beginning of another CD deal. McCarthy had taken off on something else and he was stuck with handling Rosenberg alone. How many of these scams did the goddamned government expect him to handle at once for its lousy $1,500 a month?

Weinberg picked up a pencil and scrawled Abdul's pending stings on a piece of paper:

POTENTIAL DEALS OCT 18–31

1. Edwards—German war bonds and $220,000,000 CDs
2. George (Big George) Cannon—Oriental rugs and guns and paintings and hijacked goods
3. Spencer—CDs, $25,000,000
4. Settler—drugs and guns
5. Campbell—CDs
6. Mayor —— Corruption
7. Kaye—Fence
8. Schafer—CDs
9. Riviera Hotel—Las Vegas
10. Puerto Ricco—Raphael—CDs
11. John Stowe—Richmond, Va.—$300,000,000 offshore banks

All of them were deals working in New York and Florida. His pencil had stopped for a moment at the name of Big George Cannon. Big George was a little like William Bell, who had quietly blasted a hole in his mattress, definitely not the type of person to fool with. He remembered the day he had first met Big George down in Miami. Big George had tossed two hand grenades on the coffee table in Weinberg's motel room for openers. Weinberg didn't flinch, proof, Big George said, that he had balls. After this expression of confidence Weinberg felt it would have been impolitic to inform the 460-pound omnicrook that he had been glued to his seat in terror. Instead, Big George had taken Weinberg on a tour of his marijuana warehouse.

He dropped his pencil on the desk in disgust and dismissed the thought that he could talk John Good into replacing McCarthy with another agent. He knew from his few brief encounters with Good that the supervising agent would back his own men to the hilt. An idea slowly began to percolate. He would quit.

As Weinberg's pencil thudded to the desk, William Rosenberg eased his new Chevy Camaro from the expressway onto Veterans Highway and headed toward Holbrook. Why in the world, he would later ask, would a fabulously rich Arab like this Abdul fellow want to maintain an office so far away from everything in the Long Island hinterland?

A gray-haired man with a prissy mustache and a little potbelly, sixty-one-year-old Bill Rosenberg was a picture version of the affluent swindler. A monogrammed ascot was neatly folded under the collar of his expensively tailored topcoat. He hinted of $30 cologne, wore clear polish on his carefully manicured nails and carried an attaché case of hand-tooled English leather.

His voice was syrupy, his manner polite, his demeanor ingratiating, his diction a puzzling hybrid of English affectation and Lower East Side reality. He was also insatiably greedy, in all, Uriah Heep in a trilby. A four-month stay as a government guest for stock fraud and permanent expulsion from the society of his fellow security dealers had failed to shake his firmly held belief that untold riches were always just around the corner.

Rosenberg epitomized a breed of con men known to Weinberg and his fellow swindlers as ass-kissers. "He had this sweet voice, this very polite attitude that oozed over you," Weinberg recalls. "But at the end of every conversation, he'd ask me for money. He was whiny, nervy, always pushing, pushing, pushing. He was a grabby bastard."

Resting in Rosenberg's attaché case was a typed, three-page list of potential deals that he wanted Abdul to finance. A few were legitimate; a few were outright frauds; the rest fell somewhere in between. All were impressive: $75 million for a cement plant to be built in Greece, $600 million for airport construction in Bangkok, Thailand, a $5 billion loan to Indonesia marked TO BE REPAID IN OIL.

Almost lost in the forest of dollar signs was a minor notation on the list: "Shipping Crane—used, for harbor at Camden, N.J., through Mayor Angelo Errichetti. Cost $2 million." Several other items on the list also carried advisories that they would be handled through Camden's Mayor Errichetti.

Rosenberg was loosely associated with two younger men, Bill Eden and Dan Minsky, brokering business deals from a small Manhattan office. On this day Eden had stayed in the New York office while Minsky sat next to Rosenberg in the Camaro. As they pulled into the parking space in front of the Abdul office, Rosenberg emerged from the car, and Minsky followed him into the building.

Weinberg had seen the pair entering the building from his vantage point at the window and was waiting for them as they stepped from the elevator. Instinctively, he recognized Rosenberg for what he was and developed an immediate dislike for him. The chemistry was so intense that it temporarily smothered his rebellious intent, and made him determined to hook Rosenberg and hang him out to dry.

Weinberg's pitch that day was a veritable tour de force of the Abscam inventory. He began by describing Abdul's enormous wealth and his desire to pour his money into investments in the United States. He embroidered the wealth scenario, boasting enthusiastically about Abdul's hundred-foot yacht docked at West Palm Beach and the firm's fleet of planes at nearby MacArthur: "We have a Baron there, we have a Falcon and a Lear laying over there. We do all of our own traveling and checking [on potential deals] and we don't want a nickel of front money from anyone."

He confided why Abdul was so frantic to get his money out of Arab banks and into the U.S. "They figure that in maybe ten years there'll be no more Emirs left," he said. "Let's face it. What's going on over there, they'll all be out. The Palestinians . . . take over completely. . . . Look what they're doing in Lebanon now. That's what is gonna happen to all the countries . . . and then these small Arab countries . . . you know, the five what they call the five Emirates, they will all be gone and they realize this. . . . That's why they want their money out."

He waxed eloquent about the volume of Abdul's international money deals. This was touched off by a casual question from Minsky as to whether Abdul's firm had any available Italian liras.

> *Weinberg:* No, we just pulled everything we had out of Italy.
> *Minsky:* All right.
> *Weinberg:* We were discounting our liras. For every million we were taking a thousand dollars. . . . We could have gotten $1,250 in England, but we had so much we had to take the discount.
> *Minsky:* Damn!
> *Weinberg:* We had millions, billions of it, just got finished, just got rid of the last load.
> *Minsky:* I need 250 million.
> *Weinberg:* Well, I wish you would have seen me four months ago. I was loaded with it. We were stuck with a bundle of it, all in 100,000-lira notes. What a job getting rid of it.

Weinberg was no less enthusiastic about describing the money that Abdul already had in the U.S. for immediate investment. Rosenberg sat quivering in a state somewhere between shock and ecstasy as he listened to Weinberg describe Abdul's account at Chase Manhattan.

". . . We have an adviser at Chase Manhattan Bank . . . $400 million that we use [for investments]. We try to keep it up to the $400 million mark at all times. Now, my main job here is getting it [the money] into Chase Manhattan so that . . . it stays at $400. Right now, the balance might be below $400 because we just invested quite a bit . . . I got to get it back up to $400 million; that's my main job. My next job is to okay any packages that come in [for investment]."

As Weinberg spun his web, Rosenberg mentally discarded some of his lesser, more obvious packages. This was the mark he had dreamed about all of his life. No sense risking it on a scam. He had two deals, both of which could reap a fortune. He made his move.

Mayor Errichetti of Camden, he told Weinberg, was interested in developing the Port of Camden. He also had close ties with the Campbell Soup Company, Camden's biggest employer. The Mayor, he intimated, was on the take. With the right kind of money, Rosenberg said, smart people could buy secondhand railroad cars, industrial hoists and other machinery which the Mayor would arrange to have leased by the port and the soup company.

The second package dangled by Rosenberg was even more intriguing. Atlantic City, with legalized casino gambling, was about to become the Las Vegas of the East. All the giants of Last Vegas, Caesars Palace, the Golden Nugget, Bally, plus other major investors, wanted to follow the lead of Resorts International and build multimillion-dollar hotel casinos in Atlantic City. There was one major problem, Rosenberg explained.

Because of a peculiarity in the New Jersey gambling laws, any casino had to be approved twice by the State Casino Control Commission, once before it started building and again when it applied for a permanent license. By contrast, in Nevada, he said, final approval was given by the State Tax Commission before any building started.

Potential hotel-casino owners were being asked to invest up to $80 million in construction costs in Atlantic City, Rosenberg said, without any real assurance that they would be given a permanent gambling license. Even now, he said, the state was conducting hearings on the final license application by Resorts. There were charges that Resorts had had dealings with underworld figures. If the state refused to license Resorts, the firm could lose its entire investment.

Banks and other lending institutions balked at lending money for hotel-casino construction, Rosenberg explained, because of possible loan defaults if licenses were denied. Few builders had the cash necessary to finance their own construction costs. As a result, all of them were scrambling for loans and were willing to pay top interest rates—and even to give investors a piece of the casino ownership.

Rosenberg proposed bringing construction loan packages from potential casino builders to Weinberg. Abdul could make the building loans and Rosenberg would collect commissions for putting the deals together.

Weinberg displayed cautious interest. How, he asked, could Abdul be sure that a builder would get his license after an Abdul-financed hotel casino was built? Rosenberg, careful not to show his cards, assured Weinberg that there was a way to guarantee licenses for casinos, a way so certain that maybe even Abdul himself might want to build his own casino. Minsky nodded guarded agreement. The key to that guarantee, Rosenberg hinted, was Mayor Errichetti.

"You tell me how much . . . Atlantic City," said Weinberg. "If you can show me that you got the juice, we will back you up in Atlantic City."

Rosenberg and Minsky assured Weinberg that they had the right people to handle Atlantic City. Weinberg said that he and Abdul officers would have to meet Rosenberg's Atlantic City contacts personally to make sure that they had the clout to deliver the licenses. Rosenberg eagerly agreed to make the arrangements.

Only then did Weinberg set the hook. He explained that to free up Abdul's money for investment in Camden and Atlantic City, he would need certificates of deposit, gold certificates, anything that could be sent to the Emir's Arab banks in exchange for money. The money would then be transferred to Chase Manhattan, he said, keeping Abdul's balance at $400 million. No one, he assured Rosenberg and Minsky, would ever attempt to cash the CDs—an unspoken signal to Rosenberg that they could be forgeries.

Not only would Abdul be happy to invest in Camden and Atlantic City, said Weinberg, but he would also pay for any CDs that Rosenberg and Minsky might bring in to help Abdul with his money flow.

"I'll pay you $7 million in cold cash for $100 million in CDs," Weinberg assured them.

"You'll pay $7 million cold cash?" Minsky asked incredulously. Weinberg nodded his head.

Rosenberg could barely contain his saliva. With a deal like that, he would make millions at both ends.

He bit hard. He went for the bait despite the fact that he was an experienced, professional swindler totally familiar with every facet of the trade. Within a month, he delivered $1.2 billion in CDs to Abdul, all of them forged. "The print on them was so wet they smeared when you ran your thumb over them," snorted Weinberg. And a year later, despite a series of stalls that would have discouraged the most wanton and experienced, Rosenberg still expected momentary payment from Abdul of his $7 million in cash commissions.

That Rosenberg was enormously greedy is obvious. The real reason for his gullibility, however, was that he had met his master in Weinberg. In the ensuing months, Weinberg played Rosenberg like a piano. He allowed him to catch brief glimpses of Abdul deals where money was actually paid; he praised other influence brokers, creating the subtle implication that Rosenberg wasn't performing as well; at times, he simply ignored the rapacious con man, a tactic that triggered frenzied calls from Rosenberg seeking assurances that he had not inadvertently offended anyone.

And always there was the carrot, more money to be paid if Rosenberg brought in the right packages and contacts. Rosenberg had every reason to believe. One of the first things that he had done after leaving Abdul's office that day, Weinberg later learned, was to call Chase Manhattan to check on the Abdul account.

Rosenberg was the first of four men who would play dominant roles in Abscam as it moved into its political phase. The others were Mayor Errichetti, Philadelphia lawyer Howard Criden and New Jersey building consultant Joseph Silvestri. The newspapers and, later, the Justice Department called these four the middlemen of the Abscam investigation. All were influence brokers; all wanted something for themselves; all brought in Congressmen and politicians for bribes, and none of them was ever aware that they were being scammed by the Federal government.

Over the next month, Rosenberg was on the phone with Weinberg almost every day. One of the packages he pushed was the proposed Penthouse hotel and casino in Atlantic City. Bob Guccione, owner of *Penthouse* magazine, had begun construction of the hotel casino, but needed more money to finish. Would Abdul be interested?

Weinberg pressed for a meeting with Errichetti. There was nothing to be gained from financing Atlantic City hotels, he said, unless Abdul could be guaranteed that the hotels would get gambling licenses. Rosenberg tried to play it cagey. He feared that if Weinberg and Errichetti dealt face to face, he would lose his value as a middleman and be cut out of any commissions from deals between Abdul and Errichetti. Weinberg, however, was insistent. Rosenberg was caught between a rock and a hard place. He didn't want to endanger his $7 million in owed commissions. Grudgingly, he agreed to produce Errichetti at Abdul's office on December 1, 1978.

Errichetti's impending visit to Abdul's office added a sudden new dimension to Abscam. Until now, it had been a highly productive local sting operation. Good, who had gotten it started, had assigned the project middle-level priority in the Suffolk FBI office. He was spending most of his time and most of his agents on the Suffolk County sewer investigation. Now, however, Abscam seemed headed in newer, more sensitive directions.

The mayor of a major New Jersey city might become involved. There were hints that bribery could guarantee gambling licenses for Atlantic City casinos. Maybe Rosenberg was exaggerating. Most con men did when they were making their pitch. But he seemed so certain on the tapes.

Good decided to play it safe. He made two phone calls. The first was to his old friend Tom Emory, supervising agent of the Newark, New Jersey, FBI office. Emory checked his files and reported that Errichetti had beaten an indictment for fraud and perjury several years before when he was Camden city purchasing director. The Bureau files also showed unconfirmed reports that the mob was moving in on Atlantic City. Emory promised his full cooperation if the Errichetti meeting was productive and Abscam focused on New Jersey.

The bottom line of the phone conversation between the two supervising agents was that past performance and information in Bureau files indicated the possibility that Errichetti might take bribes, might have connections in the State Casino Control Commission, and that Atlantic City might not be as pure as New Jersey officials claimed.

This was the first probability profile of the Abscam investigation. Later, as the names of Congressmen and other public officials were offered by various middlemen, each was passed directly to the Bureau in Washington. The names were checked for probability against the national FBI file system. Then the information was evaluated by top-ranking Bureau officials, including FBI Director William Webster. Webster frequently discussed these potential targets, particularly if they were Congressmen, with two successive Attorneys General, Griffin Bell and Benjamin Civiletti, both Democrats.

Only after Washington decided that the persons named by the middlemen fitted a probability profile was Good authorized to target them for meetings. This procedure, in part, explains why such a high proportion of the Congressmen sucked into the Abscam net actually took bribes. It also explains why many of the Congressmen and other public officials mentioned on the Abscam tapes were never tested.

Good's second call was to John Jacobs of the Eastern District Strike

Force. Jacobs was a brilliant trial prosecutor. He had worked closely with Good on the sewer cases and was the Strike Force liaison on Abscam. The two men discussed the importance of the Errichetti meeting. They decided to back up the standard audiotapes with videotapes. Jacobs volunteered to monitor the meeting from an adjoining room.

This phone call set another pattern for Abscam. All important later meetings with Abscam targets, when possible, were videotaped. Each of these meetings was monitored from another room by either Jacobs or another Strike Force attorney. If Jacobs felt that a target was not committing himself strongly enough in return for a bribe at one of these meetings, he would call Weinberg or one of the FBI agents present and have them frame a question to the target that would elicit the response necessary to prove a criminal case.

As the Errichetti meeting date drew near, Good and Jacobs sat down with McCarthy and Weinberg and once again reviewed the rules on entrapment. It was okay to be an attractive lure, a honey pot, they were told. It was also okay to say that money would be paid for favors, CDs, stolen art, and so forth. But, they were warned, the government should not urge unwilling targets to commit specific illegal acts or help them perform those acts. The flies would have to come to the honey pot of their own volition.

McCarthy had no problem with the rules; he had lived with them all of his professional life. But they made no sense to Weinberg. "A guy's either a crook or he isn't," he complained. "If he ain't a crook, he ain't gonna do anything illegal no matter what I offer him or what I tell him to do. If he is a crook, he will. What the hell difference does it make?" He agreed to follow the rules laid down by Jacobs, but he would trudge through Abscam with only a vague idea of the borderline, a fuzziness of definition shared by most of the nation's lawyers and courts.

On December 1, 1978, Angelo Joseph Errichetti, Mayor of Camden, New Jersey, arrived at Abdul's Holbrook office with Rosenberg and Rosenberg's other business associate, Bill Eden. Camden, the biggest city in southern New Jersey, is a tough, brawling town in the shadow of Phil-adelphia, largely supported by heavy industry and Campbell's Soup Company. As Errichetti would proudly boast more than once: "All the fuckin' tomato soup in the world gets made here."

A snappy dresser and a gray-haired look-alike to the late movie tough guy Richard Conte, Errichetti was the son of a coal-stoker and had been a high-school football hero. Brash, energetic, pungent, a man of the street, Errichetti was simultaneously Mayor at $20,000 a year, a State Senator at $18,000 a year and the most powerful Democratic leader in south Jersey.

He was a chain-smoker, a man with a vocabulary like an overflowing toilet; sometimes he would use as many as five scatological words in a simple declarative sentence, but he was earthy, funny, megalomanic, gen-erous, blunt, colorful and a crook at heart. Weinberg loved him on first sight and still regrets that he later had to testify against him. "He was a man's man, a helluva guy," Weinberg recalls. "If he had only one buck to his name, he'd give you half."

At the first meeting with Errichetti (the videotape machine wasn't delivered and the audiotape balked), Weinberg said little, taking the measure of the Mayor as he talked to McCarthy. Weinberg recollects: "He was really somethin'. He was definite about everything, no pussy-footin' around. He hadda way of sayin' things that busted us up."

Subsequent Abscam tapes are larded with examples of Errichetti's col-orful speech. Talking about a hesitant colleague, he said, "I'll hit him over the head with a fuckin' baseball bat." Speaking derisively about an asso-ciate who had conned him, Errichetti said, "After him, the shit burns out." About a fellow politician whom he regarded as dense, Errichetti said, "He's not too fuckin' swift." A favorite mobster was described as "zipper-mouthed and honest," and a favorite judge won the Mayor's admiration for having "balls as big as cantaloupes."

The Mayor characteristically minced no words in explaining his posture to McCarthy. He said, "I'll give you Atlantic City; without me, you do nothing." McCarthy wanted to know how, as Mayor of Camden, Errichetti could produce a casino license from the state and necessary approval from the Atlantic City municipal government. The Mayor spoke about his power in the State Senate (he headed several key committees) and favors owed him by Atlantic City officials. He left early, advising McCarthy: "If you people do the right thing, if you do it our way, there'll be no trouble. I'll be your rabbi."

After the Mayor left, Rosenberg told McCarthy what the Mayor had meant. It would cost between $350,000 and $400,000 in bribes passed through the Mayor for an Atlantic City casino license. Rosenberg told McCarthy that the Mayor would only deal through him and his partner and that they expected a commission on any bribe money given to Errichetti. Playing for time, McCarthy said he'd think about it.

Instinctively, Weinberg knew that Errichetti was a man who could deliver. He was right. Over the next year, the Mayor offered or gave Abscam agents hot diamonds, guns and munitions, forged CDs, counterfeit money, stolen paintings, leasing contracts, municipal garbage contracts, unregistered boats for dope-running, use of Port Camden by Big George as a narcotics depot, Atlantic City zoning changes, a list of thirteen bribable state and city officials, the vice-chairman of the State Casino Control Commission, the Chairman of the New Jersey State Democratic Committee and, directly or indirectly, five United States Congressmen and a Senator.

Good got permission from Washington to delve into Errichetti and Atlantic City. But Rosenberg posed a problem. It would be awkward dealing with Errichetti through Rosenberg. It would be expensive too. Errichetti could also later deny that he had gotten any bribe if it first passed through Rosenberg. From this problem came another Abscam precept: Always insist on dealing direct with a target when it comes to money.

Weinberg laid the groundwork with a series of cozy phone calls to Errichetti in Camden. He painted the picture for the Mayor. McCarthy was straight-arrow when it came to investing money for Abdul. But he,

Weinberg, was more elastic. He was the one checking out the packages. If the Mayor came across, for example, a likely piece of property in Atlantic City priced at $10 million, there was no reason why Weinberg couldn't add another million to the price and split the difference with Errichetti.

Errichetti enthusiastically bought Weinberg's suggestion and agreed that there was no sense in sharing the extra money with Rosenberg. He said he would deal directly with Weinberg and McCarthy. He didn't tell Weinberg that his enthusiasm was based, in part, on a phone call that he had made to Abdul's banker at Chase Manhattan.

While the Errichetti scam perked on a back burner, word of Abdul's easy cash and his elastic agent spread through the East's vast army of promoters, hustlers, swindlers, influence peddlers and fast-buck hopefuls with an immediacy usually reserved only for hot stock tips or news of a fixed horse race.

Weinberg, shuttling between New York and Florida, was juggling as many as ten packages at a time, some from Abdul, some from Florida and some that ping-ponged from one investigation to the other. Weinberg was serving two FBI masters, Good in New York and Fitzpatrick in Miami. Although the two supervising agents kept in contact, Weinberg's habit of instant improvisation made coordination between the FBI offices difficult and sometimes impossible.

Too many things were happening at once:

There was Ben Cohen, the Miami lawyer who once represented the Florida gambling syndicate and later Teamster boss Jimmy Hoffa. A friend of William Bell's, Cohen brought in CDs and was pushing for payment.

There was Ron Sabloski, star of the Abscam dress rehearsal, pushing the sale of some "warm" paintings to Abdul, and his brother Perry, regularly asking when he was going to get his money from the Iranian banks.

There was Big George Cannon, who gave Abdul a suitcase of CDs and was also looking for his money.

There was blind New York hustler Paul Roberts busily arranging still another CD deal for Abdul.

There was Marvin Rappaport of Hallandale, Florida, who was anxious to supply Abdul with sex films.

There was John Stowe, the Virginia businessman who would later deliver Congressman John W. Jenrette, Jr., to Abscam, but now was involved in still another CD deal.

And there was Alfred Carpentier, a roly-poly hustler from Long Island, who bragged of close association with some of the island's top political leaders and public officials, among them U.S. Senator-to-be Alphonse D'Amato. Carpentier and his business associate, Kenneth Boklan, had a cornucopia of packages in which they tried to interest Abdul, but Carpentier's bread-and-butter was Beefalo—a cross between a buffalo and a steer. He had a ranch in upstate New York where he supposedly kept his animals (Weinberg was never sure whether they actually existed), which he sold sight unseen as tax shelters.

Carpentier, claiming friendship with D'Amato, who was then Presiding Supervisor of the town of Hempstead on Long Island, assured Weinberg and McCarthy that D'Amato would give Abdul a choice building location on county-owned land in return for an under-the-table cash contribution. Of even greater interest to Good at the time was his offer to deliver for bribes many of the Suffolk County leaders and officials involved in the sewer scandal.

It took several months of canceled meetings for Good to decide that Carpentier was simply involved in a bait-and-switch operation, promising politicians he couldn't deliver in an attempt to sell Abdul his more prosaic packages. D'Amato has since said that he and Carpentier, a passing acquaintance, never had discussed land sales to Abdul. Carpentier was later convicted, however, of producing a U.S. Immigration agent who took a bribe from Abdul agents.

Rosenberg, sniffing Weinberg's excitement at the mention of politicians, called the government con man and offered several of his own. He said that he could arrange a meeting with "a Senator from Colorado" and Senators Lowell Weicker and Abraham Ribicoff, both of Connecticut.

The three Senators, he said, needed private financing for a much-needed water project in which they had a civic interest. Weinberg asked if they would take money. Rosenberg replied that they would not but that they might be helpful to Abdul in the future. Good wasn't interested in pursuing it. The two Senators have since denied knowing or ever speaking to Rosenberg.

At about this time, Abscam almost fell apart. To keep the New York and Miami FBI operations distinct from one another, Weinberg had invented another Arab Emir for the Florida scam, borrowing the name of Yassir Habib from his old associate at the Hotel Zurich. He flew to Florida to meet with a New Jersey swindler who had promised to give him a pile of forged CDs. FBI agents in Florida planned to arrest the swindler when he passed the CDs to Weinberg.

Weinberg got the bad news when he arrived in Miami. He was met by Miami FBI Supervisor Bob Fitzpatrick and Agent Gunnar Askeland who told him the arrest was canceled. Good, they said, had called from New York and stated that the impending arrest could expose Weinberg as a Federal undercover operative and blow the entire Abscam investigation. Since Good was Weinberg's primary control, the agents explained, they would respect his judgment.

Instant fireworks. Everything about Abscam that had been gnawing at Weinberg came rushing to the surface. The high risks and low salary, penny-pinching on expenses, the haphazard Abdul office, McCarthy's Boy Scout approach, Myron Fuller's detachment from Abscam to testify at some unrelated criminal trials, and now, what he regarded as high-handed interference with what he had come to think of as his own criminal case. He blamed it all on McCarthy.

Although McCarthy was only following Good's orders, Weinberg believed differently. To this day he feels that McCarthy disliked him, was personally cheap, and brought both of these attitudes to Abscam. Flying back to Long Island, Weinberg simmered. He recalled McCarthy's insistence that he pay his own expenses to Las Vegas and McCarthy's reluctance to pursue quickly what Weinberg regarded as hot leads. He was also firmly convinced that McCarthy had cleared his participation in the Florida arrest.

He longed to light a forbidden cigar in the plane. Instead, he chewed savagely on a giant Te-Amo Toros and soothed himself with the recollection that he wasn't the only one who thought that McCarthy was running a schlock operation.

Just the week before lawyer Ben Cohen had called from Miami, furious that McCarthy not only hadn't returned his CDs, but had made him pay for a trip all the way up to New York just to tell him that the CDs were useless. "What the hell kind of office do you run up there, anyhow?" asked Cohen. "When I call, I get a recording. There's never anyone in."

Ron Sabloski, always a man for appearances, had complained about the same thing, adding that the office looked tacky. Rosenberg echoed Sabloski and so did Mayor Errichetti. Weinberg savored the complaints. They're right, he thought, Jack is a schmuck and the office is amateur night. Abscam, he smoldered, was a joke-version of London Investors.

Confident that he was irreplaceable, Weinberg angrily confronted Good. The sandy-haired FBI supervisor was a piece of ice. He called in McCarthy and asked him if Weinberg had ever cleared the Florida arrest with him. McCarthy firmly replied that he had not. Good then lowered the boom on Weinberg.

He told the furious con man that he would do things the FBI way or not at all. This included following McCarthy's instructions, clearing all New York and Florida meetings with McCarthy and restricting his Florida activities for the Bureau. Weinberg countered that he was giving his notice. He intended to quit Abscam in February 1979, the following month.

Until then, Weinberg said, he would follow Good's instructions. He pivoted and left Good's office in what the Victorian novelists would call high dudgeon. Good sighed and sat back to think. The relationship between law enforcement officers and informants, even a special employee like Weinberg, is a very sensitive one. Professional informants are the lifeblood of police business. The informants sense this need on the part of the police and play on it to shift the balance of control to themselves.

A Bureau specialist at handling informants, Good was acutely aware that once that balance shifted, disaster was just a step away for both the law enforcement officer and his informant.

Still, he sympathized with Weinberg. McCarthy was a fine, dedicated agent. But he was inexorably straight-arrow. He would never be an actor. Worse still, McCarthy had little familiarity with organized crime as distinguished from such ordinary criminals as bank robbers and kidnappers. Abscam was shifting toward New Jersey and Atlantic City. More than any other state in the Union, New Jersey had been dominated historically by an alliance of corrupt politicians and organized crime.

He had no intention of replacing McCarthy, who had followed Good's orders implicitly, and had courageously plunged into unfamiliar situations clearly in the line of duty. Maybe he stuttered when he had to lie, perhaps he was inflexible, and certainly he dressed from the rack. But he was solid and loyal. Nevertheless, he was over his head on the subject of the mob, he could not simultaneously be in New York and Florida, and most unfortunately, he no longer commanded Weinberg's trust or respect.

What Good needed was an agent who could work out of Florida, with total familiarity with gambling and the mob, and who possessed enough flexibility and street wisdom to win Weinberg's confidence. The agent would have to be someone that Good knew personally and trusted. He would have to be experienced at handling informant situations. And he would have to be a polished actor.

Good thought for half a minute. Then he picked up the phone and was connected with the Washington office of the FBI.

"May I please speak to Agent Anthony Amoroso," he asked.

Early in January 1979, a still-obstinate Weinberg picked up Rosenberg and Eden at their New York office and drove down to Atlantic City for a meeting with Mayor Errichetti. The next day, McCarthy arrived on the Abdul plane. With him were Agent Ed Woods, the pilot; Agent Margo Denedy, a veteran of the dress rehearsal at the Plaza Hotel; and Agent Bruce Brady, a handsome, dark-eyed man with a hawk-nose and a clipped, black mustache. The other agents were introduced to Errichetti and Rosenberg as members of the Abdul staff. The stranger, McCarthy explained, was Tony DeVito, Abdul's personal construction engineer.

The entire Abdul party was booked into complimentary rooms at the Holiday Inn arranged by Mayor Errichetti. Both the Mayor and Rosenberg were pushing Abdul for a loan to Bob Guccione so that he could finish converting the hotel into the Penthouse Casino. Soon after everyone settled in, DeVito came to Weinberg's room for a talk.

DeVito quietly explained that he was actually FBI Agent Anthony Amoroso. He told Weinberg that he had been born and raised in the Bronx just as Weinberg had been. He said he had been a friend of Good's since they had both worked as summer clerks in the New York Bureau office while at college.

Quickly, he sketched his background in the Bureau including several years as an organized crime field supervisor in the Miami office. Most recently, he said, he had been working out of Bureau headquarters in Washington on the politically sensitive case of Robert Vesco, the financier who had absconded with millions and now lived in the Bahamas.

Amoroso said that he had been asked by Good to join McCarthy as Weinberg's Abscam control. He would coordinate all of Weinberg's Florida operations into Abscam and work with McCarthy on the New Jersey phase of the investigation.

Then Amoroso dropped a bombshell. He said that the Bureau was so impressed with Abscam's potential to uncover corruption in New York, New Jersey and Florida, that it had given the case top priority. From now on, the case would be run through Good out of Bureau headquarters in Washington. FBI Director Webster himself had taken charge. A planning meeting for Abscam, involving top officials of the Bureau and agents from the offices involved, was going to be held early in February in Quantico, Virginia. Good, Amoroso said, hoped to get heavier funding for the probe and a raise in Weinberg's salary to $3,000 a month plus expenses.

Weinberg was impressed by what he heard and saw. Amoroso, who would appear with Weinberg on millions of TV screens eighteen months later in videotapes of the Congressional payoffs, was an ultimately cool man. He gave the impression of a lithe cat, watchfully twitching its tail, always ready to pounce. He looked like a new-breed Cosa Nostra soldier; he talked fluent underworld argot; he dressed expensively and well.

An hour later, at the hotel bar, Weinberg got his first glimpse of Amoroso in action. Rosenberg, always pushy, sidled up to Amoroso at the bar.

"Where did you go to engineering school, Tony?" he oozed.

"None of your fuckin' business," snarled Amoroso, turning back to silent contemplation of his drink.

While Rosenberg retreated to nurse his wounds, McCarthy dined alone with Mayor Errichetti. The Mayor laid it on the line. He needed $25,000 immediately from Abdul to start the ball rolling on a casino license. He said that he would pass this money onto his contacts. The total price in bribes for the license, he said, would be $400,000. He explained that he could guarantee the license because he owned Kenneth Mac-Donald, Vice-Chairman of the State Casino Control Commission. Through MacDonald, he said, he controlled the votes of three of the other four commission members, including that of Commission Chairman Joseph Lordi.

McCarthy indicated interest, but said he would have to clear the arrangements personally with Abdul. Late that evening, Errichetti repeated the conversation to Weinberg. He also told Weinberg that he had a friend who would supply Abdul with phony CDs, securities and counterfeit money.

Errichetti offered another surprise. He told Weinberg that he had arranged for the Abdul group to go to nearby Cherry Hill, New Jersey, the next day to meet an old friend, an attorney named Alexander Feinberg. According to Errichetti, Feinberg was counsel to the Delaware River Port Authority and the "bag man" for New Jersey's senior U.S. Senator, Harrison Williams. Chairman of the Senate Labor Committee, Williams is one of the ranking Democrats in Congress and among its leading liberals.

There were hurried phone calls that night from Atlantic City to Good. He approved the trip to Cherry Hill. With the seventy-one-year-old Feinberg meeting McCarthy and Weinberg the next day was a close friend of Senator Williams, named Henry Williams (no relation). The two men explained that they were in partnership with Senator Williams and a New Jersey garbage contractor named George Katz, in a titanium mine. The government, they said, was in desperate need of titanium and the partners could make millions if Abdul would loan them money to clear the mine of mortgages and pick up a small processing plant nearby.

Feinberg indicated that the Senator would be delighted to meet personally with Abdul's representatives and discuss the partnership's financial needs sometime in the future. McCarthy and Weinberg assured them that Abdul would be most interested in helping the Senator and his friend if further investigation showed that it was a good investment.

In the hallway, Errichetti whispered to Weinberg, "Push this one. We can make a lotta bucks with the Senator."

That night, on the three-hour drive back to his home, Weinberg did some deep thinking. The idea of working for McCarthy still rankled. But he liked Amoroso. He decided to avoid McCarthy and deal with Amoroso wherever possible. If the raise came through in February, he wouldn't quit. But he was determined to keep the pressure on Good about McCarthy. He felt he had been fucked and he was going to return the favor.

There had been another incident at the hotel in Atlantic City. McCarthy, doing his best to act out his part, had boasted that he was sleeping with Margo Denedy. Taking him at face value, the Mayor had booked the two of them into the same room at the hotel. Rosenberg, who suspected that McCarthy was too Catholic for extracurricular bedroom sports, had checked with a room maid. He reported back to Weinberg that the maid told him that only one bed in the room had been slept in.

What Rosenberg didn't know was that McCarthy waited each night in Denedy's room until he was sure everyone had gone to bed. Then he would quietly slip down the hall to spend the night in Amoroso's room. "Just what every scam needs," Weinberg muttered to himself. "A no-go stud."

But Weinberg's problems with McCarthy paled when measured against Abscam's suddenly expanded horizons. A mayor, a casino commission official and, maybe, even a well-known U.S. Senator. "You know somethin', hon," he told his wife Marie when he got home. "This sonuvabitch is really gettin' interestin'."

TAPE TEN

Good: There is one basic secret to dealing with informants. You've got to give them respect. No matter what they might have done in the past, they are still human beings. These people have pride. To be called a stool pigeon, a canary, a fink is demeaning. They know what the words mean. They have to know that you are sincere, that you will keep your promises, that you value what they are doing. There's a chemistry to the relationship. It has to be based on mutual trust. They have to know that you won't let them down as long as they follow the ground rules, and the ground rules have to be clear from the beginning of the relationship. There are times when you have to bend a little with them, be a little flexible. This doesn't mean that you condone anything improper, but you have to understand that they are going against their basic nature when they cooperate with law enforcement. It isn't easy for them and they don't approach situations with your moral and professional point of view. You have to understand that they come from a different world with different codes of behavior.

Mel was that way too, although he was far more than an informant. In the beginning, we had some battles. But we got it all straightened out. Without Mel Weinberg, there would be no Abscam. He was the heart and soul of it. He styled it and made it come down. He was incredible.

Weinberg: In the beginnin', I had some problems with John Good. I didn't know him that good. When I got to know him, it was different. He fought like hell for me; he made me feel like I was part of the team with him and Tony and the rest of them. John Good would give me the shirt offa his back, and I'd go to hell and back for him. That's the way it is with John and me.

8

THE BIG BOATRIDE

The great artists of the world are never Puritans and seldom
even ordinarily respectable.   —H. L. MENCKEN

You gotta remember that I never worked for the Bureau to the
point that I knew what was goin' on. My way of work was completely different from the way they worked.   —MEL WEINBERG

Click. John Wayne peers resolutely through a submarine periscope.
"Steady as she goes . . . "

His finger paused on the TV-remote button. He liked John Wayne.
He was soothing, even on a horse. John Wayne represented honesty,
doing the right thing. People weren't like that. Still, John Wayne was
good think-noise. Like background music. His finger stayed off the
button.

Mel Weinberg, deep in thought, slumped in an armchair at his Long
Island home. Marie, hinting of perfume, brushed his arm with her
breasts as she reached over him to remove a huge ashtray littered with
cigar butts. He silently resisted the unspoken invitation. She's a helluva
woman, he reflected, but when the brain's busy . . .

Events of the past few weeks flickered across his mind. Mayor Errichetti, Atlantic City, high state officials. Rosenberg, U.S. Senators, Guccione, more Atlantic City. Feinberg, Senator Williams, the titanium mine. The good guys. Good, remote, indecipherable, no-nonsense. Amoroso, fast, tough, solid. McCarthy, square, erratic, suspicious. Fuller, creative, cautious, gone. Mayor Angelo Errichetti.

The brash, peppery Mayor would have made a helluva swindler, Weinberg mused. McCarthy thought that he might be. But Weinberg knew better. He had seen the type before. Powerful men, obsessed with money, generously sprinkling favors against the day when it came time to cash them in. Men like Errichetti might run side scams for pocket money, but never for the big score. For that, they dealt in real merchandise.

The Mayor, Weinberg was convinced, had an impressive inventory. He was the most powerful political leader in southern New Jersey. His influence pervaded the highest levels of state government and party leadership. Talking recently with McCarthy, the Mayor had boasted.

"I'm a very dear friend of the Governor [Brendan Byrne]. I call him a cocksucker, but he likes it. Very close to the Governor. Very close to his people. The Attorney General [of New Jersey] is very close to me. I spoke with him, like it was you, on a business basis."

Atlantic City, Weinberg realized, was the key. Operating on a temporary license, Resorts International, the first casino to open, was coining millions. Everybody was rushing in to grab a piece of the action. The state was already processing twelve other casino applications. Land values were soaring. The politicians and the mob were willing to deal. But there was no building money. The banks resolutely refused to loan construction funds unless a gambling license could be guaranteed in advance. The state refused to make this crucial guarantee.

To say it was frustrating was putting it mildly. Everyone could see the pot of gold. People were twenty-deep at Resort's crap tables. But there was no way to get to the pot without construction loans. No way for the politicians to earn bribes for approving zone changes, building-code conformance, extra curb cuts for parking lots. There were no new casinos in which the mob could have a hidden interest. The cash gamble was too risky.

That was the situation. Weinberg slouched in his chair, chewed on an unlit cigar, and structured the Atlantic City scam. There were two basic elements. Errichetti said that he had control of the vice-chairman of the State Casino Control Commission and enough other votes on the commission to guarantee a gambling license. Abdul Enterprises, Ltd., supposedly had millions of the Emir's money to invest in Atlantic City casino construction.

The Mayor had something to sell. He offered political influence and a guaranteed gambling license. Abdul should propose to build its own gambling casino and offer construction financing to other casino applicants. All funding would be done through the Mayor provided he could prove his ability to produce the gambling licenses.

Errichetti, Weinberg was sure, would jump at the bait. He would expect to make a fortune by taking a percentage of each casino investment package. Some of the bribe money would stick to his fingers. And, as the man who positioned the flow of Abdul's cash, the Mayor would have unlimited potential for profitable tie-in deals with potential borrowers.

The Mayor would resist any attempts by Abdul's agents to pass the bribes directly to his political and casino commission contacts. Any middleman would. The contacts themselves would want Errichetti as insulation. They knew and trusted Errichetti. Abdul was an unknown, maybe a police trap. If the bribes were passed through Errichetti, his contacts could later deny that he had given them any money. There was also another consideration. The Mayor could pocket the bribe money, claim he had passed it on and no one would ever know for certain whether he had or not.

For an airtight criminal case, Weinberg had been told, Abdul would have to pay the bribes directly to Errichetti's contacts. Errichetti must be so hooked on the scam that he would strip away the insulation from his contacts and produce them to be paid off in person.

Weinberg plotted the solution. Work on the Mayor's greed. Show him real money. Create the impression that he could tap into riches beyond his wildest dreams. If Errichetti believed enough in the illusion, he would produce his contacts in person, he would suggest anyone or anything that might earn him even more from Abdul. His greed would blind him to inconsistencies in the Abscam cover story and the improbability of the whole thing.

It was the same type of greed that Weinberg had leveraged when he had sold feetless socks in Los Angeles, when he had hustled wire glass, when he had scored millions in Swiss Bank Associates and London Investors with the promise of huge investment loans. He had so convinced his marks that they had brought in other marks. He would do the same with Errichetti. The Abdul loans would never materialize, but if the sting was properly crafted, Errichetti would be hung out to dry like a Monday wash.

It would be easier because he and Errichetti liked each other, and the Mayor, suspecting that he could make more money with Weinberg than McCarthy, would want to deal with him. He knew he could build the scam. His only concern was that the Mayor might be chilled by McCarthy's stilted approach and barely concealed distaste for corrupt politicians and all thieves in general.

He was sure that Good would buy the sting plan. Good was smart. He might even add some ribbons to the package. He would like the idea of having other potential casino owners come to Abdul for financing. If they wanted Abdul's money, they would have to disclose any hidden owners. Many of them would be mobsters. The Bureau, preoccupied under Hoover with bank robbers and car thieves, had gotten into Las Vegas too late. Atlantic City would be different. Already, Good was pushing him for information on any hidden interests that might be backing the Mayor's friend Guccione in the Penthouse casino deal.

Weinberg glanced at the TV. John Wayne stood at stiff attention as an admiral pinned a medal on him and told him that he had saved his country.

"Aw, shucks, Admiral, it was nothing," said John Wayne.

"Schmuck!" Weinberg growled at the TV. "You just sank the whole goddamned Japanese navy. Take cash!"

Errichetti took his cash at Abdul's Long Island office on the morning of January 29, 1979.

Before he arrived, a videotape camera was propped in a file cabinet in McCarthy's office. Strike Force attorney John Jacobs was hidden in the adjoining room. As the camera focused on McCarthy, he put bundles of cash into two envelopes and placed them on his desk. Each envelope contained $12,500. The amount represented the $25,000 that Errichetti had requested to start action on Abdul's gambling license.

Errichetti was chauffeured to Abdul's office by his twenty-three-year-old nephew Joseph Di Lorenzo, listed on the Camden city payroll as Director of the Bureau of Energy. FBI Agent Bruce Brady, added to the growing Abdul staff as McCarthy's driver, served coffee and left the room. Errichetti, in turn, sent his nephew outside, confiding to McCarthy that Di Lorenzo knew nothing of what was going on and was "pure as the driven snow." His nephew, the Mayor said, never asked questions.

Then the Mayor got down to business. He repeated that he could deliver Abdul's license through Kenneth MacDonald. He hinted that he was doing the same for Resorts International.

He warned McCarthy that once Abdul got into the casino business he would have to hire an expert casino manager to run matters. He said that he had convinced a friend of his, Tony Torcasio, to come from Las Vegas and work for Penthouse's Bob Guccione as casino manager. If Abdul decided not to finance Penthouse casino, the Mayor suggested that McCarthy hire Torcasio for Abdul's own complex. He was careful, however, not to push McCarthy too hard.

He said that Torcasio was interested in helping Abdul, but, if McCarthy had someone else in mind, "That's it. That's the end of the conversation. There'll be no more said and that's the end of it." McCarthy said he'd check into it.

Errichetti obviously wanted to deal with Weinberg instead of McCarthy. He knew Weinberg was a crook. And Weinberg had warned him that McCarthy was straight. He aimed the conversation in that direction.

Errichetti: . . . to implement this thing directly, is Mel the guy I wanna call?

McCarthy: Mel will be in Florida until about the first of the month. . . . He'll be leaving, so after then we'll be able to do anything you like . . . we were going to talk about buying some property down there.

Errichetti: Well, all I would like to have is whenever Mel's available. He appeared . . . he impressed me as being knowledgeable. . . . He knew what he was talking about, which is important.

McCarthy: You tell me what you need and I'll make it available to you.

Errichetti: Okay. If I have any problems, I'll call you when I need him.

McCarthy then outlined other areas of interest to Abdul. As Errichetti later confided to Weinberg, McCarthy sounded more like a priest than a hustler.

"Well," said McCarthy. "We're interested in securities . . . artwork . . . My principal [Abdul] is building a private collection in the Mideast and he takes filthy pieces of art . . . and puts them in there."

Errichetti pocketed the two envelopes and, as he left, told McCarthy he would send him some potential casino locations. "Oh, terrific," said McCarthy. "Gee, that would be terrific. Thank you. Really, that's swell."

Mayor Errichetti was the first politician to accept a bribe in the Abscam investigation. He was also the most important. He left Abdul's office convinced that the organization was safe and willing to deal cold cash for favors. Because Errichetti believed in the workability of the arrangement, he was able to convince other targets, including Congressmen, to shed their insulation and take bribes directly. He had become Abscam's Judas goat.

Weinberg had little time to gloat over the initial success of his scheme. He had been back in Florida less than a week when he had another argument with Good. It would prove to be their last argument of the investigation. But it was a fireworks display. It involved an unscheduled meeting in Florida between Weinberg and Errichetti.

Weinberg's version of the story is that he got a phone call in Florida from Errichetti who said that he was coming down on other business and suggested that they have dinner. Weinberg reported that he met Errichetti at the airport, took him to a jai-alai game and then took him home to meet his mother in Hallandale.

SCENE

Weinberg and Mayor Errichetti knock on the door of an apartment. A pleasant-faced, elderly woman answers the door, shrieks in surprise and embraces Weinberg. "Hi, Mom," says Weinberg. "I want you to meet the Mayor of Camden, New Jersey." Helen Weinberg winks affectionately at her son and replies, "Sure, and I'm Moshe Dayan." The Mayor whips out his business card. "I am, I am," he insists. "Look, I'm a State Senator too." Helen Weinberg gasps. She runs into the bedroom to put on a good dress, wailing, "My God, Mel's telling the truth."

Now, arguing over the phone, Good said that he hadn't been informed of the meeting and would have prevented it had he known about it. Weinberg shouted that he had told McCarthy about the meeting in advance. "I know differently," Good replied coldly. Weinberg lowered the boom on McCarthy. He told Good that McCarthy wasn't keeping Good fully informed and complained that McCarthy wasn't pushing hard enough for a face-to-face meeting with MacDonald.

"The Mayor introduced us to him [MacDonald] like we was a Christmas tree, and we still ain't doin' nothin'," Weinberg bitterly complained.

Good answered that the FBI preferred to take things one step at a time. "You and I are looking at this from different perspectives," said Good. "I am adamant on wanting things done my way." He again warned Weinberg that he was to hold no meetings with Abscam targets without his permission. Weinberg made another halfhearted threat to quit. But he was bluffing. Good had just gotten the Bureau to hike Weinberg's monthly salary to $3,000. And Weinberg was beginning to view Abscam as fun.

He did, however, sulk for several days. He blamed all of his problems on McCarthy. In conversations with various Abscam targets he constantly derided McCarthy and confidently predicted that he would be dumped from his post as board chairman as the result of an internal battle for control of the vast Abdul organization.

A few days later, a phone call from the unctuous William Rosenberg jolted Weinberg out of his funk. A woman friend of Rosenberg's who had accompanied him on the Atlantic City trip had seen a picture of Margo Denedy in *Newsday*. The paper identified her as one of a group of FBI agents that had arrested a female skyjacker at Kennedy Airport.

"Mel," asked a shaken Rosenberg. "Are we in trouble?"

Weinberg was caught flat-footed. He had no way of knowing whether Rosenberg's information was accurate. "Couldn't be," he snapped with the same cool he had shown when he had plunged naked through his bedroom ceiling years before. "I've known Margo for years. She's the Emir's personal secretary. It must be some broad that looks like her. Don't worry about a thing, babe." Rosenberg appeared to believe him.

But Weinberg smelled trouble. He called Good in New York and

THE BIG BOATRIDE | 175

asked if Margo's picture had been in the paper. Good said he'd check and call back. A few minutes later the phone rang. It was Good. He sounded like a beaten man. He said that Rosenberg's woman friend was right. The Bureau had desperately needed a woman agent to defuse the skyjack situation and had pressed Margo into service.

Good said that a newspaper photographer had grabbed a picture of Margo, but that no one had told him about it. It was in *Newsday*. Now, Good said, Weinberg might be exposed to extreme danger. He asked if Weinberg wanted him to abort the Abscam investigation. "Only if Errichetti suspects," Weinberg replied.

Good and Weinberg decided to test the Mayor. Weinberg called Errichetti on a pretext and made an appointment to meet him in Atlantic City. Weinberg flew back to New York and drove down to Atlantic City with Amoroso. Good and Brady stationed themselves in another room at the Holiday Inn, ready to step in if trouble developed.

It didn't. The Mayor was his usual profane, ebullient self. Either Rosenberg hadn't bothered to tell him about the newspaper picture, or he had accepted the denial that Weinberg had given to Rosenberg. The subject wasn't discussed at the meeting. Weinberg used the occasion to whet the Mayor's appetite for an even bigger score.

First, Weinberg announced that Abdul's board of directors had definitely decided to build a casino in Atlantic City and wanted Errichetti to select the site. Then he suggested that Abdul would buy all of the other choice casino sites and sell them at inflated prices to anyone who wanted to build. The Mayor would select the sites and share in the profits. In combination, Weinberg enthused, Abdul and the Mayor could offer would-be casino owners an entire package: land, financing and a guaranteed gambling license.

"We'll control all the sites," Weinberg chortled. "Anybody wants to get in here, gotta pay through the nose."

Errichetti was ecstatic and departed with the promise that he would start contacting choice property owners immediately. After he left,

Good, Amoroso and Brady gathered in Weinberg's room and toasted Abscam's narrow escape. Good was delighted at the way in which Weinberg had gilded the Abdul lily for Errichetti. "I've got to hand it to you, Mel," he grinned. "You had the Mayor drooling." Weinberg, unafflicted by modesty, glowed.

Over the next week, Mayor Errichetti was a whirlwind of activity. Almost daily, he was on the phone to Abdul Enterprises pushing the Guccione package, suggesting casino sites, boasting about his contacts. Things in Atlantic City, he said, were going well. "I sit here and tell you without any fuckin' bit of imagination or whatever have you . . . the fuckin' town is ours."

Errichetti made another visit to the Abdul office on February 12. Amoroso and Weinberg pushed the Mayor to produce Kenneth MacDonald for an eyeball meeting with McCarthy. Weinberg said that McCarthy was already in trouble with Abdul for placing some of the Emir's money in Iranian banks. McCarthy, he confided, would need personal assurances about gambling licenses from MacDonald before he committed any of Abdul's money to the Atlantic City deals.

Errichetti scribbled the figure $100,000 on a piece of paper and said that this was the amount needed to bribe four of the five casino commissioners. He said that he had discussed the figure with MacDonald, who had cleared it with the other commissioners. But, as Weinberg had predicted, he balked at producing MacDonald.

"You couldn't hand them [the casino commissioners] anything," said Errichetti. "Because, that would be the end of it. I'm their bag guy. They're gonna deal with me. I'm gonna deal with you."

Amoroso and Weinberg persisted. McCarthy should at least be able to meet MacDonald, they argued. Otherwise, all deals would be off and all of them would lose a fortune. Errichetti relented. But he warned, "The conversation's gonna be nothing but how are you, I'm fine, and goodbye. That's it."

Weinberg and Amoroso exchanged glances. The Mayor had agreed to showcase MacDonald. Nothing more. But it was a crucial move. He had compromised MacDonald's insulation. His obsession with Abdul's carrot had eroded his judgment. Now, it was just a matter of degree. Sooner or later, with the proper stimulus, he would produce MacDonald to be bribed directly by Abdul's agents.

Errichetti spoke wistfully as he departed. "Always, every time I've looked at something, there's always been a missing link . . ." he said. "This is the most fuckin' unbelievable thing I've ever seen in my whole life, and I'm fifty years old. I've seen a lotta things, and heard a lotta things, and dreamed a lotta things; but this thing just seems to be coming up."

On March 5, 1979, McCarthy had dinner with Errichetti and Mac-Donald in Cherry Hill, New Jersey. McCarthy was optimistic, but reserved in reporting the results of the meeting. The Mayor and the vice-chairman of the Casino Control Commission were obviously tight, McCarthy observed. At the Mayor's request, McCarthy had not mentioned anything about a bribe. But, MacDonald had explained the formal application procedure for a gambling license and had offered to steer Abdul's application personally.

The Mayor was far more expansive as he gave his version of the meeting by phone to Weinberg. "He [MacDonald] said he'd give Jack everything he wanted," said Errichetti. "This guy [MacDonald] came on extra strong. He said, 'We give you the word; it is done.'"

Over the next several weeks, there was a stalemate. The Mayor had baited his hook with MacDonald and asked for a $100,000 bribe. But the Mayor insisted that he must be the person to pass the bribe through to MacDonald and the other commission members. The Abdul group insisted on paying the bribe direct and stalled on purchasing any of Errichetti's suggested casino sites and acting on his other packages until he agreed to produce MacDonald for the bribe.

Handling the stall was Weinberg. He told the Mayor that Abdul's board was checking out the various sites. He blamed the delay on lawyers and title problems. He had several sessions with Guccione and reported to Errichetti that the Penthouse publisher had some previously undisclosed financial problems. He even met with Guccione's Atlantic City builder. Errichetti was convinced. He met Weinberg and Amoroso and gave them $435 million in counterfeit certificates of deposit.

The Mayor continued to boast. On March 15, 1979, on one of their increasingly frequent trips to Atlantic City, Amoroso, Weinberg and Brady (promoted from chauffeur to Abdul vice-president by McCarthy) were dining with Errichetti and his nephew in the Camelot Room at the Resorts Hotel and Casino. A gaming board decision on Resort's permanent gambling license was still pending.

Errichetti spotted Jack Davis, manager of the Resorts complex, greeting some people at another table. He called Davis over, introduced him to the Abdul group, and assured him that Resorts would get its license. He said he had talked about the situation with MacDonald and would see MacDonald that weekend to button up the decision.

After Davis left the table, Errichetti introduced the group to attorney Ray Brown, who was representing Resorts. He gave the same assurances to Brown. Later, Errichetti told his dinner companions that Brown had represented him when he had been indicted in Camden for bid fraud. In gratitude, he said, he had gotten Resorts to hire Brown and pay him a $250,000 retainer.

Little more than a year later, the attorney defending Errichetti against Abscam bribery charges in Brooklyn Federal Court would be Ray Brown.

As the Atlantic City scam developed, Weinberg kept busy with other stings in New York and Florida. Bill Rosenberg called often, expressing his concern (with good reason) that he was being cut out of the Errichetti deals; Alfred Carpentier kept promising politicians and producing packages; Ben Cohen continued to demand the return of his CDs; the Sabloski brothers were constant callers; Big George had some more deals; Paul Roberts was still promising offshore banks; attorney Alexander Feinberg wanted to talk more about the titanium mine he owned with

Senator Williams; and four or five other hustlers were bringing in millions in CDs and forged securities. It was a hectic time.

On one of his trips to Florida, Weinberg was asked for advice by Bob Fitzpatrick of the Miami FBI office, who had started a white-collar sting known as Goldcon. Weinberg told him that Abscam's private plane had been an impressive gimmick. "Down here, a yacht would go good," he said. The helpful suggestion was pure Weinberg. If Fitzpatrick got a yacht, Weinberg intended to borrow it for Abscam.

Early in March the sixty-five-foot, oceangoing yacht, the *Left Hand,* sailed into the history of Abscam and moored in a marina at Delray Beach, Florida. Originally known as the *Grand Hotel,* the yacht had been seized by the government after being discovered in 1978, anchored and abandoned fifty-five miles off Miami with 300 bales of marijuana aboard.

Amoroso, who was keeping tabs on Weinberg in Florida, immediately fell in love with the boat and virtually moved aboard. Meanwhile, Good faced two logistical problems: how to explain Amoroso's frequent presence in Florida and how to give the agent a more forceful role in Abscam. Weinberg, as usual, had a solution.

In his Florida stings, he said, he had told marks that he represented an Arab businessman named Yassir Habib. He suggested promoting Habib to the rank of Emir, giving him an investment organization in Florida similar to Abdul and making Amoroso the board chairman of Yassir's firm. Marks could be told that Abdul and Yassir were friends and frequently were partners in the same investments. Yassir and Abdul could be coinvestors in Atlantic City, Weinberg argued, and the boat could be Yassir's office in Florida.

Weinberg threw in a clincher. Sooner or later, as Abscam grew, they were going to have to produce a phony Emir to meet doubting targets. Abdul was out of the question. They didn't want a repeat of the near-disaster at the Plaza Hotel. Ron Sabloski traveled often to Florida and knew many of the Abscam targets who floated in and out of the

Sunshine State. Since Sabloski knew the Plaza Abdul, it was now impossible to pass off another agent as Abdul. But there would be no problem introducing another agent as Yassir.

Good approved the scheme. Within hours, Weinberg was on the phone with various targets, including Errichetti, enthusing about Emir Yassir and Amoroso (using the name DeVito), Yassir's newly chosen board chairman. He assured the Mayor that "Tony's just like me; he'll steal a buck." He heaped the blame for money delays on McCarthy and promised the targets that DeVito would get things moving quickly.

With the Yassir gambit set, Weinberg made another proposal. Errichetti needed a little push, something impressive, if he was going to hand over MacDonald. Why not, he suggested, throw a party on the yacht? Produce an agent acting the part of Yassir and let him impress guests like Errichetti, Feinberg, even Senator Williams. In fact, why not invite all of Abscam's targets to the reception for a mass impression.

"It's a great idea, Mel," said Good. "But we can't afford it. We've only got $750 in the budget to last for the month." Weinberg, undaunted, said, "Screw it. We'll make the guests pay for their own party. Leave it to me. Don't worry about a thing, babe."

Good said he would have to clear the party with his superiors in Washington. Meanwhile, he said, Weinberg could draw up a guest list and issue invitations. So began one of the most bizarre episodes in FBI history: a Bureau-sponsored yacht party at which a U.S. Senator and the Mayor of a major city clinked glasses with a strange assortment of swindlers, hustlers, pornographers, forgers, narcotics smugglers and professional gamblers. It was the ultimate boat ride.

Weinberg overnight became the Pearl Mesta of the swindler set. He burned the phone wires with invitations. Most of the targets said they would come. All wanted to know who was picking up the tab for the plane trip to Florida. Weinberg asked Good. Good gave him the empty-hands gesture. Weinberg called his guests back. They would have to buy their own plane tickets, he said. But he assured them it would be worth the cost. Everything in Florida would be on the house and Yassir would personally close some of their deals.

Good groaned when Weinberg suggested adding some professional hookers to the guest list. "No way, Mel," he said. He explained that there was an argument in Washington over whether even to hold the party. Hookers, he said, would be going too far. They were also illegal, he said, and the Bureau could not be involved in illegality. Weinberg was unhappy. "Whoever heard of a party without hookers?" he asked. But Good wouldn't budge.

The Abdul group huddled on a theme for the party. It was decided that Yassir was throwing the affair to honor Mayor Errichetti. The next question involved what kind of gift to give Errichetti. In the best middle-America tradition, everyone decided on a gold pocket watch. They priced watches and learned to their dismay that the cheapest one they could get would cost $600. Good turned palms up again and shook his head. Weinberg had another idea.

The next day he arrived at Abdul's Long Island office carrying a rusted, but lethal-looking dagger with an ornately carved handle. Years before, he had bought the knife on impulse at an Athens flea market for $2.75. He had retrieved it the night before from the universal repository of travel souvenirs, a cardboard box in his cellar.

"If we can get this shined up," he said, "Yassir can give it to Errichetti and tell him that it's a ceremonial knife of friendship or some kinda bullshit like that. The mayor goes ape for tradition." The agents looked doubtfully at the knife. McCarthy, however, knew of a place that reconditioned and rechromed knives. A week later, the knife came back gleaming.

"Okay, so far, so good," said Good. "But who's going to pay for all this food and booze? Even if the Bureau goes for the party, we don't have the money."

"I'm handlin' it," said Weinberg.

Weinberg called the Mayor. Errichetti was delighted to learn that

Yassir was honoring him at a boat party. He volunteered to pay for the liquor and assured Weinberg that his friend Camden produce dealer Frank Pulini would pay for the food. It was the least he could do, he explained, until Abdul and Yassir could smuggle their money out of those crazy Iranian banks.

Weinberg confided that there was a debate between Yassir and members of his staff. Yassir, he said, wanted to give Errichetti a ceremonial knife of friendship. The knife, Weinberg explained, had been in Yassir's family for hundreds of years. Yassir's staff was taking the position that the Emir should give the Mayor a gold watch because that was the American custom.

Weinberg coyly asked Errichetti which gift he wanted. He breathed an inward sigh of relief when the Mayor opted for the knife. "I will treasure it," he said, his voice choking with emotion. "Friendship is everything."

Then Weinberg called Big George, the Florida crook-of-all-trades. He told Big George about the guest list, including U.S. Senator Williams, who Errichetti had promised would fly down. Big George was impressed, and added that he knew Senator Williams. Weinberg asked Big George if he could supply a stereo set for the Emir's party. Big George said that stereos were temporarily in short supply, but that he would bring a case of Chivas Regal Salute. "That's expensive booze," Big George noted. "It costs $50 a bottle."

Alfred Carpentier, entering into the spirit of the occasion, offered to bring down a dozen Beefalo steaks. Weinberg put down the phone, laughing. "That guy is beautiful," he said to Good. "He'll probably go to Grand Union, buy a dozen sirloin steaks, and tell us they're Beefalo. Who the hell is gonna know the difference?"

His shopping list completed, Weinberg left Long Island for Delray Beach to get things ready for the party. Good, meanwhile, was taking no chances. There was still high-level opposition to the party in the Bureau.

Approval, if it did come, would be a last-minute thing. It always worked that way in government. He argued that plans had to be made early even if the party was later aborted.

Wanting no repetition of the Plaza Hotel fiasco, he asked for an Arab-speaking agent to play the part of Yassir. The Bureau agreed. Its computers turned up the name of Agent Richard Farhardt, who was assigned to an FBI office in Ohio. Farhardt had been raised in Lebanon and spoke perfect Arabic. Moreover, he exuded the presence of an Emir. He was brought east to be briefed and made ready.

It was the height of the tourist season in Florida and Weinberg initially had trouble booking rooms for his party guests. He learned that a manager of the luxury Spanish River Resort in Delray Beach was also Lebanese. He called and told the manager about the Emir's party and his room problem. Impressed by Weinberg's pitch, the manager gave him a group of rooms for himself, Amoroso, McCarthy and the important guests. "There's nothin' like OPEC clout," crowed Weinberg.

Everything was proceeding smoothly when disaster struck. Weinberg was awakened by a 3:00 A.M. phone call a week before the scheduled party. It was one of the two agents from the Miami office assigned to get the yacht in shape. There had been a fire on the boat, he reported. Weinberg dressed and drove down to Delray Beach. There was a little fire damage. But the whole yacht was covered with greasy soot. It was a mess.

The next morning, as a red Florida sun balanced on the ocean horizon, Weinberg, Bob Fitzpatrick of the Miami FBI office, and Amoroso stood on the pier gazing at the smoke-blackened yacht. "We have no money to clean it up, even if we had time," said Amoroso. Fitzpatrick, an eternal optimist, suggested that the guests might chip in $1,000 for the cleaning job.

"No way," said Weinberg. "You're not gonna get any money offa these moochers. They're lookin' to grab money offa us, not give us money." He went to a pay phone and called an old friend who had gone into the carpet-cleaning business. "Can you use them steam cleaners to get soot offa boat?" he asked. His friend said maybe. The friend agreed to come to Delray with two trucks and six men to do the job. "When ya get done," Weinberg said, "send me your bill."

Weinberg was convinced that the party would be a huge success. He was also sure that if the party produced big dividends, the government would happily pay the bills. He refused to worry about what might happen if he was wrong.

Several days later, Good called. The Bureau had finally given permission for the affair. For Good, it had been an uphill battle all the way. His confidence in Weinberg's ability had begun to verge on awe. But there were valid arguments against the party. There was no precedent for it. A United States Senator was involved. The possibility for embarrassment to the already shaken FBI was rampant. But Good believed in Weinberg's ability to work miracles. And the top brass of the Bureau, after long consideration, had backed him.

Good flew in that afternoon with Jacobs and several of the agents assigned to Abscam. He set up a command post with Fitzpatrick at the Hawaiian Village Motel several miles away from the marina. Fitzpatrick ordered the rental of impressive dress-white uniforms for his agents assigned to act as captain and crew of the Emir's yacht. Another agent was assigned to be the Emir's official photographer.

Everyone was ready.

Errichetti arrived two days early on March 22, 1979. He had with him his nephew and Tony Torcasio, Guccione's casino manager. Carpentier, lugging two big bags of steaks, came in later that day with Kenneth Boklan, his business associate, and several other hustlers that they had invited on their own. Some of the other guests began to filter in. Weinberg, Amoroso and McCarthy moved from room to room in the hotel, greeting the new arrivals. The tape recorders started turning.

Much of the time was spent talking to Errichetti. He was obviously impressed by the luxury of his surroundings, and allowed that both he and Senator Williams had canceled scheduled appearances at an important New Jersey political affair to come to Florida. Amoroso and Weinberg nudged him to have MacDonald come to Abdul's office on Long Island to accept the $100,000 casino commission bribe directly.

Relaxed and expansive, the Mayor agreed to strip another layer of MacDonald's insulation. He said he would have MacDonald come with him to Long Island. But MacDonald would wait out in the parking lot in the car while he, Errichetti, came upstairs and accepted the bribe for MacDonald.

Once the bribe was paid, the Mayor told them, Abdul's casino gambling license would be assured. "That place [Abdul's casino] should move like lightning," said Errichetti. "If it's fucked up, I wanna know. You're buying the whole fuckin' town. You got four fuckin' guaranteed commissioners . . . Ken MacDonald; that's his job. Whether he keeps all his profit [the bribe] . . . whether he splits it up . . . I don't give a fuck."

There was another long taping session with Errichetti and Torcasio. Both wanted Abdul to invest in the construction of the Penthouse casino hotel. As Weinberg and Amoroso listened in fascination, Torcasio, the former casino manager of the Tropicana in Las Vegas, described various ways he could skim huge sums of money off the casino without Guccione being aware of it.

Earlier, Errichetti had told Weinberg and Amoroso that if Abdul financed the Guccione casino, Torcasio had promised to skim the weekly profit and split it with the three of them. Torcasio now added some substance to Errichetti's promise.

He said, "I never lie to my friends. When we break bread, hear, you guys will never have to work . . . if you come up to me and say . . . we gotta have $80,000 taken off . . . it'll be there. You know what that is? Eighty thousand without any taxes!"

Weinberg later edged the conversation into the next night's presentation ceremony, when Yassir would arrive to give Errichetti the knife.

Weinberg: No fuckin' around. That knife I told you, that is a knife of friendship, he's givin' ya. That's a ceremonial knife. That means more than the watch.

Errichetti: Well, I'm gonna pick it up as such.

Amoroso: Yeah.

Errichetti: The fact that I understand this is a symbol of friendship, is one that's meaningful to your religion, and I accept it in that same fashion, of one of true friendship; and I welcome the opportunity to be your friend.

Weinberg: He's [Errichetti] gonna get a nice key to the city [Camden]. He's gonna mail it to New York for us to give it to him [Yassir].

Amoroso: Yeah.

Errichetti: I'd like, I'd prefer to go to the jewelers and have a key made especially, ya know, with my name on it to him. But [inaudible] what about the engraving? Well worth its weight; it's a gold key that would be [inaudible]. Dollar-wise, it may cost two or three hundred bucks.

Amoroso: Yeah.

Errichetti: It's more than . . .

Amoroso: It's an insignificant amount, but the sentiment is more.

Errichetti: Yeah.

Emir Yassir arrived magnificently the next day. He was driven by a chauffeur in a large limousine, accompanied by crisp, efficient aides and two tough-looking bodyguards. The Emir strode down the pier with an imperious wave to the assembled guests, followed by his entourage, which included Weinberg and Amoroso.

The yacht gleamed. The captain, impressive in his whites and gold braid, saluted the Emir aboard as the crew stood at respectful attention. The tuxedoed bartenders, courtesy of Errichetti and Pulini, stood ready to set out the food and drinks, supplied by the Mayor and his friend.

Carpentier's mystery steaks sizzled on the aft-deck. Big George's Chivas Regal Salute was prominent at the several bars.

Weinberg went to the bridge and peered down appreciatively at the panoply. The guests moved one by one up the gangplank where they were met by Amoroso and escorted over to meet the seated Emir.

Errichetti, eyes glistening, accepted the knife of friendship from the Emir. He gave his short rehearsed speech, concluding in a voice choking with emotion: "Friendship is everything." Then the Mayor, Senator Williams, Carpentier, Torcasio and other key guests posed individually with Yassir for pictures taken by the Emir's official photographer. Exercising royal prerogative, the Emir then departed in a flurry of excitement, bidding his guests to drink and make merry.

They did. The booze flowed freely and so did the guests.

One of Carpentier's guests, a New York hustler called Prince Forte, surveyed the yacht and sneered: "This yacht is a dinghy. My yacht is 150 feet long." The impact of his boast was lessened by the fact that his fly was open at the time and he had been trying all evening to sell memberships in the Knights of Malta for $25,000 each.

Miami lawyer Ben Cohen trailed McCarthy through the entire party, demanding his CDs back and accusing McCarthy of being a cheapskate. The pair almost got into a fistfight.

Big George Cannon, accompanied by his bodyguard and a business associate, introduced as New York Al, proposed to borrow Yassir's yacht for a week to make a narcotics run. He greeted Senator Williams effusively. The Senator stared at him blankly. "You gotta remember me, Senator," insisted the 460-pound hustler. "When I lived in New Jersey, I delivered a car to your house."

A Florida lawyer who moonlighted as a dope smuggler asked the Senator for help in getting back one of his planes that had been seized in a raid by the government. He roamed the party offering his fellow guests free snorts of cocaine.

"There were forty guests there," recalls Weinberg. "Everybody was trying to promote a deal. Ya know, on TV they got this thing called the love boat. Well, this was the con boat. It was like a convention of swindlers. Everybody was connin' everybody, includin' us."

Later that night, and again the next morning at the hotel Weinberg and Amoroso worked on Errichetti to strip further the insulation from Kenneth MacDonald. The Mayor, now conned beyond redemption, agreed to bring the vice-chairman up to Abdul's office for the bribe. He insisted, however, that the money should be handed to him. The Mayor called MacDonald from his room and arranged the trip to Long Island.

In another taped conversation, Senator Williams told of his interest in the titanium mine, but cautioned Weinberg and Amoroso that they should deal entirely with the attorney Feinberg, who would front for him. Weinberg caught Amoroso's eye. More insulation to be stripped.

The next day, the last guest was poured onto a plane, and the Abdul group took stock. There were the telltale tapes on Torcasio, Carpentier, Feinberg and Williams. MacDonald apparently flushed from cover. Errichetti in deeper. Offers of more CDs from Big George and a number of the other guests. An Emir convincing in every respect whom they could use in the future. Amoroso displayed and accepted. They all decided, though, that the most important result of the party was increased credibility for the entire operation.

The Bureau agreed. After analyzing the tapes and studying Good's reports, Washington Telexed "well done" to all involved. Suddenly, no one had ever opposed the idea. Success had created its thousand fathers.

The next week, on March 31, Errichetti brought MacDonald to the Abdul office. Once again, the videotape camera was propped in McCarthy's file drawer, while John Jacobs monitored the scene from an adjoining room. McCarthy's job was to get MacDonald on record as to what he was going to do for the money and then pass the $100,000 to him. This, Jacobs said, would make the perfect case.

The event turned into another near-disaster.

Errichetti did most of the talking. MacDonald did assure McCarthy that if Abdul had no criminal background and followed standard procedures, it would have "no trouble" getting its license. The Mayor, in MacDonald's presence, was much stronger. Eventually, while the Mayor droned on, MacDonald walked over to the window and stood there gazing over Veterans Highway. McCarthy opened an attaché case and displayed the bribe money. The Mayor reached for it.

McCarthy quickly snapped the case shut and pulled it back. He wanted MacDonald to take it, not Errichetti.

A few moments later, McCarthy opened the case again, showing the money. MacDonald looked at him in surprise, but made no move toward the case. Once again the Mayor reached for the case.

McCarthy flipped it shut and pulled it back again. The conversation continued, never mentioning the near tug-of-war going on at McCarthy's desk. MacDonald turned back toward the window again. Then he gazed back at McCarthy. The agent, making the best of the situation, chose that moment to give the case to Errichetti. The two New Jersey men left.

Several miles away, at a Holiday Inn just off the Long Island Expressway in Hauppauge, Errichetti and MacDonald kept a prearranged meeting with Weinberg and Amoroso. MacDonald was fuming. He said that the display of the money by McCarthy was crude and insulting.

Errichetti agreed, enlarging his attack on McCarthy. He recalled that McCarthy had marred the glitter of the boat party by dressing "disgracefully" in dungarees and a sports shirt. He complained that McCarthy was a stiff and said that he would not deal with him again.

Amoroso and Weinberg spent an hour smoothing MacDonald's ruffled feelings. Meanwhile, the attaché case containing the $100,000 bribe sat outside in Errichetti's locked car. Amoroso told MacDonald and the Mayor that he would shortly be taking over the entire Abdul-Yassir operation. When that happened, promised Amoroso, he would give MacDonald a top job at Abdul's planned Atlantic City casino. Mac-Donald, perking up, said he'd like the challenge.

The Mayor beckoned Weinberg to follow him outside the motel restaurant for a private talk. When they were alone, he handed Weinberg a brochure containing the names and pictures of all the members of the New Jersey State Legislature. He put a check mark against thirteen of the names, among them some of the legislature's most prominent members, and told Weinberg that all of them could be bribed. He also wrote out a separate list of Federal, state and local officials who could be bought. He offered to introduce all of them for payoffs.

Errichetti called Weinberg the next day. "Thank God for you and Tony, because, very honestly, he [MacDonald] was quite shook up; there's no question about it," reported the Mayor.

". . . Just to show you what kind of guy he is. When he had the case in his hand [on the trip home] and he started counting it [the $100,000], and I explained to him Tony's plight with the boat, that he needed the $25,000, he didn't hesitate one little second. Just whipped it right out and said, 'Give it to Tony,' and, uh, I've got it right here and I wanna know . . . what to do with it."

The Mayor was keeping a promise he had made to Weinberg and Amoroso in Florida at the yacht party. The pair had invented a story that Amoroso would be discharged by Yassir if he learned about the fire on the boat. The fire, they confided, had happened because of Amoroso's neglect. It would cost $25,000 to fix the engine-room damage secretly. Errichetti, radiating goodwill, had offered to kick back the repair money from the MacDonald bribe.

Abdul's new vice-president, Bruce Brady, picked up the $25,000 kickback from Errichetti and returned it to Good. The money more than covered the government's costs for feeding and lodging the party guests, including the $800 worth of phone calls that Carpentier had made from his Florida hotel room and tabbed to Yassir's bill. Even Weinberg's friend, the rug cleaner, got his promised check. The entire cost of the party had been paid by Abscam's targets. Weinberg winked at Good and bragged, "I told you not to worry about a thing, didn't I?"

There was, however, a postscript to the affair. As Good listened to the tapes, it was apparent that Errichetti no longer would deal with Mc-Carthy. Some of the other targets were also complaining about him. It was a unique problem. McCarthy's integrity was too obvious. He could not act what he was not. Good retired McCarthy from the field and put him in charge of logistics for the mushrooming investigation.

TAPE ELEVEN

Weinberg: Angie Errichetti was one helluva guy . . . I really liked that man. He was a sport and whenever he had a buck, he spent it. He wasn't no Bill Rosenberg . . . Rosenberg has his first nickel. He was always buggin' me for free hotel room, free meals, free everything. Not Angie. There's no fishhooks in his pocket. He always looks relaxed, but his mind's goin' a mile a minute. He's got deals goin' all over the place and he's always lookin' for a new one. He told me that if he talks to a hundred people and he makes money with one of them, then it was worthwhile talking to the other ninety-nine. I think the two things he loves most in life be-sides makin' deals is money and his daughter. He really worships her. There's somethin' else about Errichetti. He loves people to recognize him. It's an ego thing. I remember one night we was walkin' on the boardwalk in Atlantic City. Up comes this sloppy drunk, I mean, the bum was falling over. But he sees us and he shouts, "Hey, ain't you Mayor Errichetti?" The Mayor's face lights up and he spends twenty minutes bullshittin' with this lush. Another thing about Angie. He likes to win. I remember one night we was sittin' around a hotel room in Cherry Hill, playin' gin rummy. There was me and the Mayor and a coupla agents, who were posin' as Abdul people. We played for hours and he won $40. The way he bragged, you woulda figured he'd won ten grand.

9

HOOKING THE BIG FISH

A man lives not only his personal life, as an individual, but also, consciously or unconsciously, the life of his epoch and his contemporaries. —THOMAS MANN

New Jersey stinks. All the politicians steal. I never met a straight politician the whole time I was in New Jersey. They must hafta screw 'em in the ground when they die. —MEL WEINBERG

Whir. Buzzz. Click.

Telephone propped to his ear, Mel Weinberg glared malevolently at the tape recorder on his desk at Abdul's Long Island office. The tape was at an end. Shit! He fumbled, one-handed, to insert a new cassette.

"What was that noise?" asked his caller, New Jersey lawyer Alexander Feinberg.

"Nothin'," Weinberg replied quickly. "The microwave oven just went off. Them damned things make a lotta noise."

"You have a microwave oven in your office?" Feinberg asked incredulously.

"We gotta," Weinberg assured him. "We got packages comin' in from all over. Sometimes me and Tony is here until midnight workin'. We get food sent in and warm it up in the oven."

They went on to other subjects, among them the financial enrichment of Feinberg's close friend and business partner, Harrison Arlington (Pete) Williams, Jr., the senior United States Senator from the state of New Jersey.

The conversation concluded, he hung up and loosed a torrent of invective at the tape recorder. Always breaking or screwing up. Either the damned machines didn't start until partway through a conversation, or they stopped just when things were getting interesting. And those warning buzzers . . . ! How in hell did the government expect someone to think, talk and change tapes, all at the same time? Cheap fuckin' equipment, he mumbled to himself. Nixon didn't have to get up every half-hour and change the Watergate tapes. He got the good stuff and we get the crap. Idiots!

Weinberg had been irritable lately. For most of his life, he had called his own shots. Now, he had the uneasy feeling that events were beginning to control him. He had been forced to put his Long Island house on the market. Too many hoods had visited his home during the earlier stages of Abscam. Good was concerned that Marie and his son might be in danger when the investigation finally surfaced and arrests were made.

Another thing bothered him. Too many bosses were horning in on Abscam. John Good and Tony Amoroso had won his complete trust. So had Eastern Strike Force boss Tom Puccio and his aide John Jacobs. With them, he felt part of a team. No favorites, no punches pulled, let's get off our asses and get the crooked bastards. But, as the investigation moved into New Jersey, the Justice Department had ordered Puccio and the Bureau to coordinate with U.S. Attorney Robert J. Del Tufo in Newark. Del Tufo, a Democrat, had sent two of his assistants to a recent Abscam coordinating meeting. Weinberg had felt hostility. After the meeting he had prophesied to Jacobs: "Watch out for them. They're trouble."

Deep in thought, Weinberg swiveled in his executive chair and stared out the window. He felt a sense of déjà vu. How many Abscam gambits had he plotted gazing out the same window? Spring 1979 was flipping her skirts. The geese overhead were honking their way back north. There was a soft green on the trees. The thawed earth in the fields had a smell to it. But the change in season passed unnoticed by Weinberg.

Senator Harrison Arlington Williams, Jr. He rolled the name over in his mind, savoring it. Waspie, educated, powerful. A biggie. He dredged the Senator from his memory of the Florida boat party. Very proper, concerned with appearances, quiet, almost vacuous. Weak personality, a piece of fluff, vulnerable to dominant people and ambitious friends. Typical of many former alcoholics, warm wax waiting to be impressed. But the Senator was hungry. Weinberg had smelled it that night.

Washington had given the green light on Williams. There were enough indications, the higher-ups had decided, that the Senator might not be as pure as his publicity releases painted him. Weinberg mentally ticked off the indicators as he doodled on a scratch pad.

The introduction was key. The introduction had been arranged by Mayor Errichetti, clearly a crook. Alexander Feinberg had been identified by Errichetti as Senator Williams's front man. The Mayor had been right. At his first meeting with the Abscam group at Cherry Hill, Feinberg admitted that he was fronting the Senator's interest in a Virginia titanium complex. In Florida, Feinberg had done most of the talking for Williams. The insulation was obvious.

Another factor was the context in which Senator Williams lived and worked. Weinberg had learned to his advantage as a swindler that people frequently tailor their moral standards to the level set by their friends and business associates. The first step in this process was known as "going along." Later, it would be explained as "just doing what everybody else is doing." The more widespread the corruption, the more businessmen and politicians claimed justification to be corrupt.

Senator Williams, Weinberg knew, was a total creature of the New Jersey Democratic organization, one of the most corrupt political parties in the country. Good and some of the other FBI agents had given Weinberg a sketchy outline of the system. Errichetti and other New Jersey politicians were completing his education.

The New Jersey Democratic organization, which the Senator represented, had been molded in 1949 as an alliance between the party and the mob by former party boss John V. Kenny of Jersey City. Kenny had shaped and ruled the party for nearly twenty-eight years. While he held power, the state was for sale. The mob moved at will. Kenny had finally been jailed for corruption during a brief period of reform along with his political satraps, Mayor Hugh Addonizio of Newark and Thomas Whelan of Jersey City. But he had set the tone of the interaction between mobsters and politicians for years to come.

Following Kenny's demise, the reformers had quickly been absorbed and digested by the organization. Now, things were back to normal. Many of the thirteen high state, legislative and city officials on the bribe list that Errichetti had given to Weinberg had been handpicked for office by Kenny. Other Kenny men were now judges, prosecutors and Congressmen. Just last week, Weinberg recollected, Errichetti had offered to bring in the state Democratic chairman for a bribe. Senator Williams had been Kenny's man in Washington.

Another indicator, Good had told Weinberg, was the proposed mining deal itself, and the people apparently involved in it with Williams. Particularly interesting to Good and the Bureau was the Senator's association in the package with New Jersey garbage contractor George Katz, a known bag man for corrupt officials.

To Weinberg's practiced eye, the Virginia titanium deal looked like a scam. The mine and processing plant were located at Piney River in the foothills of the Blue Ridge Mountains. Both had been sold out cheaply to other parties years before by the American Cyanimid Corporation. The current ownership and option agreements were murky. On paper, the two principals were Katz and Henry (Sandy) Williams III, who was a close friend of the Senator's. Secretly sharing their interest, at no cost, were Senator Williams and Alexander Feinberg, who was handling the legal work.

The four men proposed that Yassir lend the group $100 million to purchase American Cyanimid's huge processing plant in Savannah, Georgia, and for clear title to the mine and smaller processing plant at Piney River. This deal, they claimed, would give them a virtual monopoly on titanium in the U.S. The Senator, himself, had said that the rare metal was vitally needed by the government for the construction of submarines and other defense projects. With the titanium monopoly, they predicted, they would make a fortune.

Weinberg quickly dismissed Sandy Williams as a loser. He had been the publisher of a newspaper that went under; he had tried to build a gambling casino on an offshore barge that sank; and he had been beaten up by two hoodlums who were his associates in a platinum importing scheme after he had balked at their attempt to shake him down for $100,000. Then, he had gotten involved in a company known as Biocel.

Sandy Williams had sold stock in the company, which proposed to build a new kind of waste disposal plant in northern New Jersey. He even got an $18 million loan for the project from the state economic development agency. But he was enjoined from selling more stock after the proposal went belly-up because of community opposition. A campaign opponent later charged that Senator Williams personally cleared the way for the state development loan to Biocel. He also revealed that the Senator's wife, Jeanette, held stock in the firm given to her at no cost by Sandy Williams.

George Katz, however, was a different matter. The aging businessman had become a millionaire through a series of corrupt deals with New Jersey Democratic officials spanning thirty years. He had only been indicted once, for fraud on state highway contracts. Katz had earned a solid reputation as a stand-up man with New Jersey politicians, when he had refused to testify against his partner, a county political leader, in a deal that could have spared him indictment. The charge was later dropped on a technicality. Since then, Katz had harvested a bonanza of municipal contracts, including a scandalous kickback deal with Kenny and Jersey City Mayor Whelan.

Katz had another business edge, as he later disclosed to Weinberg on tape. He was a close friend of underworld financial wizard Meyer Lansky and Pete La Placa, who at the time was a leading figure in the New Jersey Cosa Nostra. Katz's firm handled garbage collections in Newark, Jersey City and a number of other New Jersey communities. He told Weinberg that he had garnered his municipal contracts by paying bribes to elected officials. He termed the practice "doing the right thing."

Strange business partners, thought Weinberg, as he sat gazing out his office window. His mind flashed back to the scene on the boat. He had been talking to the attorney Feinberg and Senator Williams in the spacious forward stateroom of the *Left Hand* at Delray Beach.

> *Weinberg:* One fellow [in the mine venture] I don't know, uh, and I don't want to say yes and no, 'cause I'm not sure.
> *Senator Williams:* Georgie?
> *Feinberg:* Georgie Katz?
> *Weinberg:* Yeah.
> *Senator Williams:* He's the guy . . . he's got the resources.
> *Feinberg:* He's got the money.
> *Weinberg:* Yeah, but unfortunately, he's also got a bad reputation.
> *Feinberg:* Well, he . . .
> *Senator Williams* (**laughs**): Ahhh.
> *Feinberg:* You know . . .
> *Senator Williams:* He lived . . . I'll tell ya. I don't know George very well. I know quite a bit about George.
> *Feinberg:* He's really a nice guy.
> *Senator Williams:* Uh, he is a nice guy and he's a generous guy and he, uh, he was in a business in a community and he was

doing business the way business is done in a community in
that business. I mean nothing venal.

Feinberg: He's in the garbage business.

Senator Williams: Yeah, nothing venal, you know. But, uh, now
and again, uh, people, you know [inaudible].

There had been considerable head-scratching about the Williams situation after the Florida party. Why was the Senator keeping his interest in the mining venture secret? Why was a corruptor like Katz keeping the venture afloat with his own cash? The Senator had put in no money; he had rendered no services. Why had the other partners given him an equal share in the deal?

The team—Tom Puccio, John Jacobs, John Good, Tony Amoroso and Weinberg—went back to the tapes. One thread, it was discovered, ran through the tapes: The government was in desperate need of titanium. Williams was the fourth- or fifth-ranking Democrat in the U.S. Senate and had the ear of President Carter and Cabinet members. Slowly it dawned on the small Abscam group. Senator Williams was the key to government contracts and defense contractors who worked for the government. That was why he had been made a partner in the deal. And that was why his interest had to be kept secret.

Williams would be committing a Federal crime if he had agreed to use his position as a Senator to help the mining venture in return for a share in it. Now there were two major problems facing the investigators. It would be difficult to prove Williams's actual interest, which was hidden by his attorney Feinberg, whose interest was also hidden. The second problem involved legal proof that the Senator had actually taken his interest in return for using his influence on government. It was one thing to know that something was corrupt, reminded Good, but quite another to make a criminal case.

Weinberg had wrestled with a solution. "Let's form a new corporation to handle all of their mine deals," he suggested to Good. "We'll tell them that Errichetti is our partner in everything and that me, Tony and the Mayor won't get Yassir to come up with the bread unless we get a piece of the action. That way, we can issue some of the corporation stock to the Senator and we can ask him what he's gonna do for us with the government. He'll have to tell us why he deserves a free ride. With something like that on tape, the Pooch has it made."

The audaciousness of the idea appealed to Good. Many of the details would have to be worked out in the future. For example, if the Senator accepted the stock in his own name, he would expose his interest and lose his value to the corporation as an influence peddler. Still, Good thought, the idea was basically sound. And it was typical Weinberg. Impale the mark on the spike of his own greed.

"Let's try it," said Good.

Now, Weinberg stared blankly at his office window and plotted his moves. He had just given the good news to Senator Williams's attorney and front man Alexander Feinberg. Yassir would loan $100 million to a new corporation that would buy the American Cyanimid plant in Georgia and own the Piney River property. But the loan would be made only if Weinberg and Amoroso approved it. The price for approving the loan, he told Feinberg, would be a secret interest in the corporation for himself, Amoroso and the Mayor. Yassir, he warned, would not know about the kickback.

Feinberg, as Weinberg had predicted, was delighted. Weinberg had frosted the deal by agreeing to give highest priority to another package being offered by Feinberg. The lawyer wanted Abdul to handle the financing for the construction of the proposed Dunes hotel and casino in Atlantic City. The key person in the Dunes package was Morris Shenker, owner of the Dunes in Las Vegas, who had gotten his money in the past from Jimmy Hoffa's scandal-scarred Teamster welfare fund.

Deciding to give the Mayor a share in the mining corporation had been a master stroke, Weinberg mused. Now Errichetti would be on the hook for nearly $17 million—his share of the Yassir loan to the new corporation. Already, the Mayor was on the phone with Feinberg and Sandy Williams. He'd get everybody moving. Oops! He'd almost forgotten. He made a note on his pad. Good was interested in learning more about the garbage rackets. He'd introduce George Katz to Errichetti. It might be rewarding.

As spring quickened, so did Abscam's pace. Packages were flowing in from New York, Florida, Long Island, Atlantic City and the rest of New Jersey. Feinberg and Errichetti wanted Abdul or Yassir to loan money to the Garden State Racetrack in New Jersey. Errichetti said he would get a law through the legislature granting the track special tax relief.

In Florida, Weinberg went house-hunting. On Long Island, Marie complained that the volume of calls to the house from Abdul clients had turned her into a switchboard operator. In one phone conversation, Errichetti pushed loan packages for the track, Bob Guccione's penthouse casino, the titanium mine, and a waterfront condominium project in Camden. He also said he had more casino sites for Yassir in Atlantic City and he wanted to set a date for a meeting with the state Democratic chairman.

Flying back from Florida, Weinberg arranged a meeting between George Katz and Errichetti at the Holiday Inn in Atlantic City. Errichetti agreed to give Katz the Camden garbage collection contract and Katz agreed to "do the right thing" by the Mayor. (Katz later told Weinberg he had loaned the Mayor $20,000.) Errichetti had an even bigger proposal for Katz. He said that he was close to incoming Philadelphia Mayor William Green and City Council President George Schwartz. How about, he asked, a garbage district that would involve all of Philadelphia and southern New Jersey?

Errichetti intimated strongly that Schwartz's support for the project could be bought. Abdul or Yassir could finance the waste-disposal facilities for the huge district and Katz's company would hold the collection contract. Philadelphia, the Mayor admitted, would have to fire its municipal sanitation employees if it wanted to switch over to private collection. Katz, Weinberg, Amoroso and Errichetti would share in the profits.

Weinberg groaned when Good told him that copies of the garbage tape would be forwarded by the Justice Department to the United States Attorney in Philadelphia. "Not another boss," he complained. "That's the problem with you, Mel," grinned Good. "You're too good at your job." But he calmed Weinberg with the assurance that all Abscam assignments would still flow through Puccio and himself.

One of Abdul's persistent callers was the man who had brought the Mayor to the attention of the team in the first place, Bill Rosenberg. He continued to worry that he was being cut out of his split on deals involving Mayor Errichetti. He was right, but Weinberg gave him the stall. One of the deals that Rosenberg complained of was the mining venture with Senator Williams.

> *Rosenberg:* That's a beautiful deal. How the heck do you pay off these guys . . . ?
> *Weinberg:* What do you mean, pay off the guys?
> *Rosenberg:* Pay off Errichetti and Williams.
> *Weinberg:* Well, they get pieces of it [the corporation].
> *Rosenberg* (**pregnant pause**): I see.
> *Weinberg:* And, ah, you know, this is one of the things that we gotta work out.

Alexander Feinberg called several days later and said it was important for Weinberg to tour the American Cyanimid plant in Savannah which they intended to buy. Sandy Williams and Katz would make the trip with him. Weinberg didn't want to go. "What the fuck do I know about chemical processing plants?" he asked Amoroso. "Fake it," said Tony. "You're good at that."

SCENE

Weinberg stands in the huge shipping yards of the American Cyanimid Corporation in Savannah. He is dressed in a rubberized hat, coat and boots. He wears a huge pair of goggles. All are required protection against poisonous fumes. He chews on his unlit cigar. He has just completed a tour of the processing plant with his two companions. Making a huge show of taking notes, he has asked to see the company books and has been told he must put up $50,000 for the privilege. Now he watches the final product being packaged for shipment. The only company employee in view is a black laborer filling sacks. He nudges George Katz.

"Hey, George, if this plant's such a big deal, how come they got only one schwartzer doin' all the packagin'," he asks.

"How do I know," answers Katz. "Maybe it's the off season. Maybe it's like the garment industry."

"Screw them, then," exclaims Weinberg. "If an outfit this big has an off season, I ain't payin' no fifty grand to see the books. What do they take us for, schmucks?"

The Mayor was on the phone nearly every day bubbling with projects and ideas, all designed to flow money his way. He constantly urged a meeting of the principals in the mining venture so that a corporation could be formed and the Yassir loan processed. He nagged for a meeting with the state chairman and offered to introduce Weinberg to some of the state and city officials on his bribe list. He was particularly insistent that he meet Jersey City Mayor Thomas Smith.

From the moment Errichetti had given Weinberg the bribe list, members of the Abscam team had pondered possible approaches to the state and local officials. Errichetti had been bribed for his help in getting a casino license. So had Kenneth MacDonald. It would seem reasonable to the targets that Abdul or Yassir would pay bribes for assurances on that score, given the New Jersey state laws. Everyone wanted to get into the casino business. But what could the two Arabs want in the other New Jersey cities, such as Jersey City? In other words, what pretext was needed to widen Abscam's horizons?

One of the team members had the answer: approval from both the state and various cities for check-cashing businesses. The team would let it be known that they wanted the businesses to wash money skimmed from the casinos or used to bribe public officials. Weinberg had passed the message to Errichetti, who had scouted the state and returned with the names of more officials who would take bribes to smooth the way. At the top of his new list was the name of State Democratic Chairman Richard Coffee.

On May 23, 1979, Weinberg and Amoroso met at the Holiday Inn in Atlantic City for a long conversation with George Katz and Mayor Errichetti. It was a wide-ranging discussion of the garbage business, the mining corporation, political corruption in New Jersey and the proposed check-cashing business. At one point Katz discussed his warm relationship with Jersey City Mayor Thomas Smith.

> *Errichetti:* How do you get along with Tommy Smith?
> *Katz:* Fine. I just got another five-year contract with him.
> *Errichetti:* Tommy is pretty close to me. Dave Friedland [State Assemblyman] and I are pretty close. Wally Shiel's [Hudson County Democratic leader] pretty close to me. Yeah [inaudible], we got a good alliance going . . . Well . . . that's where Alex [Feinberg], Pete [Senator Harrison] Williams, and the whole bunch [inaudible]. True professionals. Today you got a bunch of cocksuckers. Okay.
> *Katz:* Everybody is trying to put the other guy in jail today. See . . .
> *Errichetti* (**interrupting**): Unbelievable!

A week later, the prospective partners in the titanium venture held their first meeting in an elegant setting over luncheon at New York's

Hotel Pierre. Much of the meeting was spent discussing ways in which a corporation could be set up and shares issued. Senator Williams wondered aloud as to whether he should openly declare his shares.

Senator Williams: My situation is this. I've got to, uh, under the law disclose an interest when I have an interest. But, up until now, there's been no defined interest [in the original mining venture]. In what? In ideas basically. We've dealt with no corporate stock.

Katz: But when and if you do.

Senator Williams: When that happens that's part of my law [inaudible].

Feinberg: Well, that's what you . . . and I have to discuss. We have to examine. We're going to do that.

Senator Williams: But there's no sense doing anything yet before we really know. No reason for me to do it [inaudible] May fifteenth because it's just for the record.

Everyone: No! No!

Weinberg: You can put anybody down.

Feinberg: I know that. I understand that. Don't worry. I'll take care of [inaudible].

Weinberg, mounding butter pats on his fourth hard roll, was expert at cutting through verbal garbage and fixing on the real meaning of what had been said. He thought about the conversation that had just taken place. The Senator didn't want to declare the shares, but he needed assurance from his partners that he was acting correctly. He had gotten it. And Feinberg, the foxy old lawyer, had smoothly telegraphed the Senator's course of action.

The Senator said little else at the luncheon, deferring to Feinberg when questions were asked. At one point, as several conversations went on at once around the table, Weinberg asked the Senator if he would use his influence to get government contracts for the fledgling firm. The Senator, Weinberg insisted, said that he would.

Elated, Weinberg returned to the Abdul office. "He went for it," he told Good. But the luncheon tape was a nightmare. Time and again, simultaneous conversations on the tape made parts of it inaudible—including the Senator's answer to Weinberg's crucial question. Weinberg was outraged. "I'm gonna make a bonfire of them fuckin' [tape] machines," he threatened. Good and Amoroso calmed him. There would be other opportunities, they said.

In a telephone critique of the luncheon to George Katz, Weinberg complained: "I think the Senator's a little punchy." Weinberg repeated to Katz Williams's promise to go after government contracts. "But, you know, he don't put no oomph into it when he says it . . . When the Senator says it, you know, you look at him and say, 'Hey, schmuck! Do you really mean it?'"

The Abscam team held another strategy session. The problem was clear: It was not enough to have Feinberg's word that Williams would use his influence with the government. If there was to be a criminal case against Williams, the Senator would have to say it on tape. The solution: tell the partners that Yassir would not finance the corporation unless Williams personally made such a promise to Yassir himself. The FBI would videotape the meeting.

The success of the sting, Weinberg knew, depended on greed. If the Yassir loan came through, the Senator, Feinberg, Sandy Williams, Errichetti and Katz would each own a $17 million share in a $100-million titanium complex. Amoroso and Weinberg had pretended that they would share the remaining $15 million interest in the venture. This would represent the bribe paid to them by the Senator and his partners for persuading Yassir to approve the loan.

Each of the partners, except for Senator Williams, had done something to earn his share in the venture. Sandy Williams and Katz had put together the original package. Feinberg was doing the legal work and fronting the Senator's interest. Errichetti had introduced the group to Weinberg and the other Abscam agents, making the Yassir loan possible.

Senator Williams was in the deal because of an implicit understanding. Weinberg was sure he would use his influence with the government to help the new corporation in any way possible, including contracts for the titanium. This assurance, however, had not yet been made by the Senator. Such discussions, Weinberg had learned, are considered boorish in the world of political corruption. If a government official accepted a free interest in a firm that depended on government-related contracts, his agreement to help get those contracts was understood.

Boorish or not, Weinberg had been told, the Senator would have to spell out personally his agreement to use his influence with the government in return for his interest in the corporation. Otherwise, no criminal case.

All of the Senator's partners in the deal were hungry men, Weinberg calculated. And they were crooked. Neither the Senator nor his partners had batted an eye when Weinberg had demanded the kickback for getting the loan approved. If they were told that the loan was conditional on the Senator's spoken promise to get government contracts, they would make Williams spell it out.

Meanwhile, however, there had been a strange phone conversation with Feinberg. The attorney said that the Senator had been thinking about holding his stock in his own name. What did Weinberg think? The question fortified Weinberg's conviction that the Senator was not operating with all of his marbles. If he were publicly associated with the titanium venture, how could he approach the government for contracts?

> *Weinberg:* He can't report [his interest] . . . if he reports, then he can't do nothin' for us.
> *Feinberg* (**thoughtfully**): That's correct, right.
> *Weinberg:* I mean that. What the hell we got him in there for?

Feinberg: That's right . . . Okay . . . I'll take care of it. I'll work it
out another way. Okay.

Then Weinberg called the Mayor. He reminded Errichetti how much
money was at stake in the deal for all of the partners. He said that it was
vital that the Senator state exactly to Yassir what he was going to do for
his part in the business.

Weinberg: Right . . . now we just want . . . you know, he's getting
twenty percent. What's he going to do for it?
Errichetti: Okay. . . . I'll get hold of Pete right away . . . I'll talk
to him myself . . . head-to-head.

Immediately afterward, Weinberg called Feinberg. He told the lawyer
that he was relaying a message directly from Yassir.

Weinberg: He says without Pete Williams, we got no deal because
the whole thing is gettin' . . . them government contracts.
Feinberg: Uh, ah, okay. You don't have to discuss that any
further. I understand that.

The next day, Weinberg was back on the phone with Errichetti. Again
he stressed the importance of Williams and the contracts to the entire deal.

Weinberg: But we wanna make sure that the Senator knows,
[even] if he did say it in front of us [at the Hotel Pierre], that
this is where he's gettin' his twenty points for.
Errichetti: Pete, I can talk to Pete, like I'm talking to you.
Weinberg: Well, you should get hold of Pete and straighten
him out.
Errichetti: All right, sure.

Weinberg smiled as he hung up. He could picture the scene. Phones jangling in Senator Williams's office as one partner after the other called demanding that he lay it on the line for Yassir. At this point, he was sure, none of them worried about stripping the Senator's insulation. They just wanted a shot at Yassir's millions. So did Williams.

This would be the test, thought Weinberg. He was totally convinced that the Senator was a crook. But until now, he had been a timid, sneaky one, hiding behind Feinberg and others. There would be a difference this time. Williams would have to stand bare-assed naked in Macy's window and do his own dirty work. It made no difference if Williams didn't keep his promise to Yassir. It was enough that he make the offer. That was the crime.

George Katz reported back in mid-June. Feinberg, Sandy Williams and Errichetti had all talked to the Senator. He would personally promise Yassir that he would work to get government contracts for the corporation. He would do better than expected. Weinberg still worried. He was convinced that the senior U.S. Senator from the state of New Jersey was a klutz.

Weinberg set the meeting with Yassir for June 28 at a Marriott Hotel in Arlington, Virginia, just over the Potomac River from Washington, D.C. He orchestrated the suspense. Yassir would fly in the night before on his own jet and secrete himself in the hotel, registering under an assumed name. Weinberg told a grateful Feinberg that Yassir wanted to protect Williams at all costs. Only Yassir, the Senator, Amoroso and Errichetti would be present. It would be a meeting both discreet and safe.

Once more FBI Agent Farhardt was flown to New York from Ohio and briefed on the impending encounter at Abdul's Long Island office. As in Florida, he would pretend to understand English but speak it poorly. That way, Amoroso could ask the key questions and Senator Williams and Errichetti would have to do most of the talking.

Weinberg, always the detail man, argued that Farhardt needed a more expensive suit to play the part of a wealthy Emir like Yassir. Good had seen it coming and groaned. But before Good could respond, Weinberg was out the door with Farhardt in tow. He took the agent to Marsh's, a luxury men's store in nearby Huntington, where he outfitted him in a $500 suit and matching accessories, and charged the purchases to the Suffolk FBI office.

As the day of the meeting approached, Weinberg fretted that Williams would blow his speech to Yassir. So did Errichetti who had had long talks with the Senator. They discussed it on the phone.

> *Errichetti:* What you have to do is get back to me to give me the proper speech. Now, he [Williams] knows he's got to guarantee. He knows he's got to say that.
> *Weinberg:* Right.
> *Errichetti:* He knows he's got to say "I'm the man or this thing doesn't move or work . . . I guarantee all the contracts, guarantee it's going to be successful."

The day before the meeting, Feinberg, Weinberg, Errichetti and Katz gathered in a room at the Marriott and made final plans. Feinberg called Williams at his Senate office and told the Senator: "We're looking forward to seeing you tomorrow . . . You'll get your briefing as you've already gotten your briefing from Eric [Errichetti], and that's the key to the whole goddamned thing . . ."

He promised Williams, who expressed concern, that none of Yassir's staff would be present at the meeting. He added: "You don't want anybody around, okay? Eric will talk to you before you go in, and just like he said, it's a bullshit speech. Do you know what I'm talking about? But it's the key and they're really excited . . . I'm telling you, it's gonna [be] beautiful. Life's gonna be beautiful, pal."

After Feinberg hung up, the four men once again discussed the necessary elements of the Senator's speech to Yassir:

Errichetti: He better [be] bright tomorrow.

Weinberg: He doesn't drink anymore, does he?

Feinberg: No.

Weinberg: Maybe we should give him a marijuana to pep him up.

Errichetti: Oh, no. I'm gonna be next to him. I got the fuckin'
  pin [to jab the Senator]. He knows I got a pin next to him. I
  told him, you make a fuckin' speech or I'll pay for the fuckin'
  baseball bat.

Later in the conversation, the Mayor told Katz and Weinberg about a
recent meeting he had with Senator Williams:

Errichetti: When I went there, he didn't say two fuckin' words. I
  got Pete by the fuckin' throat . . . Let me tell you something,
  cocksucker, don't you go fuckin' this thing up. I got a chance
  to make a million fuckin' dollars, you prick. All you're gonna
  do is give a fuckin' speech, like, give 'em your life. Not much
  left to say. You're gonna fuckin' say it. I don't give a fuck.
  Never mind about doing it. You're gonna fuckin' say it . . .
  And he turned fuckin' white and I revived him. Okay. And
  I'm gonna be sitting next to you, put a fuckin' pin up your ass,
  and you're gonna tell him [Yassir] that without you, there ain't
  no fuckin' mine. Forget it, I'm the fuckin' man. You gotta say,
  "I, not me, me, I, you, and nobody else, and I'm gonna be
  your fuckin' bird dog."

Errichetti was exaggerating the physical aspects of his session with
Senator Williams, Weinberg suspected. But he had told Williams what
to do and he was going to sit at his side in the meeting with Yassir and
make sure he did it. Williams had been primed by his own partners to
pander his Senate seat for money. And he had agreed to do it. That's why
he was coming to meet Yassir at the Marriott the next day.

Weinberg slept fitfully that night. He got up at 3:00 A.M. and flipped on the TV. Nothing. Shit! He'd forgotten that the nation's capital is a tank town. Despite assurances from all the partners, Weinberg worried that the Senator would blow his pitch, even with Errichetti at his side. Sitting on the edge of the bed, he made an unusual decision for a man who had always warned his fellow swindlers never to overplay their hands. He had intended to say just a few words to Senator Williams before he went upstairs to meet Yassir. Now, he decided to give the Senator a last-minute review of the instructions he had already gotten from Errichetti.

When Senator Williams and Errichetti arrived at the hotel, Weinberg was waiting for them downstairs. The ensuing conversation would return to haunt him through the Abscam trials. Defense lawyers, complaining of entrapment and governmental misconduct, would charge that Weinberg had put incriminating words into the Senator's mouth. If he had done this with Williams, they argued, he must have done the same with the other defendants. Ironically, in his pitch to Williams that morning, Weinberg only suggested that the Senator do what he had already been advised to do by his business partners and Feinberg, his own lawyer.

The conversation began with Weinberg's instructions to the Senator that he should tell Yassir that he was in the corporation to get it government contracts and without his participation there would be no government purchases. The Senator replied, "Well, that's why it comes down to metal [titanium] is the big thing. That's the government's area."

Weinberg pressed on: "He's [Yassir] only interested in you. You gotta tell him how important you are, who you are, what you can do, and you tell him in no uncertain terms: 'Without me there is no deal. I'm the man. I'm the man who's gonna open the doors. I'm the man who's gonna do this and use my influence and I guarantee this.' Follow me? All bullshit."

Strong language from an obvious hustler to a member of the United

States Senate. But Senator Williams signaled his agreement, rode up the elevator with Errichetti to room 1104, to perform as promised.

Farhardt, looking appropriately wealthy in his Arab headdress and new $500 suit, sat regally in an armchair with Amoroso at his side.

The conversation moved quickly. Amoroso said that he had background-grounded Yassir on the history of the project and told the Emir that its success depended on the power of the Senator and Mayor Errichetti. He asked Williams to explain it personally to Yassir. Williams replied that titanium was in short supply and that the U.S. desperately needed the metal for submarine skins and other defense-related projects. He added: ". . . if this [titanium deal] can be put together, in my position . . . within our government . . . and knowing, as I do, the people that make the decisions . . . when we got it together, we move. We move with our government."

Almost, but not quite, thought Amoroso. He asked Williams what he would do specifically.

Errichetti primed the pump:

> *Errichetti:* Well, without the Senator, there is no . . . forget it.
> There's no . . . mines and nothing . . . the Senator had the
> know-how in his position as a United States Senator. You're
> what? Chairman of the Labor . . .
>
> *Williams:* Yes . . . I've been there for decades, and, uh, in that
> position, you come up to those positions and you work with
> the people that make the decisions.
>
> *Amoroso:* Right.
>
> *Williams:* Very close to them. Uh, very close . . . I just
> completely believe in this one, this whole situation we've
> presented through the mine. With great pleasure, I'll talk to
> the President of the United States about it and, you know, in a
> personal way, and get him as enthusiastic and excited, because
> we know what our country needs.

The Senator cited his other connections, Vice President Walter Mondale, the Secretary of State, the Secretary of Defense. With these contacts, he said, getting contracts would be no problem. Amoroso skillfully drew the rest out of him. Yes, agreed the Senator, he wanted Feinberg to front his stock in the corporation so that he could not later be charged with a conflict of interest. Yassir beamed his understanding, but said nothing.

The next day Feinberg called Weinberg and reported the Senator's enthusiastic reaction to the meeting:

"You know, the Senator seemed to get a kick out of his own performance. Because, when he related to me what he said, after each statement he said, 'And it's all true.' He was very excited. Like a kid. He was pleased with himself."

There was no time for a celebration. Weinberg and Amoroso flew back to Long Island for the long-awaited meeting with Errichetti and New Jersey State Democratic Chairman Richard Coffee. Errichetti had told Weinberg that Coffee could facilitate state permits for Abdul's planned check-cashing business in various New Jersey cities. He could also, the Mayor said, reach the highest officials in the state for anything the Abdul group might want in the future. The agreed bribe was $50,000, half of which was to be kicked back to Errichetti, who promised to split his half with Weinberg.

Once again, members of Puccio's staff monitored the meeting from another room. The videotapes whirred. Coffee quickly explained that he was also the paid state official in charge of the State Assembly. He said that he had run the past two campaigns for Governor Byrne and was the Governor's closest adviser. That wasn't all, said Coffee. "I walk right in and out of the White House like you walk into your own home." Pointing to Errichetti, Coffee added, "You know him. He's given you the word on me. You've got to understand, okay. I can deal in anything."

Amoroso played unconvinced. The proposed bribe was mentioned twice in the conversation. Once Amoroso told Coffee that he was attempting to buy his influence. Later, he said that he was prepared to pay the $50,000. Coffee clearly understood from Amoroso that Abdul wanted the check-cashing licenses to launder the source of money skimmed from the casinos. But he told Coffee that it sounded like it was easy to get such licenses, implying that it was not worth the bribe. Amoroso's skillful baiting had provoked Coffee's boasts of influence.

Both Amoroso and his Strike Force adviser in the next room were uncertain as to whether Coffee had violated any Federal law in promising to use his influence with the state banking commissioner to get the check-cashing license. Amoroso was startled when the phone rang on his desk. "Don't pay the cash; stall him until we check it out," said the Strike Force attorney. Much to the Mayor's disgust, the meeting ended with no bribe paid and an agreement to meet again at an unspecified later date.

When the pair left, Weinberg turned to Amoroso and exclaimed, "This guy just offered to sell us the whole state. They're unbelievable over there. Everybody steals."

Fresh in his memory was a series of conversations with George Katz. The garbage contractor had said that he was friendly with Mayor Kenneth Gibson of Newark, whom he had rewarded for helping Katz win the city's garbage collection contract. He said that Gibson had promised him that he would arrange the necessary municipal approvals for Abdul to open a check-cashing service in Newark.

Weinberg had proposed paying Gibson a $50,000 bribe immediately, but Katz cautioned him that it wasn't done that way in New Jersey. Bribes, he said, were only paid *after* the favor had been delivered. Katz assured Weinberg that Gibson always kept his promises and always delivered. Weinberg was excited at the information. He had read that Mayor Gibson would be an important leader in President Carter's approaching reelection campaign. He also had learned that Gibson was under Federal investigation for possible income tax evasion involving his Swiss bank account.

Several days later, Good sat Weinberg down for a talk about a sensitive subject. The United States Attorney's office in Newark had routinely been getting copies of the Abscam tapes through the Justice Department in Washington. Most of the officials named on the tapes were from New Jersey, including Williams and Gibson. Robert J. Del Tufo and his aides wanted Weinberg to come to New Jersey and work for them directly. Would he?

Weinberg asked if Good would still be his boss. Good hedged. Not as directly, he said. What about Puccio and John Jacobs from the Strike Force? Good explained that Weinberg would primarily be working under the direction of Del Tufo's assistant Edward Plaza. Weinberg did some fast thinking. He didn't know anything about Del Tufo or Plaza. But he had learned about New Jersey and its Democrats. And he knew that Senator Harrison Williams had nominated Del Tufo for appointment to his job as United States Attorney for New Jersey.

He told Good: "Tell those shits in Washington that if they send me to Newark, I'll quit." Good breathed what Weinberg interpreted as a sigh of relief. "Okay, Mel," said Good. "Let's get back to work." Neither Good nor Weinberg could know that Weinberg's refusal to work for Del Tufo and Plaza would eventually result in another major crisis for the Abscam investigation.

But there was a more immediate crisis to take their minds off the subject. On July 6, just a week after the meeting with Senator Williams and his state party chairman, Weinberg got an anxious call from Mayor Errichetti asking for an immediate meeting. He met the Mayor at Kennedy Airport.

The Mayor looked frightened. When Weinberg heard his story, he understood why, and almost swallowed his cigar. The Mayor said that a Florida swindler had visited Tony Torcasio, Guccione's Atlantic City casino manager, the day before. The swindler said he had sought out Torcasio because he had seen him at the Florida boat party. The swindler said he had been working as an informant for the Miami FBI office and had been smuggled aboard the boat for the party by local FBI agents to wander among the guests and pick up information on Florida crime.

The whole party, the swindler told Torcasio, had been an FBI sting. One of the key people involved in the sting, he had reported, was an FBI agent called Tony (Amoroso). Torcasio had asked the informant about Mel Weinberg. Was he an FBI agent? The swindler said that he had asked Tony about Weinberg at the party. He said that the FBI agent had snapped, "He's just another thief." Thank God for Tony's cool, Weinberg thought to himself. Now he was under fire and had to think fast.

The swindler was obviously telling tall stories to get attention from Torcasio, Weinberg told the Mayor. He had known Tony for years and knew he wasn't with the law. Weinberg suggested that the Mayor warn Torcasio that his source was probably trying to set him up for some kind of scam or shakedown. After all, Weinberg asked indignantly, wasn't the source a big swindler? The Mayor obviously wanted to believe Weinberg. He promised to warn Torcasio right away. "I'll tell Tony [Torcasio] to stay away from this guy," said the Mayor as he left smiling.

For the second time, Weinberg's instant alibi had saved Abscam from collapse. Errichetti, a streetwise political hustler, had been so artfully hooked by Weinberg that he worked with the Abscam group for eight more months despite a firm warning that he had been sucked into an FBI trap.

A furious Weinberg confronted Good later that day. Good told Weinberg that he had been unaware that the Miami office had sneaked the informer into the party. It had been a mistake and he would have forbidden it, if he had known about it. There had been, he said, a communications breakdown. Weinberg barked profane derision. First Bill Rosenberg spots Margo Denedy's picture in the newspaper and now this bush league fuck-up. The FBI wasn't supposed to make mistakes.

The sandy-haired FBI supervisor suddenly looked tired. Almost single-handedly he had sold the Bureau on Abscam, fought for it battle by battle and ruffled some bureaucratic feathers by insisting on a direct line of command to the Bureau's top brass in Washington. The FBI was the best law enforcement agency in the country, he told Weinberg. But this wasn't a TV show. The FBI was composed of human beings. Occasionally, they made mistakes. But not often. It wouldn't happen again.

Staring at Good, Weinberg felt the stirrings of a rare emotion. Compassion. He had come to trust and respect Good more than anyone since his father. He shrugged his shoulders, dropped the subject. "So, what do we do next?" he asked. Good told him. There were some odds and ends on Senator Williams that had to be locked up. Alexander Feinberg was fronting the Senator's stock in the titanium deal. It would be necessary to show that the Senator had actually gotten his stock shares.

On July 11, 1979, Weinberg, Amoroso and Errichetti met Senator Williams at the Northwest Airlines lounge at Kennedy Airport and gave him his unsigned shares representing an interest of $17 million in the new corporation. The Senator and his wife were about to depart for a three-week tour of Scandinavia and Italy.

Weinberg had done some fancy footwork. He had first called Errichetti and fibbed that a second Arab group believed that the titanium corporation was already in operation and wanted to purchase it at a $50 million profit to Errichetti and the other partners. As soon as Yassir's loan came through, said Weinberg, they could sell to the second Arab group. It was important, Weinberg confided, that Yassir not be told of the impending sale. Otherwise, he would insist on part of the profits.

Errichetti whooped at the prospect. He was too dazzled by greed to question Weinberg's fuzzy reasons for wanting the stock shares personally handed to Senator Williams. Once again, the Mayor dominated the Senator. He called him and told him to accept his shares directly. Now, sipping tomato juice in the airport lounge, Williams thawed a little. He said that he was already using his influence for their corporation. He said that the chairman of a large firm had recently come to his office seeking a government favor. The favor-seeker was in a position to do things for the corporation. Williams said that he had granted the favor and used the occasion to express his senatorial interest in the success of the corporation. Gottcha, thought Weinberg.

Things were moving, particularly in New Jersey. Weinberg and Amoroso, faking expertise, pored over prospective casino construction packages from eager builders sent by Errichetti and Feinberg. The Mayor had offered to produce some Congressmen. George Katz was pushing the deal with Mayor Gibson. The forgotten Bill Rosenberg was still on the phone daily, anxious not to be forgotten. The Mayor was making appointments with other New Jersey mayors and reaching out for more casino commission members.

Robert Del Tufo, Weinberg learned, was angry. His assistant, Ed Plaza, had written directly to the Attorney General. The gist of the letter was that unless the United States Attorney's office in Newark could take over Abscam in New Jersey, he and Del Tufo would regard it as a vote of no confidence. Good replied that Weinberg hadn't changed his mind. He wouldn't work for Del Tufo and Plaza. Moreover, he didn't trust them.

SCENE

It is a sultry August day. Weinberg and Amoroso have come to Atlantic City to discuss a casino builder at the request of the resident FBI agent. They buzz his apartment door and enter. Inside, they find Assistant U.S. Attorneys Ed Plaza and Robert Weir, Jr., from Del Tufo's office. There is no polite chitchat. Plaza has read the tape of Weinberg's prep-talk with Senator Williams at the Marriott the month before and angrily accuses Weinberg of setting up the Senator and putting words in his mouth. There is a heated argument. Plaza will later testify that Weinberg claimed there would be no cases unless he put words into the mouths of witnesses. Weinberg and Amoroso will deny it. Plaza demands details on other New Jersey Abscam operations. Both Weinberg and Amoroso suffer instant memory lapses. As Plaza grows more insistent, they stalk out, slamming the door.

Back on Long Island, Weinberg steamed as he related the incident to Good. "What the fuck are these guys, the Senator's defense lawyers?" he asked. "Those bastards ambushed me and Tony. They're out to get our asses. No wonder New Jersey is such a mess. Those fucks can't tell the difference between black hats and white hats. Ain't we supposed to be the good guys?"

Apparently there was also consternation at the highest levels in the Department of Justice, but for different reasons. Senator Williams was one of the highest-ranking Democrats in the U.S. Senate. He was a close friend of Senator Ted Kennedy, who obviously was going to back President Carter in the primaries. Williams's support was up for grabs. Any case against Williams, the word filtered down, had better be airtight.

Once again, Weinberg and Amoroso went to work. Weinberg arranged for Errichetti to call a meeting of the corporation stockholders on September 11 at the Hilton Inn at Kennedy Airport. Senator Williams was present. Weinberg proudly reported that his imaginary new Arab group had raised their offer for the titanium corporation. They would pay $70 million over the $100 million corporate loan from Yassir. The difference would be clear profit for the partners.

Then Weinberg gave the details. The new Arab buyers had one major condition. Senator Williams must retain his 18 percent interest in the corporation after the new Arabs bought it. He would keep his interest at no cost in return for his promise to continue getting government contracts for the firm.

Weinberg turned to Williams and said, "I'm gonna be honest with ya, Pete. That's the only way I'm gonna deal with ya. You're the one that's gotta give us the okay . . . If ya have any qualms about it, ya wanna keep [inaudible] makes no difference to me either way. But the whole thing depends upon you to work in the same capacity as ya working for us to get us government contracts . . . Ya do it for them."

Perhaps the most ill-timed knock on the door by a waiter in the history of law enforcement interrupted the Senator's answer. But, after a long discussion of tax consequences, it was Senator Williams who made the motion to sell to the new Arab group under the conditions given by Weinberg. His motion passed unanimously. It was agreed that Yassir, who would make the whole deal possible with his corporate loan, would not be told about the impending sale. As the meeting broke up, Williams told Weinberg:

". . . Communicate with my friend Yassir, who I like. I thought a great deal of Yassir . . . I just have the feeling that we weren't communicating."

"I get the same feeling with him sometimes, so don't feel bad."

"I like the guy," Senator Williams said.

"I know ya do."

Alone with Amoroso later, Weinberg remarked, "This guy Williams is unbelievable. Twice he's with Yassir. Twice Yassir is a dummy, he don't say nothin'. If the Senator likes Yassir after that, he must have wet-dreams over Charlie McCarthy." They returned to the office, convinced that the government now had all the evidence it needed on Williams.

Washington, however, was still nervous. It wanted even more evidence against Senator Williams. "I can't believe those assholes," Weinberg complained to Good, recalling that in Pittsburgh, he himself had pleaded guilty to a far weaker government case. But he tried. He told Errichetti that the new Arab buyers wanted a letter from Williams assuring them that he would continue to get government contracts for the firm after they had taken it over.

He had not reckoned on Errichetti's aptitude for crime. At a later meeting with Errichetti, the Mayor produced the requested letter which he had written on Williams's Senate stationery, forging Williams's name. He boasted that a friendly printer had counterfeited the stationery. Weinberg was stymied. He certainly couldn't tell Errichetti that it was wrong to forge the Senator's name. Not after all they had done together. He took the letter back to Good. "What a set of balls," he marveled.

Early in October, Weinberg was half-dozing in a suite at New York's

Plaza Hotel as George Katz droned on about New Jersey politics. Suddenly his eyes snapped open. Katz was talking about a White House attempt to squelch the Federal income tax investigation of Newark's Mayor Gibson. Amoroso was staring at Katz saucer-eyed.

Katz said he had gotten details of the fix directly from Mayor Gibson. He said that Gibson had discussed his case with the White House and that President Carter had sent him to then Attorney General Griffin Bell for help. The Gibson probe, Katz explained, was being conducted by the tax division of Bell's office in Washington. According to Katz, Bell told Gibson that he might be criticized by the Republicans if he killed the case in Washington. He said he would transfer it to Del Tufo's office in Newark where it would be killed quietly.

The strategy, Katz said, was for Del Tufo to invite Gibson in front of a Federal grand jury in Newark without a subpoena and allow him latitude to answer all of the evidence against him. Del Tufo, Katz said, was to "chill" the tax case so that the grand jury would return no indictment. He said everything had gone as planned and Gibson told him that there would probably be no indictment. Katz was pleased at the outcome.

After Katz left, Strike Force attorney John Jacobs bounded from the other room, where he had been monitoring Katz's taped conversation. "My God," he exclaimed. "Do you hear that?" Jacobs grabbed the phone and dialed Tom Puccio. He told the Strike Force director to come to the suite immediately. Puccio arrived a few minutes later and played the tape. His face was grim. Orders were immediately issued that the tape was not to be included in the batch of Abscam tapes routinely delivered to Del Tufo's office.

Weinberg nodded to Amoroso. "I told you so," he said.

Weinberg had a chance meeting with Mayor Gibson a few weeks later at a cocktail party Abdul held in Atlantic City for New Jersey politicians. Weinberg was outfitted with a "body-tape," and for once, it worked. Gibson allowed that George Katz was a good man. The Mayor acknowledged that he planned to run for Governor in 1981. Weinberg suggested that the Yassir-Abdul group would help him in the race, and Gibson agreed to the offer. There was a brief conversation about possible Arab investments in Newark and Gibson agreed to a meeting with Weinberg and Amoroso to discuss the matter further.

Mayor Gibson: Okay, we got to start talking about something.
Weinberg: You know, the Arab way.
Mayor Gibson: Oh, yeah.
Weinberg: Well, all right, as long as you understand. I can work
    any deal you want.
Mayor Gibson: Okay.

The meeting was never to come about. Good, Weinberg and Amoroso were discussing possible approaches a few days later with Puccio, when Ed Plaza from Del Tufo's office came in. He said that his office had an income tax case against Mayor Gibson and was going to indict him shortly. Any Abscam meetings with Gibson, he warned, might compromise the tax case. After he left, Puccio, helpless to do otherwise, ordered the Abscam team to stay away from Gibson. They were boxed.

No tax indictment was ever returned against Gibson.

It was also during the fall that Senator Williams and his attorney Alexander Feinberg visited Amoroso and Weinberg at the Plaza Hotel. They wanted a $70 million construction loan for the proposed Ritz hotel casino in Atlantic City. The Senator's wife was a paid consultant to the company that wanted to build and open the casino. Williams said that he had overcome opposition by the Casino Control Commission to the construction plans by secretly visiting Commission Chairman Joseph Lordi, whom he described as "my man." Feinberg admitted that he had helped by making a similar visit to Errichetti's pal, Commission Vice-Chairman Kenneth MacDonald.

Weinberg and Amoroso said they would urge Yassir to make the construction loan. Between the titanium corporation and the Ritz casino,

Williams and his associates were now expecting a total of $180 million in loans from Yassir. Citing the usual problems with Iranian banks, revolutions, strikes, Arab lassitude and lazy lawyers, Weinberg easily stalled actual execution of the loans until the entire Abscam investigation ended.

But the Department of Justice, expressing increasing nervousness over the Williams case, insisted on one more shot at the Senator. The pending casino loan was used as the excuse. Once again, Farhardt flew in from Ohio with his $500 suit to play Yassir for Senator Williams. On this occasion, he was elegantly situated in a suite at the Plaza. Because an understanding had to be precisely articulated his English had also improved admirably.

Once again Farhardt reclined in an easy chair to hold court. With him was Amoroso. There was no Weinberg lurking in the lobby. He stayed away entirely. Farhardt, pretending to use Berlitz English, would ask the questions directly.

Williams arrived with Katz and Feinberg. The date was January 15, 1980, just two weeks before Abscam ended. All greeted Yassir, who assured them first that the $180 million loan money had just arrived in the United States. Yassir then said that he planned to come and reside in the United States in the near future. He asked Williams if he could arrange legislation to give him permanent status or citizenship. Williams said that it could be done and that he would do it. He added:

". . . We met in April of last year in Florida. And, er, er, I was impressed with you as a person . . . reserved, er, moderate, thoughtful, and I read sensitivity. Qualities that I had . . . associated . . . with, er, er, good character, and, er, er, interesting and, er, pleasing personality . . ."

Yassir, who graciously told the Senator that he could call him Sheikh, said that he would be willing to pay for the legislation. But Williams, who was eagerly pressing for the loan money, said that he would not take Yassir's money for pushing his citizenship. He said he would personally steer the necessary legislation through Congress.

The sting had been a masterpiece. Drawing upon his fertile imagination, Weinberg had relied on a lifetime of experience to build the illusion. Time and again he had conjured the targets to jump through hoops, reverse direction and turn inside out. He had created corporations, issued stock shares, inspected books, toured plants, hired hotel suites—all to flush Senator Williams from cover. And he had done so. Now, as he viewed the final videotapes from the Plaza Hotel, he chuckled. Senator Harrison Arlington (Pete) Williams, Jr., had indeed been left standing bare-assed in Macy's window.

New York Times, Jan. 6, 1981. Following are excerpts from the guidelines issued today by the Justice Department to govern undercover operations by the Federal Bureau of Investigation:

AUTHORIZATION OF THE CREATION OF OPPORTUNITIES FOR ILLEGAL ACTIVITY

1. Entrapment should be scrupulously avoided. Entrapment is the inducement or encouragement of an individual to engage in illegal activity in which he would otherwise not be disposed to engage.
2. In addition to complying with any other requirements, before approving an undercover operation involving an invitation to engage in illegal activity, the approving authority should be satisfied that:
   a. The corrupt nature of the activity is reasonably clear to potential subjects.
   b. There is a reasonable indication that the undercover operation will reveal illegal activities; and
   c. The nature of any inducement is not unjustifiable in view of the character of the illegal transaction in which the individual is invited to engage.

3. Under the law of entrapment, inducements may be offered to an individual even though there is no reasonable indication that the particular individual has engaged, or is engaging in the illegal activity that is properly under investigation.

   Nonetheless, no such undercover operation shall be approved without the specific written authorization of the Director, unless an Undercover Operations Review Committee determines . . . that either

   a. there is a reasonable indication based on information developed through informants or other means that the subject is engaging, has engaged, or is likely to engage in illegal activity of a similar type; or

   b. the opportunity for illegal activity has been structured so that there is reason for believing that persons drawn to the opportunity, or brought to it, are predisposed to engage in the contemplated illegal activity.

4. In any undercover operation, the decision to offer an inducement to an individual, or to otherwise invite an individual to engage in illegal activity, shall be based solely on law enforcement considerations.

TAPE TWELVE

Weinberg: I don't understand all this entrapment bullshit from the defense lawyers. Like . . . I'm supposed to have told the Senator what to say in the hotel. He's a United States Senator. Why's he takin' orders from a hood like me? He always coulda said "No." Nobody twisted anybody's arm to take the bread. We said it was there if they wanted it. They knocked each other over tryin' to be first on the bread line.

10

CONGRESS FOR SALE

It could probably be shown by the facts and figures that there is no distinctly native American criminal class except Congress.

—MARK TWAIN

Most of them [Congressmen] curse like mad and drink like fishes; they're not too bright.

—MEL WEINBERG

It was a picture-book panorama. Palm fronds rustling in the vagrant breeze, vivid green in the afternoon sunshine. Pastel mansions and hotels in wedding-cake white. Tropical blue-green waters, sleek yachts bobbing at anchor, and bikinied young ladies waving hello as they flashed by on water skis. A time to be burned in memory as insurance against the certainty of life's lesser moments.

Click. Click. Mel Weinberg leaned over the rail of the *Left Hand* and captured the idyllic scene on film. Gottcha! Great boobs, mused Weinberg, as he oogled the shapely blonde he had just photographed gliding down the inland waterway. Nice ass too. Broads stuck out in all the right places when they leaned back against a tow rope.

He dismissed the image. Weinberg already had his hands full. He'd

sold the Long Island house a month ago and moved with Marie and their
son to Florida. Now, it was less than an hour's drive from his new condo
to the trailer home where he kept Diane. The matinees were killing him.
He was actually anticipating his return to New York.

The Long Island house had been sold at a $40,000 loss and he was
lucky to get that in the depressed sales market. Buyer interest in the
house had only turned brisk, he reflected, after Marie told the neighbors
that he lost a valuable diamond from his ring under the kitchen stove.
Well, he had lost a small diamond chip. Name of the game, he shrugged.
Back to business.

As the Abscam yacht slowly cruised north of Fort Lauderdale,
Weinberg turned toward the group of men who sat in deck chairs, sipping
iced drinks. Tony Amoroso and Mayor Errichetti were deep in conversation with two newcomers. One of them was Howard Criden, a portly,
owlish, Philadelphia attorney. The other was his law partner, Louis Johanson, a Philadelphia City Councilman. The Mayor had brought them
to Florida to discuss Arab financing of an Atlantic City casino for one of
their clients.

The pitch had been made; the proposal would be studied. Artists'
conceptions, construction plans and cash-flow charts had all been neatly
folded and returned to leather attaché cases. Now it was time to relax,
savor the present, and pleasurably anticipate the future. The conversation
turned general, the lawyers shed their vests and loosened their neckties.
The booze flowed.

FBI Agent George Allen, playing the role of Yassir's yacht captain,
gestured toward a sleek cruiser berthed at a hotel pier. He said that the
boat was under charter to General Anastasio Somoza, who had just fled
to the U.S. after being ousted as President of Nicaragua. Amoroso had a
sudden idea. He turned to Errichetti, who was dressed in the Camden
version of gentlemen's yachting attire: a screaming sport shirt and crepe-
soled sneakers.

Amoroso told the Mayor that Abdul and Yassir were concerned about unrest in their homeland and would probably have to flee to the United States in the near future. He said that the two Arabs were worried that they would not be allowed to remain in the United States. Errichetti eagerly replied that he had the political connections to handle the Arabs' residency problems. After all, he winked, Abdul and Yassir had plenty of money to cover the expenses. He'd go to work on the problem as soon as he returned to New Jersey.

The date was July 26, 1979, and, at that moment, began a phase of Abscam that would dominate the nation's headlines seven months later. Six United States Congressmen would be charged with bribery. A seventh would win immunity as a prosecution witness. And twenty-three others, some of them totally innocent, others less so, would be named as potential targets on the Abscam tapes. Errichetti would get it started; Criden would expand it, and Johanson would become ensnared in it.

Three days later, Errichetti called Weinberg in Florida as the pudgy con man prepared to fly to New York. Marie carefully folded and packed his shirts while he talked with the Mayor on the master-bedroom phone. Errichetti discussed arrangements to meet United States Senator Harrison Williams at Kennedy Airport and deliver the Senator's stock in the titanium corporation. Then he switched to the subject of asylum for the Arabs. He said that he already had lined up two Congressmen, Michael (Ozzie) Myers and Raymond Lederer, both of Philadelphia.

"Quick, gimme a pencil," Weinberg called to Marie as he hung up. She made a hurried search of the room, eager to please. Finding none, she opened her bag and handed him a ballpoint. He scratched the two names he had gotten from the Mayor onto a notepad and then read them aloud. The names meant nothing to him. He didn't follow politics, regarding politicians with the disdain that professionals have for amateurs in their chosen field. The names meant nothing to Marie either. He'd pass them on to Good tomorrow.

A week later, he sat in the Long Island Abdul office talking on the phone to Bill Rosenberg. The oily swindler complained that he needed money and wanted to know how much longer he'd have to wait for his percentage on the CDs he had supplied. Weinberg gave him a double-talk stall:

> *Weinberg:* So, ya gotta have patience. I know ya need bread, but ya need patience.
> *Rosenberg:* All right; patience we got.
> *Weinberg:* Ya know, you're not dropped outta anythin'.
> *Rosenberg:* All right, good. I'd like to be a little closer to the picture, if I could be.
> *Weinberg:* Well, ya know, ya stay closer to the picture—I don't think anybody is close to the picture.
> *Rosenberg:* Yeah.
> *Weinberg:* Ya know, one minute you're close, the next minute you're standin' on the outside.

Weinberg smiled as he put down the receiver. He always enjoyed shafting Rosenberg. If the greedy bastard really knew the whole picture, he'd be running for a criminal lawyer as fast as his chubby little legs could carry him.

It had been a busy day keeping all of Abscam's balls in the air. He had already told the Mayor that Abdul wasn't going to finance Guccione's Penthouse casino. And he was subtly souring Errichetti on Tony Torcasio. The Mayor wanted Abdul to hire Torcasio as a casino manager if the Penthouse deal fell through. Weinberg reminded Errichetti of Torcasio's promise in Florida to skim Guccione's profits when the Penthouse opened. "He'll do the same thing to us," Weinberg warned. The Mayor finally agreed. "I'm jerkin' him off, keepin' him in limbo," said Errichetti.

Weinberg worked at keeping the Mayor happy. Errichetti was vital to the Abscam case against Senator Williams, he was the entrée to political corruption in New Jersey and now he was offering to deliver Congressmen. Weinberg called the Mayor almost every day. Abscam files would eventually reflect 173 taped conversations between the two men. And now, he was arranging to send the Mayor a fake deed for an ocean-front condo in Florida as a gesture of gratitude from Abdul and Yassir.

The phony deed had been arranged through a builder friend of Weinberg's. The apartment actually existed in a complex under construction. It would be another six months before the building was ready for occupancy. Weinberg fervently hoped that Abscam would be finished before the Mayor, luggage in hand, walked into his condo and found the real owner living there. Errichetti, for his part, had been very grateful.

The Mayor had needed some sweetening. As a packager of casino financing, he was batting zero with Abdul. Errichetti and his contacts had been bringing prospective casino builders to Abdul for the last six months. All of them wanted financing in the $60- to $80-million range. Errichetti had been promised a cut of each successful deal.

The government, however, in the guise of Abdul, had no intention of making the loans. The endless hours of meetings with various builders and promoters had only one purpose: to build the FBI files on underworld investments and political corruption in Atlantic City. Once this information was extracted from a hopeful borrower, it was Weinberg's job to stall for a few months and then invent some reasonable excuse for Abdul's "financial advisers" to turn down the loan application. He had done this with Bob Guccione.

While he was stalling, Weinberg would keep borrowers' hopes high with glowing reports on the progress of their loan applications through the complex Abdul bureaucracy. "I just heard from Abdul's people in the Mideast and they had a very favorable impression of the package," Weinberg would whisper. Confident of success, the borrower would spread the news of his impending good fortune and other builders would get on line for loans. It was London Investors all over again.

The hostage crisis in Iran, headlined daily, was a perfect rationale for the stall. Occasionally, Weinberg would vary the excuse, explaining to Errichetti that Jack McCarthy, demoted in an Abdul corporate power struggle, was trying to sabotage every casino loan package approved by Amoroso. Weinberg took savage delight in blasting McCarthy, knowing that the FBI agent was assigned to listen to replays of each day's tapes. The end result, however, was that Errichetti was living on promises.

John Good wandered into Weinberg's office. He said that Washington was interested in Errichetti's offer of the two Congressmen. The crime would occur, he said, if the Congressmen offered to use their government positions in return for money. It was the same premise as the Williams case, but this time it would be a straight cash deal. He asked Weinberg to get some basic answers from the Mayor: what, where, when and how much.

The hard-nosed FBI boss and the unrepentant swindler talked familiarly. Each had come to admire the other's unique ability and mutual admiration had bridged the way to friendship. Good firmly dominated the relationship and Weinberg had learned to obey orders implicitly, a lesson learned solely out of respect. In the privacy of the Abdul office, Good dispensed with formalities and they talked and counseled as unlikely equals.

The same attitude prevailed through the growing Abscam team. If Weinberg had been a praying man, he "would have knelt on nails to thank God for Tony Amoroso." He respected Amoroso as a smooth professional and enjoyed him as a person. Quickly, they had evolved into a nice-guy tough-guy team. Weinberg would tell targets that both he and Tony were willing to skim side money from Abdul and Yassir. But he would explain that Tony had to insist that certain rules were followed, such as taking bribes directly, or he would lose his job and be replaced by an honest man.

FBI Agent Steve Bursey had joined Agents Haridopolos and Brady as an Abdul chauffeur. The organization now boasted two limousines, a Caddie and a Lincoln, and two smaller cars, all leased cut-rate by Weinberg from an auto-dealer friend. "Everybody used to fight to sit in the back seat and play big shot," Weinberg recalls.

Since Abscam had moved into the political arena, expense money had loosened up considerably. Tom Puccio had added assistant U.S. Attorneys Ed McDonald and Larry Scarf to help John Jacobs coordinate the unfolding cases. And the Strike Force boss himself was meeting regularly with John Good. Things, Weinberg reflected, were definitely going well.

There was a flurry of conferences among Puccio, Good, Weinberg and Amoroso to develop a scenario for the proposed meetings with the Congressmen. The bribes must be paid in the actual presence of the Congressmen. The Congressmen would first have to pledge the use of their offices to help Abdul and Yassir stay in the U.S. And they would have to acknowledge that they were getting the bribes for that reason. Weinberg then passed along the ground rules to Errichetti. He agreed. The price for each Congressman, the Mayor said, would be $100,000 in cash.

The Mayor had good news. He said Congressman Myers would be the first and that he had "five or six others" lined up besides Lederer. The Mayor said that his contact, whom he would only describe as "my man," had also arranged meetings with U.S. Senator Herman Talmadge of Georgia and two Congressmen from President Carter's home state. He later identified the Congressmen as Elliot H. Levitas and Wyche Fowler, both from the Atlanta area. He was particularly enthusiastic about Talmadge.

Even Weinberg had heard of Talmadge. He had read that the Senator was currently under Senate investigation and might face official Senate censure. He suspected that the Mayor might have pulled Talmadge's name out of the newspapers, but the Bureau traced the name of the Atlanta lawyer named by Errichetti as his contact with Talmadge and the two Georgia Congressmen. According to Good, the lawyer's name checked out.

On August 8, Weinberg and Amoroso were talking in a hotel suite to Errichetti about their progress on the Williams titanium deal. Errichetti switched the subject to the proposed meeting with Congressman Myers:

Errichetti: I will naturally talk to Ozzie [Myers] first; I was just tryin' to grasp as to what he'll say. Ozzie's got balls, that's for openers. Ozzie is the same kid, so you know, the night they gave the swearin' in [Congressional oath of office] in Washington, he's that Congressman that got locked the fuck up . . . for punchin' a waitress in the mouth . . . he's crazy; he's got balls; the man's got balls.

Weinberg: Don't give him nothin' to drink that day [of the Abscam bribe].

Errichetti: No, he got balls.

Weinberg: All you gotta do is punch Yassir in the fuckin' mouth and we'll all be lookin' for jobs.

Errichetti: He [Myers] represents all Italians. You gotta be a pretty decent guy, be Irish and be [act] fuckin' Italian like him in South Philly. Like [former Mayor Frank] Rizzo, [he] thinks he's [Myers] the greatest thing since fuckin' sliced bread; he's got fuckin' balls.

Weinberg: Then who would be the next one after him?

Errichetti: I guess it would be Lederer, Congressman Lederer, okay? Next I guess is the two from Georgia and Talmadge. Now, I don't [inaudible] with Talmadge. Talmadge has already been talked to.

Weinberg: That's one I'm surprised at, that guy's gotta be . . .

Errichetti: Now, he's reachin' out for two in Florida, and hopefully, in California [inaudible]. Now the other one would be Frank Guarini, the Congressman from Hudson County [New Jersey] . . . that will all be resolved after Labor Day.

Howard Criden now called Weinberg frequently at the Abdul office. For the record, he was asking about the progress of the casino loan that he and Louis Johanson had requested. But in almost every conversation, he would discuss Errichetti's quest for bribable Congressmen. Gradually,

Weinberg and Amoroso came to realize that Criden was the Mayor's secret contact man. It was he who was actually finding Myers, Lederer and the other Congressmen for Errichetti.

Final plans for the Myers bribe were set with the Mayor. The meeting would be in a suite at the Travel Lodge Hotel at Kennedy Airport on August 22. Yassir would not make it because of a fast-breaking "Mideast crisis." Good had decided that Yassir, who had met Senator Williams two months before, should not be exposed too often. Errichetti would come to the room with Myers. Amoroso and Weinberg would handle the payoff. Errichetti would take a $15,000 split of the money from Myers.

There was a rush of preparations. The government, Weinberg decided, was finally going for a buck. New sound-recording equipment suddenly appeared. An FBI electronics specialist flew in from Washington. A three-room suite was hired. Room 381, the living room, was designated for the meeting. One of the two bedrooms leading off the living room was left in its normal state. The door to the other bedroom was to be closed and locked. The fish-eye camera would be aimed into the living room through a screw-hole in the locked bedroom door.

TAPE THIRTEEN

Weinberg: We got there . . . two days aheada time. It takes a day or two to set the cameras up. . . . Now everything is all set. We went over what we was gonna say to him [Myers]. Everybody was nervous. Be careful [they said], don't say nothin' that will hurt us later on. We had ninety bosses tellin' us what to do. John Jacobs, the Strike Force attorney, was with us. So was Good. The way it was supposed to work, the Mayor was gonna come first and Ozzie Myers was gonna meet him downstairs. Me and Tony is alone in the livin' room. All of a sudden Tony says to me, "Tell the Mayor we're only going to give $50,000." I says, "Tony, you're liable to blow it." But he says we're throwin' too many $100,000 prices around. We're givin' away too much. We're gonna run into trouble with the Bureau and the Justice Department with all these $100,000s. Well, Tony is a pretty smart agent and he worked in Washington for a while. So I says, okay, we'll try it. . . . He says when the Mayor comes, I should go down and tell him we only got $50,000. He says if the Mayor gets hot, I should think of a good story to tell him. . . . After, I went down and seen the Mayor. I says to him it's gotta be $50,000, no $100,000. Well, he's gettin' hot and he hems and haws. So I says to him, we're runnin' into a problem because of Jack [McCarthy]; we was blamin' everything on Jack. I tell the Mayor that Jack is screamin' that he couldda got the guy [Myers] for $50,000, that me and Tony was throwin' the Emir's money away. I says I know it ain't true, but Jack is causin' a problem and we gotta make Tony look good, 'cause, otherwise we're killin' the goose that laid the golden egg. Finally he goes for it.

There was a sharp rap on the door. Weinberg opened it and Errichetti entered with Congressman Myers, a youthful-looking former long-shoreman who spoke in the argot of the Philadelphia docks. Weinberg steered the Congressman to the couch where he would be in direct view of the hidden camera. The scene has since become familiar to millions of television viewers.

From the moment he began speaking, Myers left no doubt that he knew he was there to take a bribe for arranging to get permanent residency in the United States for an Arab. He boasted that he controlled a bloc of four other Philadelphia-area Congressmen and that they would back a residency bill for Yassir which he would introduce in Congress.

Amoroso handled the key questions, as he would in all the future

Congressional payoffs. He asked Myers if he could guarantee that Yassir would have no problems getting refuge in the United States.

> *Myers:* Well, let me say this to you . . . I'm gonna tell you right now without any qualms about it. With me in his corner, his chances are hundred percent [more] than they would be without somebody in his corner . . . but, uh, the point I'm making to you, without someone in my position, okay . . . you're in deep trouble. People wouldn't even want to deal with you. You gotta use connections to make connections.
>
> *Amoroso* (later): And, you know, you are talking about a lot of money, okay.
>
> *Myers:* Tony, you're going—let me just say this to you— you're going about this the right way . . . I'm gonna tell you something real simple and short. Money talks in this business and bullshit walks. It works the same way down in Washington.

Myers added that there were many others in Congress who shared his business philosophy. While the Mayor beamed approval, Myers told Amoroso:

> ". . . There's a lotta action there [Congress] if you know how, if you have the right connections . . . I gotta lotta guys who is willing to do business—you know, work with you. Different states. Guys right off the [House] Judiciary Committee. You know, key people, key staff guys, show you how to stall things, how to lay things out. But [in] each case, you know, you just have to have these people there . . ."

He said that he was friendly with Congressman Peter Rodino of New Jersey, Chairman of the Judiciary Committee. He strongly hinted that he could arrange for Rodino to be helpful. Weinberg listened fascinated. He remembered white-maned Congressman Rodino from the televised Watergate impeachment hearings.

Amoroso handed over the briefcase containing the $50,000 bribe. Myers would complain much later that he thought the briefcase held the $100,000 promised by Errichetti. The Mayor hadn't warned him about Amoroso's sudden change of signals. There were a few lines of parting chitchat and Errichetti and Myers left together. Then there was silence for a moment. Gazing thoughtfully out the window, Weinberg saw the Congressman emerge alone at a dead run from the hotel's rear exit.

Then the door of the locked bedroom burst open and jubilation reigned.

Weinberg: We were very happy, I remember that. We knew we had him. Everybody was happy. All the people from the bedroom, all of us. It was so easy, we couldn't believe it. In a way it kinda threw us off. Some of the others wasn't that simple. We was pattin' each other on the back. Tony was tickled pink, he couldn't believe it. John Good came into the room and he kept repeatin' he couldn't believe what a crook this guy was. Jacobs was jumpin' up and down. He called the Pooch on the phone and told him that we got what this guy said and did. I guess we was all jumpin' up and down. That night we went out and celebrated. It ain't every day that you tie the can to a Congressman. I kept thinkin' about Myers runnin' out the back door. Bein' from the other side, I know how he felt. He was scared. You never worry about comin' into a room until you take the money. That's when you expect the feds to bust in. Once we gave the money to Angie for him, he was nervous. He couldn't wait to get outta the hotel. I guess, knowin' how he felt, once he got in his car

and got away from the fuckin' place, saw he wasn't bein'
tailed, he felt much better.

Much later the Abscam team would learn that Myers got only
$15,000 of the bribe money. The rest was split by the middlemen. They
were Errichetti, Criden, Johanson and Robert Cook, a member of
Criden's law firm. Myers would complain bitterly about his small cut in
future months when he took more bribes in an offshoot of the Abscam
operation run by the Philadelphia FBI office. Middlemen didn't come
cheap.

It had been perfect. All the criminal elements. A Congressman had
accepted cash to perform specific official acts. He had frosted the cake by
offering to make similar deals with his colleagues and Congressional
staffers. The video and sound had been on the button. Myers had minced
no words. He was a flat-out crook. And his description of how things
really worked in Congress had an unmistakable ring of authenticity.

The same scenario, with slight variations, would be played for the rest
of the Congressmen snared in Abscam. Some of them were more skittish
than others. Myers would prove to be the frankest of them all in laying
it on the line. But they all promised. And they all took the bribes.

The script was standard. Weinberg would handle the preliminary contacts with the middlemen, all of whom had other financial deals hanging
fire with the Abdul organization. Amoroso would dominate the actual
payoff meetings, asking the essential questions necessary to establish a
Federal crime and handling the bribe money. Weinberg was his genial
helper, freshening drinks, handing out cigars, vouching with the names of
mutual friends, and hinting at great fortunes for all involved.

The bribed Congressmen always left with the promise of even more.
As a further reward, Amoroso and Weinberg would promise each of
them substantial Arab business investments in their home districts.
These investments, it was suggested, would give the Congressmen an

excuse to be concerned publicly with Yassir's welfare. And the jobs generated by the investments would help create voter goodwill.

Weinberg was a prodigious spender of Yassir's Monopoly money. He would promise investments of $50 million in a Congressional district without blinking. Most of the Congressmen passed up the chance to funnel Yassir's expected investments into projects that would help their constituents. They eagerly suggested that the money be put into businesses owned by themselves or their friends.

The Myers sting was bittersweet for Weinberg. He was troubled by the fact that he had just helped the FBI nail his lawyer and old drinking buddy Vince Cuti. Good was still juggling Abscam and the Suffolk sewer scandal. He had asked Weinberg to check with Errichetti and learn if the Mayor had ever had any business dealings with Bowe-Walsh, the private engineering firm supervising construction of the ill-fated Suffolk sewer system.

The Mayor said that he was mad at Charles Walsh, the managing partner of the firm, because he had never gotten his part of a $50,000 bribe paid by Bowe-Walsh for a minor contract in New Jersey. The attorney for Bowe-Walsh was Cuti, who still lunched frequently with Weinberg at Orlando's in Huntington. Cuti was impressed with Weinberg's position at Abdul and pleased that his client was making big bucks with the Arabs.

It was a simple matter to tell Cuti of Errichetti's displeasure. There were several meetings, one at the Plaza Hotel involving Walsh, Cuti, the Mayor, Weinberg and Amoroso. Errichetti had agreed to settle for $10,000 which Walsh had paid and Cuti had delivered. Good had been ecstatic.

Errichetti blew his top at Weinberg for the first time on August 25, three days after the Myers payoff. The Mayor was still upset at the last-minute shaving of the bribe money. Moreover, Weinberg had just told him that another casino loan package had been thumbed down by Yassir's viziers. And now Weinberg was telling him that Abdul and Yassir couldn't possibly send several million barrels of oil to one of the Mayor's personal friends.

The Mayor announced that he was "totally pissed." He launched into a scathing complaint about withered deals. "I'm stone broke; eight months runnin' around like a goddamned nut," Errichetti complained. "You know what I do. Then it's another story the next time, then another, then another." Weinberg calmed the Mayor with a promise to try to get some oil. But he privately warned Good that Errichetti's patience was beginning to run thin. Good told him not to worry. Abscam would be closed down on October 1. "We'll take what comes along until then," he said. "But we can't keep all these stalls going forever."

Congressman Lederer was a piece of cake. It was a replay of the Myers bribe. Again it was a hotel suite at Kennedy. Again the Congressman came accompanied by Errichetti. He promised to push a bill to give Yassir asylum and he took the $50,000 bribe. Amoroso told Lederer what was expected of him and the former head of the Philadelphia Probation Department replied, "I'm no Boy Scout." Lederer also coyly suggested that Congressman Rodino could be of assistance to Yassir. After Lederer had left the room, Weinberg asked Errichetti about Rodino. The Mayor smiled enigmatically and joked about going to jail. But he was strangely taciturn.

The Mayor's mood turned cheery after the Lederer meeting. Perhaps it was because, as later testimony would show, part of the Lederer bribe money was neatly tucked in his wallet. He met during the next week with Weinberg and Amoroso at Cherry Hill for a wide-ranging discussion of the titanium corporation, underworld interests in Atlantic City, casino financing packages and the next batch of Congressional bribe-takers.

He started the meeting with a surprise offer to sell munitions to Abdul and Yassir. He had read that the Arab countries were having problems getting guns. He had, he said, a friend in the business. He could even supply the Arabs with Israeli-made Uzzi machine guns. The Mayor whipped out a pad and pen and asked Weinberg and Amoroso what kind of guns the Arabs needed and how many they wanted to buy. The two Abscam agents stared at each other wide-eyed. "This guy was unreal," Weinberg recalled.

They told the Mayor that they'd check with the home office and asked Errichetti whether he had any new "candidates," the Mayor's term for bribable Congressmen. He said that Senator Talmadge and Congressman Fowler of Atlanta were definite. He estimated that his contact (whom Weinberg and Amoroso knew to be Criden) could eventually produce at least ten more. Weinberg was interested in newspaper stories he had read about Talmadge's impending Senate censure. What did it mean, he asked the Mayor?

"They [the Senate] read a statement to him: 'You done wrong, prick,'" explained Errichetti. "He says, 'Thank you very much, goodbye.' It's all bullshit."

> *Errichetti* (later): He's [Talmadge] got the biggest balls in the world, right?
> *Weinberg* (persisting): But, what does that mean when they say they're censuring him?
> *Errichetti:* Slap on the wrist.
> *Weinberg:* I hope they don't slap him on the wrist that takes the [Abscam] money . . . If he drops it, I'll pick it up.

The Mayor offered to produce three candidates for bribes on Wednesday, September 19. He named them as Senator Talmadge, Congressman Fowler and U.S. Deputy Immigration Commissioner Mario Noto. Talmadge's price, Errichetti said, was $100,000. Fowler and Noto were to get $50,000 each. The Mayor casually added that he might be accompanied to the payoffs by Howard Criden. Weinberg and Amoroso exchanged glances. He was surfacing his contact man.

Weinberg did some quick addition. The Mayor was proposing that

Abscam pay a total of $200,000 in bribes on a single day. Errichetti had been bitching lately. Was he testing their ability to come up with big bread? Weinberg automatically shifted into a semistall. "That's $200,000," he said. "That may clean out the vaults. I'll call the bank and get back to ya." The Mayor said he'd wait on Weinberg's call.

Good sent a skyrocket to FBI Supervisor Mike Wilson in Washington. Wilson was the next man up in the FBI's Abscam chain of command. He was a strong supporter of the project and had followed its progress on a daily basis. Wilson bucked the decision upstairs, asking for a fast response. He got it. Pay the $200,000. Pictures and descriptions of the three targets were given to Weinberg and Amoroso. This was standard practice. The government didn't want to be swindled out of its own sting money by a ringer.

There would be a new location for the meetings, Good informed Weinberg. He said that the Bureau had a townhouse on W Street just off Foxhall Road in Georgetown, the exclusive, old section of Washington, D.C. The house was already being used for another FBI sting, Good explained, and was completely wired for secret filming and recording. There was even a hidden camera in the TV set. The place, said Good, was furnished.

Good expected that Weinberg would flip at the chance to add the exclusive, four-bedroom townhouse to the Abscam illusion. He had been enthusiastic about the plane, the cars, the *Left Hand,* the stepped-up hotel suites, and the recent condo that the Bureau had sublet for Abscam in Ventnor, New Jersey, next door to Atlantic City. But Weinberg shrugged noncommittally and said, "Let me take a look at it."

The brick house, built in Williamsburg Colonial style, was a swindler's dream. It had the aura of old money, conservative, tasteful, solid. The furnishings reflected exquisite taste, Oriental rugs, authentic antiques, delicate, translucent china. There was even a completely stocked wine cellar offering the best of the French and California vintages. Hidden cameras were everywhere, all of them controlled from a huge electronic panel in a locked basement room.

The townhouse, Weinberg was told, was being used to entertain clients of a construction firm set up by the Bureau to uncover bid-rigging in the Washington area. The firm was named Olympic Construction Company and was actually involved in the building business. The president of Olympic was Richard Muffoletto, a contractor from Locust Valley, Long Island.

Though impressed, Weinberg still felt uneasy. Both Abscam and the Washington sting could operate out of the townhouse, Good suggested. Different sets of agents could move in and out as needed. There might be, for example, an Abscam meeting in the townhouse on a Thursday and a Washington sting meeting on a Saturday. Besides, said Good, Abscam could push Olympic Construction with the mayors of the New Jersey cities. A construction contract was far more liable to elicit kickback demands than a check-cashing license.

From other sources, Weinberg discovered that the Washington sting had been operating since 1978 and was regarded as an expensive flop. The Bureau had invested $6 million in setting up Muffoletto in Olympic, which he was going to keep as his own company, paying the government back gradually out of profits.

Meanwhile, Muffoletto was being paid $7,000 a month as company president—more than twice Weinberg's Abscam salary. The actual targets of the sting were the members and staff of Congress's District of Columbia Committee and Washington city officials. The sting had gotten such poor results, Weinberg learned, that the Bureau worried over how to justify the money it had laid out.

Weinberg reported back to Good. It would be dangerous for Abscam to push Olympic with the politicians, he said, because Muffoletto was a known informer. The Bureau, he added, wasn't doing Abscam any favors offering the townhouse for meetings. Abscam was a winner, he said, and the Washington sting was a loser. By moving Abscam into the townhouse, the Bureau was covering some of the financial losses on its other sting by charging off the townhouse to Abscam.

There was some merit to Weinberg's argument. His motives however, were more complex. He was seething at the fact that he was being paid so much less by the FBI than Muffoletto. And Muffoletto would wind up owning the construction company. All of this money to Muffoletto while Weinberg had been using his own furniture, paying for his own tapes, flopping in cheap motels, and scrounging money for the Florida boat party. It was, he steamed, unfair.

But Good turned flinty when Weinberg knocked the Washington sting and questioned the Bureau's motives. "We'll use the townhouse and I don't want to hear any more argument," he snapped. Weinberg shrugged, picked up the phone and called the Mayor. The meeting with the Deputy Immigration Commissioner, Talmadge and Congressman Fowler would be at a Washington townhouse that the Arabs had just bought. Errichetti seemed impressed. Weinberg laid it on.

The meeting arrangements were set. Then Weinberg got a call from Howard Criden. Errichetti was on the phone a few minutes later with the same message. The Atlanta lawyer who had arranged for Talmadge and Fowler to take the bribes had just called with an urgent bulletin. Talmadge and Fowler were canceling out. The lawyer reported that Talmadge felt the timing wasn't right in view of his recent Senate censure. Fowler, the lawyer alibied, had a death in the family. No mention was made of Levitas, the third Georgia Congressman promised earlier by Errichetti.

Talmadge and the two Congressmen have since denied knowledge of the proposed meetings. All three were first named on the Abscam tapes early in August 1979. They are mentioned several times on the tapes through August and early September, either by name, position or both. U.S. Attorney General Griffin Bell left office on August 16, 1979, and was succeeded by his assistant Benjamin R. Civiletti. In 1980, Bell served as a manager of Senator Talmadge's unsuccessful reelection campaign.

Both Criden and Errichetti agreed, however, that the Mayor would still bring Deputy Commissioner Noto to the townhouse. Errichetti had been promising Noto for a month. He had said that he didn't know him personally, but that a mutual friend had vouched for Noto, promising that he would take the $50,000 bribe and guarantee Yassir would be issued the necessary immigration permits to remain in the United States.

The Mayor omitted only one important detail from his report on the proposed bribery. It was a scheme that he had hatched with Criden to swindle Abdul out of $50,000.

The Mayor arrived at the townhouse with a man whom he introduced as Commissioner Noto on September 19, 1979. Weinberg met them at the door and escorted them into the study. The Marx brothers would have burned with envy at the ensuing scene as recorded on videotape.

Amoroso, his cigar clenched at a jaunty angle, was waiting for them. Weinberg steered the guests into seats facing the camera hidden in the TV and unobtrusively placed the attaché case containing the $50,000 bribe on the floor near the supposed immigration official. Casually, he glanced at Amoroso, shaking his head slightly. Amoroso nodded. The man brought in by Criden and Errichetti was definitely not Deputy Immigration Commissioner Mario Noto. They had screened pictures of the real Noto.

"Do you have a card, Commissioner?" asked Amoroso.

The ersatz commissioner, later identified as Robert Cook, one of Criden's law partners, replied that he rarely left his office and had no reason to carry business cards.

Amoroso looked at Errichetti. Then he rose and walked toward another room, calling, "Mayor, let me see you outside a minute." Errichetti followed Amoroso out and the door closed behind him. Weinberg made small talk for a few minutes with Cook and then said, "I didn't get your name."

"Nopo," fumbled Cook. "N-o-p-o."

"We understand that Mr. Nopo is a much older man," said Weinberg gently. "We're afraid that someone might be throwin' in a ringer. . . . We have to be careful." Cook nervously replied, "If it's a bust today, it's a bust." Weinberg told him not to worry and left the room.

SCENE

Cook sits alone in a chair. He stares, unknowingly, at the hidden camera. He is motionless, a frozen man. Slowly, three minutes and twenty-six seconds pass by. The only sounds are in the background. A plane flies over, birds chirp, a church bell tolls, the clock ticks. Cook seems scarcely to breathe. An FBI agent enters the room and gazes around. His eyes lock on the attaché case with the money sitting at Cook's feet. "Is this yours?" the agent asks as he picks it up. "No, of course not," croaks Cook, swallowing hard. The agent carries the case out of the room. More background noise. Cook remains in the chair, unmoving, unblinking, etched in time and place.

In the adjoining room, Amoroso carefully picked his words as he talked to the Mayor. Errichetti was Abscam's most important middleman. Amoroso shrewdly realized that he might lose Errichetti forever if he accused him of trying to put over a ringer. The volatile Mayor would save face by turning on his accuser. He would leave in a rage, taking all of his contacts with him.

Amoroso quickly backtracked his memory. The Mayor had told them he didn't know Noto personally. He said that the immigration official had been obtained through a mutual friend. Amoroso decided to use the Mayor's phony story for leverage. He asked him what he knew about the friend who had arranged the meeting. Errichetti, sensing something amiss, said he only knew the friend casually. His answer gave Amoroso the opening he had needed.

Amoroso whispered to the Mayor that the man sitting in the other room was an impostor. He said that he was worried both for the Mayor and for his own group. Maybe, he speculated, the impostor was an FBI agent sent to trap them. And maybe the Mayor's casual friend was also part of the FBI plot. Errichetti exhaled slowly. Then he bit. The Mayor was a good actor. His face turned scarlet and his eyes bulged with righteous indignation. "I been jack-potted," he hissed.

The Mayor quickly agreed to Amoroso's suggested counterplot. Errichetti would tell the impostor that there had been a mistake about the purpose of the meeting. He would stay supercool. He would drop the impostor off at the government building where he had originally picked him up. Later, when the Mayor returned from a scheduled Florida trip with Weinberg, he would cautiously check to learn whether the whole thing had been an FBI sting.

Errichetti left with Cook. He had taken the face-saving way out. He traveled to Florida the next day and attended several taped meetings there with Weinberg and Amoroso. After that they would not see him again. Weinberg is sure that the Mayor knew he had been compromised and was too embarrassed to face them. Over the phone, he correctly accused Weinberg of dealing with rival New Jersey politicians, complained that none of the promised deals had ever materialized, and raged that his integrity had been challenged as a result of the ringer deal.

Weinberg worked desperately to win back the Mayor. The Abscam group even transferred $1 million into an Atlantic City bank that Errichetti had been touting for months. The Mayor had claimed that Steven Perskie, the State Senator who fathered casino gambling in New Jersey, had an interest in the bank. But the Mayor had turned his back on Yassir and Abscam for good.

SCENE

Weinberg and Errichetti are sitting on a plane headed for Florida. The Mayor is unusually quiet. He is, in fact, sulking. His scheme to steal a fast $50,000 with the Noto ringer has been blown. Weinberg tells a few sure-fire dirty jokes. The Mayor doesn't laugh. He doesn't even smile. Weinberg spots a pretty black hostess coming down the aisle. He decides on a play to the Mayor's economy-sized ego. Weinberg loudly tells the stewardess that the man sitting next to him is the Mayor of Camden, New Jersey, and a state Senator. "Really?" she asks. Weinberg introduces her to the Mayor, who instantly brightens. Errichetti boasts of his power and influence. The stewardess interrupts the Mayor in midparagraph. "Who gives a shit," she whispers sweetly and moves away. The Mayor looks like he has been smashed with a brick. "Those damned niggers are all alike," he mutters. He slouches back into his sulk. Weinberg gives up.

SCENE

Amoroso, trailed by Weinberg, walks importantly into Atlantic City's Boardwalk Bank. He is about to open an account with the bank for $1 million. The money has secretly been transferred from FBI operating funds. Mayor Errichetti has been advised and has indicated through his secretary that Amoroso will get a fitting reception from the bank officers. Amoroso clears his throat noisily and a young lady looks up from her desk. Amoroso gives his name and says he is there to meet a high bank official. The young lady replies that the official is tied up. She asks if she can help. "I want to open an account with $1 million," Amoroso states imperiously. "Fill these out, please," says the young lady, handing him a batch of routine application forms. Amoroso looks at Weinberg. Weinberg looks at Amoroso and lifts an eyebrow. Both shrug. Amoroso fills out the forms as the young lady busies herself with other work. He finishes and hands the forms to the young lady. "Thank you," she says and hands Amoroso his temporary checkbook. They leave the bank. Weinberg calls the Mayor. The Mayor is out.

Errichetti was replaced as Abscam's key middleman by Howard Criden. Weinberg is convinced that both Errichetti and Criden designed it that way. From the first, as Criden later admitted, it had been he who had been reaching the various Congressmen to take bribes. He continued to do so. But he would later add another dimension to the investigation: direct contact with a key representative of the national gambling syndicate.

Precise, intelligent, low-key, Criden fitted the classic stereotype of the influence peddler far more exactly than talkative, impetuous Mayor Errichetti. It is axiomatic in the business of selling politicians that known middlemen are watched middlemen. Although he had been an assistant district attorney in Philadelphia and later an assistant state attorney general, Criden was unknown to the usually astute Philadelphia press corps. He was, however, an integral part of the corrupt Philadelphia Democratic machine and used the organization's political clout to forge relationships with the vast network of similar influence peddlers in virtually every city and state in the nation.

Known in the gray world of political corruption as bag men, people like Criden provide the same type of insulation for crooked politicians that Errichetti was supposed to give to Kenneth MacDonald of the New Jersey Casino Control Commission and lawyer Alex Feinberg to Senator Harrison Williams. Most of them are lawyers, buying and selling public and party officials under the cover of apparently legitimate legal representation or lobbying activities. If a lawyer in Philadelphia, for example, wants to buy a Congressman from Georgia, he calls his counterpart middleman in Atlanta and the deed is set in motion.

Like most middlemen, Criden had survived and prospered by being careful. He preferred not to talk on the telephone, always suspecting a law enforcement tap. But he often broke his own rules. A former army intelligence officer, Criden frequently implied that he had current CIA ties. Weinberg found himself constantly fending off Criden's questions about Abdul, Yassir and the entire Abscam cover story.

Criden and Weinberg are in deep conversation. The heavyset lawyer is persistent. He wants to know exactly where Yassir comes from. Weinberg is evasive. Any country he names can be immediately checked by Criden.

Criden: What country?
Weinberg: Who the fuck knows.

Criden: But, I want to know what country he's from.
Weinberg: One of them . . . what they call emigrant.
Criden: Arab Emigrants?
Weinberg: Yeah.
Criden: Emirates?
Weinberg: Emirates. Yeah, one of them.

Criden also questioned Amoroso's cover as a former CIA agent. He said that CIA agents recognized one another through a system of conversational buzz words and recognition signals. Weinberg stalled a moment while he thought it over. If Criden actually was connected with the CIA, he would know Amoroso was fake and the whole scam would be endangered. He had spent months selling Amoroso's CIA cover to Abscam's targets. He had even countered the Mayor's complaints about Ernie Haridopolos with the invention that Ernie had once been on a CIA assassination squad and still had bad dreams about all the people he had killed.

Still, Criden could be lying. It was possible that he was merely testing the Abscam cover. Weinberg played both ends against the middle. He told Criden that he had only known Amoroso for a year. He said that he believed that Amoroso had been in the CIA, but it was possible that he had not been. Maybe, he said, Amoroso had fabricated his CIA background to get his job with Yassir. He said that he really didn't care if Amoroso had lied to Yassir. In the year that he had worked with him, Weinberg said, Amoroso had proved to be smart, safe and a compatible crook.

Ironically, the Cook fiasco with the Mayor may have been the clincher for Criden. Since Criden had secretly teamed with Errichetti to cheat Abscam with a ringer, he knew that Cook, his law partner, wasn't part of any FBI trap. But the very fact that Amoroso had voiced that fear to Errichetti may have convinced Criden that Abscam was for real. Anyone suspicious of an FBI trap had a head start on credibility.

Once convinced, Criden literally gushed the names of Congressmen he said he was approaching to come in and take bribes from the Abscam agents. From bits and pieces of his taped conversations, it was apparent he was arranging for these Congressmen through other middlemen. Some of the prospects named by Criden included House Majority Leader James Wright of Texas, House Majority Whip John Brademas of Indiana, Senator Bill Bradley of New Jersey, Congressman James Howard of New Jersey and Congressman Jim Mattox of Texas.

The names sent a shockwave through the FBI and the Department of Justice. Wright and Brademas, who had also been suggested earlier by the Mayor, were the two most powerful members of Congress behind House Speaker Thomas O'Neill. Senator Bradley was a respected former Rhodes scholar and NBA star. It was also just at this time in the history of Abscam that Bill Rosenberg, the persistent Long Island swindler who earlier had been sidestepped as a middleman, chimed in with the names of two Senators and a Congressman.

Weinberg had kept him current on the Myers and Lederer bribes as a way of keeping Abdul and Yassir's credibility alive. Rosenberg was still waiting for money on the CDs he had given Weinberg a year before, so was still very much in touch. He called Weinberg in the fall of 1979 and said that he had access to several people in Congress who would assure asylum for Yassir. He said they were Senators Jacob Javits and Daniel Moynihan and Congressman Norman Lent, all of New York.

He called back a short time later scratching Moynihan from the list. "He was very cold," complained Rosenberg. However, he said, he was sure that Javits and Lent would help. "Can we meet 'em and say, 'Here's $50,000, take it and run,'" Weinberg asked. "Oh no," replied a shocked Rosenberg. He suggested that Abscam contribute $100,000 to the GOP Congressional Committee through its executive director Steven Stockmeyer. The money would be a campaign contribution. The GOP candidates, if elected, would help Yassir. Weinberg told Rosenberg to forget it. To himself he added: Campaign contributions weren't crimes.

The names of Wright and Brademas are not mentioned again on the tapes. Weinberg shrugs and explains, "Nobody [in government] told me to push it." He was referring to the basic Abscam routine. If a name was mentioned on tape as a potential bribe target, Weinberg was usually told to explore the bribe possibility further in conversations with the middleman. Approval for the actual bribe meeting also had to come from Washington.

Nor did Howard Criden push it. It is quite possible that his contacts told him that the two House leaders could not be bought. It is also possible that he was merely throwing their names into the hat to impress his newfound associates. Weinberg did ask him about Bradley at a later date and Criden replied that he couldn't be gotten. Criden was also complaining at this time that many of the Congressmen he reached were wary about coming to the townhouse for their money.

There was no problem getting bribable Congressmen, said Criden, adding, "I can get you almost anyone you want." But he complained that the Congressmen were a wary breed. "In the first place, when you lay the [Abscam] story on the guy, he don't believe it," said Criden. "Because right away he thinks he's being [inaudible] someone trying to middle or something like that. He's [the Congressman] got to do it with someone [a middleman] he trusts implicitly, otherwise he ain't going to do it. Okay?"

Another time, Criden complained: "There are some problems on our side. Okay, I understand that you needed a candidate [Congressman], okay, but, you know, let me tell you, to convince those guys to do this number is not as easy as you think it is. They are so—drive me bananas— you don't have to deal with these guys like I do. They drive me fuckin' bananas with their intrigue. They're in the middle of the goddamned— they make a commitment to you, they get chicken feet and they say they don't want to do it. Or they want to do it this way or they want to do it that way or they don't want to do it at all. Okay, I go nuts."

The middleman's tirade came shortly after arrangements had collapsed for a meeting at the townhouse with Congressman Howard of

New Jersey. Criden called saying that Howard had switched signals. He said that Howard would meet only in the safety of his own Congressional office. Criden explained that the Congressman was skittish about security at the townhouse. Howard's name was scratched from the Abscam target list.

Some Congressmen, however, were apparently willing to take the risk. After several weeks of negotiations, Criden made an appointment for two of them to come to the townhouse on October 9, 1979. They were Frank Thompson of New Jersey, Chairman of the powerful House Administration Committee, and Jim Mattox of Texas. Amoroso once again reviewed the bribe conditions with Criden. The Congressmen must agree to use their offices for Yassir and accept the bribe money directly. Criden agreed.

A schedule was set. Criden would hire a limousine and drive from Philadelphia to the Capitol, where he would pick up Thompson and return him after the meeting. Then, at the end of the day's Congressional session, he would return to the Capitol, pick up Mattox, and bring him to the townhouse. Criden said that both Thompson and Mattox had been fully briefed. About Mattox he said, "Don't worry about Jim, he's a thousand percent." He added that Mattox wanted to come in the evening so that the meeting would not show in the daily schedule that his secretary logged.

On the appointed day, the Abscam team sat playing poker in the townhouse, waiting for Thompson and Criden to arrive. Thompson, the fourth or fifth-ranking House Democrat, was heady game. There was an air of excitement. Good was there with Jacobs from the Strike Force. Weir had come down from Del Tufo's office in New Jersey to observe. Haridopolos was there, and Brady and Bursey, and the FBI electronics technician. "Nobody wanted to leave," recalls Weinberg.

It was a convention, which Good set about to disperse. Only those absolutely necessary to the scam could remain. Haridopolos and Brady were to leave as Thompson entered. Bursey would stay to serve drinks and be on call. Good took Jacobs and Weir in tow and went down to the locked control room with the electronics specialist. They would monitor the meeting by TV from there.

Weinberg and Amoroso sat expectantly at the round table in the study. As usual at such meetings, they were dressed casually. Weinberg wore a sports shirt, slacks and no socks. Amoroso was similarly dressed, but he wore socks. It was part of the sting atmosphere orchestrated by Weinberg. Formality, even business suits, put people on their guard, he had explained to Good. Everything, even the offer of the bribe, had to be done casually. As Weinberg explained it: ". . . like we couldn't of cared less. Like, hey, ya wanna take the money, ya don't wanna take the money, fuck it."

Thompson and Criden arrived. The Congressman admired the house and asked for a tour. Weinberg led the way, carefully avoiding the locked control room. The Congressman, boasting of his wine expertise, browsed through the wine cellar and pronounced it quite acceptable. The ice broken, they gathered around the table. Thompson began by describing his enormous power as Chairman of the Administration Committee.

The subject then swung to the Arab's plight. "We represent Yassir Habib and Kambir Abdul Rahman," explained Weinberg. "The problem is what happened to Somoza and the Shah of Iran, that God forbid, if anything happens over there, and they want to come to this country, they want to be sponsored. And they want us to meet people that will sponsor them. And Howard [Criden] said you could do something for us."

Amoroso embroidered the details and asked Thompson if he would introduce a bill to give the Arabs refuge in the United States. Thompson said that he would, but he warned that a bill was not a sure guarantee of success. Amoroso replied, "Well, that's what the money's for."

Thompson's answer was a shock. "I'm not looking for any money, and, uh, it depends on the circumstances," he stammered. "I mean not a Communist and not a known criminal." He asked the origin of the two Arabs. Criden quickly volunteered, "One of the Emirates."

Weinberg took a stab. "You see, Abdul married one of the king's or sheikh's daughters and he became an Emir, all right? And they realize over there eventually the guerrillas are going to take over. The Palestine guerrillas are, well, it's just a matter of time and they want security. They're puttin' millions and millions of dollars into this country, all right? And they just want to know that they have the right people behind them when the time comes."

The Congressman said that he would welcome investment of the Arab's money in his district and suggested several businesses owned by his friends and law partners. He again promised to introduce a bill for Abdul and Yassir. Amoroso wanted to reoffer the payment to Thompson but stopped when Criden kicked him under the table. He thanked Thompson, and, as Weinberg listened slack-jawed, suggested that Criden drive the Congressman back to the Capitol. No bribe had been passed.

As soon as the door closed behind the departing Congressman, Weinberg asked Amoroso why he hadn't just given Thompson the money. "Only if he spells out why he's taking it," said Amoroso. "Don't worry, he'll be back."

Criden rushed back to the townhouse in near apoplexy. Why hadn't Amoroso given the money to him? He would have privately given it to Thompson. Those were the arrangements that Thompson had made with him. Thompson didn't want to take the money directly from Amoroso. The lawyer was so frustrated that at one point tears streamed from beneath his horn-rimmed glasses. He said that Weinberg had told him that the indirect payment was acceptable. Weinberg pleaded a misunderstanding.

At one point Criden begged Amoroso to drop his insistence on direct payment. He said, "I made a commitment to the man [Thompson] . . . and the man delivered. Okay? His end of the bargain, and then you tell him he didn't do something right. He ain't gonna buy it. This guy's been around too long for that." Amoroso wouldn't budge. Criden tried again. "Listen," he said. "This cocksucker needs money worse than anybody in this fuckin' room." Amoroso shrugged and suggested if Thompson needed money that badly, "Let him get into the fuckin' water with us."

Nearly an hour passed in argument. Amoroso agreed to pass the bribe money to Criden only if Thompson witnessed the event and agreed that the money was being paid to him for his official acts. Criden sighed deeply and accepted the crumb. He left for a talk with Thompson at the Capitol.

TAPE FOURTEEN

Weinberg: After Criden left, we was discussin' it. John Good said Tony done the right thing. Jacobs got all excited and said I don't think he's comin' back. Tony says he'll be back. I really didn't know. I was greatly upset. I actually thought we blew it because we pushed Criden to a point of no return, as they say. . . . I just didn't think we was gonna make it. But then, like I say, I take my hat off to Tony again. He pushed him [Criden] to a point, and you gotta remember, Tony was under great pressure. If he paid the guy and the guy didn't say anything, everybody in the place woulda said he shouldn't of paid him. . . . The pressure on Tony was incredible. You know, my pressure was bad, but not that bad. I didn't have to make any decisions [about payment]. Tony had to make the decisions. Tony worked for the FBI, and if he made a bad decision, it was his ass. Me, I couldn't give a shit less.

Criden returned later with Thompson. "Okay, Frank understands the situation now," said Criden.

"You know, and you know," Amoroso replied, holding out the money-filled briefcase to the two men, "I just wanna make sure, you know, [that] you understand. There's the briefcase."

Thompson turned to Criden. "You look after that for me, will you," he asked. Criden took the briefcase.

"Well, as long as I know, now," Amoroso added. "Okay, I think he [Criden] explained it to you."

Thompson held up his eyeglasses. "I got these, all right—fine," he replied.

It was done. The Chairman of the House Administration Committee was in the bag. It was late. Criden dialed Congressman Mattox's office and canceled out. They parted with Thompson's promise to bring in more Congressmen, particularly a good friend of his from New York. He did. And the parade continued.

TAPE FIFTEEN

Weinberg: Me and Tony made a great team. We were meant for each other. He was an easygoin', cool-headed guy and he learned fast. At the beginnin' he didn't talk as much as I did, and in the end he was doin' more talkin'. The guy learned fast; he was a quick picker-upper. He just knew how to handle [things]. If I got into a spot, he would jump in. If he got in a spot, I would jump in. We even had a system to keep each other from dozin' off during some of them long boring sessions. The team was good, the guys [FBI] around us was good, Steve, Ernie, Bruce, we was all good together.

11

MESSING WITH THE MOB

It helps to know the wise guys, but don't go into business with
'em. You'll wind up either screwed or dead.   —MEL WEINBERG

He slept fitfully on the king-sized bed. The dreams were bad. They had
no beginning, no end. Faster and faster, they flickered from scene to
scene. All had the same theme. He was being murdered.

Somehow, he had crossed the wise guys. No hard feelings, they said.
Nothing personal. Boom—you're dead. He moaned and slammed a fist
into his twisted pillow. The executioner was always a polite goy in a
Brooks Brothers suit. But inventive. Already the bastard had strangled
him with piano wire, punched an ice pick into his brain, buggered him
with a cattle-prod and mashed him in a compactor.

Weinberg came awake shouting. He shook his head. *Aggghh!* More of
those damned dreams. The morning sunlight shafted through the
windows. He sat up in bed and shook his head again. Got to get oriented.
Check it off. Morning. September 20, 1979. Holiday Inn, Hallandale,
Florida. He had flown in the night before with Mayor Errichetti. Lousy
trip. The Mayor was annoyed, probably because he hadn't ripped them
off the day before with his phony immigration official. Nice try, though.

Click. They were here to meet with Alvin Malnik, the apparent heir to mob financial wizard Meyer Lansky.

Okay. That explained the dreams. He didn't mind scamming politicians. The only weapons they had, he thought, were wise-assed lawyers. But the mob was different. No sense of humor. Just a dead fish on your doorstep, a red snapper, maybe, to let the family know that you're not coming back and the local undertaker is going to get stiffed because you're under eighteen inches of concrete and a permanent part of the new interstate highway system. He shuddered at the thought.

He'd always stayed on the right side of the wise guys. When he bellied up to the bar at Orlando's with Tony Ducks Corallo and Neil Migliore, he always bought. When Jimmy Nap called for a favor, he always did it. And once or twice, when he needed something small like vouching, they'd help him out. But he always showed respect. Hadn't he walked away from the gambling casino on St. Martin when Meyer Lansky called him and told him to bug off?

Now John Good wanted him to take on Lansky's number-one man. At least, that's what the Bureau said. The fact that he was a government crook wasn't going to help him with the mob. Sure, Amoroso would be with him. And Good and the rest of the team were in rooms downstairs, ready to back him up if there was trouble. But that wasn't going to help five years from now when the government had sucked him dry and tossed him away like it did all of its informants. The mob had a long memory. And Meyer Lansky was something special.

Why the hell was he doing this? It sure wasn't for the money, although he couldn't complain lately. Good had gotten him a $15,000 bonus last spring after Mayor Errichetti and Kenneth MacDonald had taken the bribes. The Bureau had given him another $10,000 in relocation expenses. And Good said that when the entire investigation was over, he would push to get him a lump-sum bonus for his work. But nobody could pay him enough to do this. He was doing it because John Good had asked him to do it. He shrugged. That was enough.

As far as the Bureau was concerned, Alvin Malnik was the key to Lansky, the wispy, seamed old man, who lived in a modest Miami apartment, walked his dog every night along Collins Avenue, and was the mob's expert on bookmaking, gambling casinos and washing dirty money. And Lansky, Weinberg reflected, still ran Las Vegas and collected the skim for the real owners of the multimillion-dollar casinos that lined the fabulous Strip. The list read like a Who's Who of the American underworld.

Good wanted some answers. What, if anything, did Malnik have to do with the Aladdin Hotel in Las Vegas? How strong were his ties with Caesars Palace, another of the huge Strip casinos? Was he connected with Resorts International or the Boardwalk Regency, the two Atlantic City casinos that had already opened? Would he be involved in some of the others? How did the Lansky-Malnik relationship work? And, Good added, get it all on tape.

The same theme had dominated Weinberg's recent talks with Amoroso. The mob, Vegas, Atlantic City, Meyer, gambling. The swindler and the FBI crime expert, swapping notes. Both knew a lot. Weinberg's love of gambling had lured him to Vegas more times than he could remember. Friendly wise guys would always call ahead to make sure that he got the best of everything. He went big at the crap tables and bought big for his wise-guy hosts. He was a good listener. For his part Amoroso's information had come from informants and hundreds of FBI bugs and telephone taps.

Weinberg sat on the edge of the bed, feet braced on the floor, and thought about getting dressed. He quickly rejected the idea. Diane was driving down to meet him and would be here in an hour. He'd take a quick shower. . . .

He climbed out of the shower and spent fifteen minutes carefully cleaning his nails. He hated people with dirty nails. The sight of them, for some peculiar reason, made him feel sick. He rubbed dry, plodded back to the bed and lay down on his back, hands clasped on the pillow behind his head. It was a good time to think things out.

He pondered the mob. Mostly Italian. Families running the rackets in most of the country's major cities. Five families running New York and New Jersey, a real mess. Most other places had only one. It was just like *The Godfather*. A boss at the head of each family, each boss had his *capos*. Underneath were the soldiers. If you were invited into a family, you were a man of respect.

But the old Jewish mob wasn't dead yet. At least Meyer Lansky wasn't. Everybody in the mob needed Meyer. The wop hoods could talk gambling until they croaked, but they didn't know shit about it. Most of them couldn't even count good. They depended on Meyer and his boys to handle the credit, set the odds, run the casinos, deal the cards. Only Meyer could give you a casino crew that wouldn't rip you off, boys who knew how to make money.

And it was Meyer who could get your money in and out. Wise guys couldn't get licensed in Nevada. So if you wanted a piece of a casino, you had to own it in secret. Each casino was broken down into a hundred secret ownership points. The cost of a point in one of the bigger operations like Caesars Palace could be $100,000 and up. Your name didn't appear anywhere as an owner. They had stiffs fronting the license. But if you owned a point, you were an owner. Moe Dalitz, Meyer's man in Vegas, kept track of everybody's secret points. The points were bought and sold between the wise guys and Dalitz kept track of everything. Nobody cheated. That's why Vegas ticked.

There were lots of ways for points to make money in Vegas. The points themselves were like shares on the stock market. They were shares in the skim. Las Vegas, except for the high rollers on credit, is a cash business. Lots of cash. A certain amount of that cash each night never got to the counting windows and wasn't recorded on the books. This was skim. Then there were the vendors, suppliers of liquor, food, laundry, you-name-it, who gave cash kickbacks. That was skim.

Each week, the skim would be divided by a hundred points. Each point owner would get his share of the cash. The money would be picked up by couriers and deposited in Swiss bank accounts or flushed through a series of corporate fronts and offshore banks operated by Lansky. Since the skim money was cash and Uncle didn't know about it, it was tax free.

Nothing changed when the big gambling corporations like Caesars World and some of the others went public. The wise guys simply had banks, corporations and other nominees hold their stock. And they still got their points of the skim. Legitimate profits from the casinos were so huge that the average sucker who bought his stock through a brokerage house never realized that he should be making even more. The difference was the amount skimmed off each week by his unknown silent partners.

The Italian mob, the Cosa Nostra, needed Meyer very badly. And Meyer needed the mob. A good marriage. Both Las Vegas and Miami were known as open cities. No family owned them. Everyone could suck at the teat as long as they had the money and went by Meyer's rules. Now casino gambling was coming to New Jersey. The mob had declared Atlantic City an open city. Meyer's boys, as usual, would provide the know-how. But Angelo Bruno, boss of the Philadelphia family, didn't want to play by the rules. He wanted most of the city for his family. The other wise guys were pissed. Bruno was a dead man. He just didn't know it yet.

Meyer was getting old. He was nearly eighty. Too old to take jail time. Each year he added another layer of insulation. His old buddy and closest friend Sam Cohen was getting old too. That was the reason for Alvin Malnik, a clever lawyer in his late forties, who knew how to grease and when. He also knew how to count. Meyer still called the big shots. But Alvin was being groomed. He'd wheeled and dealed the Teamster pension fund for so many loans that Jimmy Hoffa was cross-eyed when they stuffed him in a barrel.

Good's interest in the mob and Atlantic City had ballooned the day Mayor Errichetti ambled through Abdul's door. And it hadn't let up since. If anything, it increased when Senator Williams's partner George Katz came into the picture. Katz knew Lansky, and he was an asshole buddy of Sam Cohen, Lansky's top lieutenant. Good had pushed both

Weinberg and Amoroso to get everything they could on the mob from Katz and the Mayor. They hadn't done too badly either.

The Mayor was the first to bite. He said that he had his own connection with the mob. According to Errichetti, his man in the Cosa Nostra was Paul Castellano, the new boss of the old Carlo Gambino crime family in New York. Early in the game, when Weinberg and Amoroso had pushed the Mayor for assurances that Abdul's casino wouldn't be bothered by the mob, Errichetti told them that he had Castellano's personal blessing.

Another powerful mobster in Atlantic City, the Mayor had said, was Gerry Catena, semiretired boss of the old Genovese crime family. Errichetti said several times that Catena owned Joseph Lordi, Chairman of the State Casino Control Commission. The Mayor was echoed by Tony Torcasio, the veteran gambler from Las Vegas who had been hired to run Guccione's proposed Penthouse casino in Atlantic City.

Both Errichetti and Torcasio had said that Gerry Catena spent most of his time in Florida, but still represented his crime family's casino interests in Atlantic City through his control of Joseph Lordi, who was also the former district attorney of Essex (Newark) County. Catena was a regular at the Boca Raton Hotel in Florida, owned by the contractor who was supposed to be building the Penthouse for Guccione. The contractor himself had come to Abdul and guaranteed a casino license if Abdul wanted to cut Guccione out and finance the casino itself.

Standard mix of wise guys and politicians, Weinberg thought. The ankle bone's connected to the leg bone and so on. A huge circle-jerk. This guy knows that guy who is connected to this guy. In almost any other walk of life it didn't mean anything. But in this game it meant everything. Because these guys didn't bother knowing each other unless they could make money together. Social friendships were for golfers and Rotarians.

The Mayor had described his meetings with Castellano. Phone calls from public booths, switched cars, a pat-down at the gate from

Castellano's bodyguards. The Mayor, who delighted at playing hood, had offered to bring Amoroso on his next visit to the mob boss. From Errichetti's description of Castellano's security drill, Amoroso knew he might have to go in without cover and a tape recorder. Too big a chance of being compromised. He shrugged off the invitation and Errichetti forgot about it.

SCENE

Weinberg is eating breakfast at a hotel in Mount Laurel, New Jersey, with Mayor Errichetti. Lurking someplace near is Agent Steve Bursey, Weinberg's cover for the day. There is no tape of the meeting. Weinberg has forgotten to bring down the attaché case with the tape recorder inside. He is too tired to go back and get it. Fuck it. The conversation is dull anyhow. Errichetti on Errichetti. The Mayor stops in midsentence and leaps from the table. He brings over a man who has just entered the dining room, "Mel," beams the Mayor, "I want you to meet my good friend Joe Gambino."

Weinberg gulps. The name is Gambino. And the man shaking his hand has the smell of a wise guy. There is some quick chitchat and Gambino is escorted to another table. As soon as he sits, two men arrive and sit down with him. He is holding court. He is a wise guy. The Mayor confirms it. "Joe runs a lot of things around here. He reaches into Atlantic City too." The Mayor says that Gambino will give them an audience in a half-hour. Errichetti is glowing. Weinberg looks frantically for Bursey. He knows he is in the background but he can't see him. Besides, he doesn't have his tape recorder. Weinberg slowly releases a stream of cigar smoke at the Mayor. "Screw Joe Gambino," he says. "He's shit. He's nothing." The Mayor is shocked. He protests Gambino is important. Weinberg, rising from his chair, tosses a contemptuous look in Gambino's direction and whispers to the Mayor, "If he's so fuckin' important, how come he don't clean his fingernails?" As they leave the dining room, the Mayor is scratching his head. His look says he isn't sure whether he has heard Weinberg correctly.

It had been in early August, while they waited at Kennedy Airport to give Senator Williams his titanium stock, that the Mayor had first mentioned Meyer Lansky. It was the same day that Errichetti confirmed the arrangements for the bribery of Congressmen Myers and Lederer, so it had slipped by in the conversation. But the Mayor had returned to the subject more often as the days passed. His interest, undoubtedly, was stimulated by his budding friendship with Howard Criden.

The Mayor met frequently with Weinberg and Amoroso that August. He bubbled with plans to perfect the titanium deal with Senator Williams and the payoffs to the two Congressmen, Myers and Lederer. George Katz was present at a few of these meetings. The Boardwalk Regency, a sibling of Caesars Palace, had opened in Atlantic City with a temporary license. There were newspaper stories reporting that the casino might have problems getting its permanent license because of past business connections between Alvin Malnik and Caesars' board chairman Cliff Perlman.

Both Errichetti and Katz confided that Perlman still had close ties with Lansky and Malnik. Now that Abdul was preparing to build an Atlantic City gambling casino, what Abdul needed, Weinberg insisted, was a connection with Meyer Lansky. Without such a protector, he argued, other mobsters would muscle into Abdul's proposed casino operations. Besides, he added, only Lansky could provide the gambling experts needed for the casino.

Errichetti had considered the problem. He said that he didn't know Lansky, but was close to someone who knew him well. "This guy [Lansky] is gonna be very fuckin' careful," Errichetti cautioned. "He ain't been in trouble." Using one of his favorite expressions, Errichetti said that he had already been "head-to-head" with his Lansky contact. He described the contact as "a guy [who's] . . . pretty high up there." Then the Mayor dropped a few tidbits.

He reported that he had asked his contact to speak to Lansky and determine whether he would get involved in Atlantic City. There were rumors, he said, that his associate Malnik was already active in the area.

The Mayor had another hot item. He said that members of the Detroit Cosa Nostra family had a heavy point interest in the Aladdin Hotel in Las Vegas. Weinberg steered the conversation back to Lansky, and asked the Mayor to get specifics from Lansky on what he might do for Abdul's proposed gambling interests. "Give us the rules, who controls what and who's gonna sit with whom and what's he [Lansky] gonna ask . . . okay?" The Mayor agreed.

Early in September, the Mayor reported that the meeting between Lansky and his contact had been arranged. He also seemed to have more information about the mob money genius. The quickest way to Lansky, he confided, was through his stepdaughter-in-law Susan. She was the widow of Lansky's stepson who had been murdered in a parking area near his Miami restaurant by mob gunmen. The murder, said Errichetti, was a matter of underworld honor. The stepson apparently had killed the son of a Cosa Nostra soldier in a drunken argument.

Weinberg shuddered. The Mayor, despite his fluency on the subject, was a man with secondhand knowledge. Weinberg had personal reasons for his reaction to Errichetti's recital of the contract killing. A year before he had been reached by Lansky's brother and asked if the Abdul operation was for real or just another one of Weinberg's scams. He had assured him that Abdul was legitimate.

This contact had occurred in Miami while Weinberg was working on a CD sting for the local FBI. A Miami businessman had visited him and suggested he call Jake Lansky. Weinberg knew Jake. He treated the request like a royal command and called Jake from a public phone. Afterward, he scrawled a brief account of the conversation on a piece of paper and threw it into a box with his expense-account receipts.

It read (in part): "Jake Lansky and —— told me that he wanted to know . . . Abdul. Mentioned Meyer wanted to know about it . . . told me that they [Lansky group] are trying to move them out of Atlantic City—Bruno family—'we could do big things if you're for real'—problem that Abdul is for real."

Lansky's brother was testing, Weinberg reasoned. If Abdul was legitimate, Meyer Lansky intended to use its money to buy up Atlantic City, shoving out Angelo Bruno of the Philadelphia family with the sheer weight of Abdul's cash. Weinberg had lied when he told Jake that Abdul wasn't a scam and stalled further discussions, pleading that he would get back to Jake when the Abdul operation was fully organized.

He might have been excused for lying, he thought, if nothing further had happened and the Lansky group lost neither time nor money. Now, however, he was pushing Abdul directly at Meyer Lansky and as a consequence would be scamming one of the most powerful men in the American underworld. That was a mob no-no. Lansky was, he had reflected, a deadly sonuvabitch.

In mid-September, Errichetti enthusiastically reported that his contact would be sitting down with Lansky the next day. He no longer referred to the mobster as Lansky. Now it was just plain Meyer. The Mayor said his contact was giving Meyer the following message on behalf of the Abdul group: (1) they didn't want any trouble; (2) they didn't want to die; (3) they didn't want to be ripped off; and (4) they wanted to run a profitable business and not be killed [financially]. Mournfully, Weinberg assured the Mayor that he had sent exactly the right message to Lansky.

Several days later, Errichetti summoned Weinberg to New Jersey for a meeting with his Lansky contact, Howard Criden. Later investigation would show that Criden had been closely associated with the Lansky group for a number of years. He had, in fact, been a business partner of Lansky's protégé Alvin Malnik in several Florida deals. Weinberg had a sudden thought when the Mayor revealed Criden's role. It would return frequently over the following months: Howard Criden, who delivered the Congressmen, was more than a bag man. He was also Meyer Lansky's man. The mob, he reflected, had a long reach.

Criden wasted no time. He said that he had lunched with Meyer Lansky and reported that Lansky would work with Abdul. Further, he had sent Criden to Malnik to arrange the details. Lansky, said Criden, was already involved in Atlantic City.

> *Criden:* There's nothing gonna happen anywhere [without Lansky]. The two joints that are functioning [in Atlantic City] are his joints. Resorts is originally his, through the Mary Carter Paint Company. Cliff Perlman [Caesars Palace and Boardwalk Regency] Mr. Lansky owns lock, stock and barrel. He put him in business.
> *Weinberg:* . . . Well, I know he put him in business, and I knew [bluffing] that he had a piece of Caesars. How much he owned, I never knew.
> *Criden:* Do you think that Cliff goes to the fuckin' bathroom without talking to Malnik?

Weinberg later returned to the subject of Lansky's interest in Atlantic City.

> *Weinberg:* May I ask you a question? How are these other casinos that are opening here gonna operate?
> *Criden:* Where in Atlantic City, I didn't ask. I didn't go into details [with Malnik] . . . I know that he [inaudible] . . . desk in the penthouse was about three messages. One was from Crosby [Resorts]. One was from Jack Davis [Resorts] and the [number] three was from [inaudible]. Okay. I know he [Malnik] talks with Crosby every day. Now, how the rest of these things—I don't know. I know that as far as Resorts is concerned, they check with him [Malnik]. I know that as far as Cliff is concerned, they're partners.

Criden produced mortgage documents for the Cricket Club in Miami, a swank condominium complex owned by Alvin Malnik and

Lansky's buddy Sam Cohen. Perlman appeared on the papers as a guarantor of mortgage loans to the club complex.

Criden said that Malnik wanted to deal. The Lansky aide proposed that Abdul buy the Aladdin Hotel in Las Vegas and the Cricket Club in Miami. Abdul could either buy both outright or Malnik would share Abdul's interest. He would handle the management of both through front men. He would also provide staff and management for Abdul's planned casino in Atlantic City. Again and again, Criden stressed that Malnik was Lansky. And he warned that nothing would happen in Atlantic City unless Lansky was part of it.

The middleman became expansive as he talked about Lansky's power in Las Vegas. He boasted: "They own [inaudible] commissioner in Vegas in Nevada [inaudible], they own him lock, stock, and barrel, okay? If they tell him to shit, he squats. Now if the Stardust [casino] is [inaudible] they [Nevada authorities] tell 'em they have to sell it. They were supposed to close the place down, and wound up with a $100,000 fine."

> *Weinberg:* You're sayin' on Vegas—I know the Italians own Vegas—all the families out there.
>
> *Criden:* The way it works is this. Everybody's got their sphere of authority. Their joint. Their split of the cut, including Atlantic City. Okay? If every [mob] family had to watch every other family, it would be fuckin' warfare.
>
> *Weinberg:* Bloodshed.
>
> *Criden:* Okay, cause nobody would trust anybody . . . So early in the game it was decided that they had to have somebody that everybody had implicit trust in. That guy became Meyer. Absolute unequivocal law when it came to cutting up the pot okay. If a dollar came in and he [Meyer] was entitled to three dollars and you were entitled to six dollars, he got his three and you got your six and I got my five, whatever was the arrangement . . . there were no excuses . . . if you were to be

delivered your six dollars Thursday at noontime, you got your six dollars. Okay. That's the way it went for years and that's the way it still goes. . . . There was a dispute several times. . . . A guy would say I don't think I have the right count. . . . They [the mob] would have a meeting. . . . The top guy would say: Meyer's word is law. We will hear from Meyer. He will give us an explanation and that's it. . . . Now what did that . . . accomplish? First, it put the whole fuckin' . . . on a businesslike basis. There was no killing there, no shootings there . . . no fighting, no arbitration, nothin'. . . . Now they had to be able to trust this man [Meyer] implicity, right? Cause he had control over hundreds of millions of dollars. But he never fucked anyone.

Weinberg, sighing inwardly, pressed for a meeting with Malnik. He hoped that Criden was exaggerating, but knew he wasn't. Criden's inside knowledge was too exact. And his track record so far had been 100 percent. Criden picked up the phone and dialed through to Malnik's penthouse. Arrangements were made with Malnik to meet for dinner at the Forge Restaurant in Miami on Thursday night, September 20. Criden said that Malnik owned it.

As the meeting ended, Criden took Weinberg aside. "The most important thing," he warned, ". . . we can't jerk Alvin off." Weinberg deadpanned his reply: "We told him the way it is . . ."

Criden had still worried. It was obvious that the jowly lawyer was just as concerned as Weinberg about upsetting the mob, although for different reasons. He told Weinberg: "We have the opportunity of a lifetime with this guy Malnik. Okay? He can do things and open doors for us that you never dreamed existed. However, the minute our credibility is dead, we're dead." There goes that word again, thought Weinberg.

A knock on the door brought Weinberg abruptly back to the present. He was in Florida to meet Malnik. He answered the knock. It was Diane. He forgot about the mob.

That evening, as Weinberg and Diane walked through the lobby on the way out to dinner, they were greeted by Criden and the Mayor who insisted on taking them to a restaurant they had discovered. He sensed that the two had been waiting in ambush. He nodded to Diane and played along. Criden drove. They pulled into a restaurant parking lot and got out. This was where Lansky's stepson had been riddled with bullets, announced Criden. Weinberg winced.

Inside, a table was already set for six. There were several platters of onion-board, Weinberg's favorite. An attractive woman accompanied by a strange man sat down at the table with them. Criden introduced her. She was Susan, Meyer Lansky's stepdaughter-in-law, the mother of his four grandchildren. Weinberg watched carefully. He knew what was happening. Criden was proving his connections. And Weinberg was being measured.

It was a careful conversation. The stranger with Susan said little. Weinberg has never identified him. Criden and the Mayor burbled politely with Diane. Susan concentrated on Weinberg. She's the pump, he decided. She asked him about Europe and the places there he had been and seen. It was a subject he had often mentioned to the Mayor and Criden. Susan had traveled extensively. He passed her testing easily. He gently probed her family life. She was friendly but vague. Suddenly it clicked. Susan was looking him over before Alvin Malnik decided whether to keep his dinner appointment the next night at the Forge.

Weinberg ate and drank little. He said just enough to appear open and unconcerned. On the way back to the motel, Criden told him that everything was set for the next night with Malnik. Evidently, he had gotten a good report card from Susan. There was another plus. His Abscam partner Tony Amoroso would be at the Forge. He was flying in that night.

Even so, dinner with Alvin Malnik was a letdown. He kept the subject general, discussing the Cricket Club, his efforts to get casino gambling in Florida, and the Aladdin. The meeting wasn't taped. Good had decided that body-tapes in this league with these players would be too dangerous. And people didn't bring attaché cases to dinner. Malnik invited them to his penthouse the next week. Afterward, he said, they would take a cruise on his boat.

Malnik was cute, Weinberg told Good later that night. He didn't talk in front of witnesses. He would choose his own time and place to talk business, Weinberg predicted. It happened the next week.

The following Saturday, accompanied by Amoroso, and his own teenaged son, Weinberg visited Malnik at his penthouse. It was impressive. Malnik explained that each of the club's condominium units went for $350,000. But Malnik was putting in some improvements. He escorted them to the roof where he was installing his personal swimming pool and helicopter pad. Important for privacy, he explained. He introduced the group to a teenaged girl whom he identified as his daughter. There were several other guests. After a half-hour of chitchat, Malnik invited everyone for a cruise.

Malnik's yacht, berthed at the nearby marina, was a hundred-footer with a uniformed crew. The guests boarded and the craft sailed out into Biscayne Bay.

SCENE

Malnik's cruiser cuts swirls of white foam as it purrs past Fisher Island and into the Atlantic. The guests sit with drinks in hand, making polite conversation. Weinberg's son is playing backgammon with Malnik's daughter. Weinberg's son is winning consistently. Weinberg watches fondly over his son's shoulder. His son wins again. Weinberg leans forward and whispers into his ear: "Lose, schmuck! Don't ya wanna marry into the family?"

Halfway through the trip, Malnik made his move. He took Weinberg and Amoroso to a deserted part of the deck and laid it on the line. He could get them the Aladdin, he said. It would require an under-the-table payment of $10 million to buy out the mob point-holders from Detroit. The price on top of that, he said, would be $105 million, part of it an assumed Teamster mortgage. He would arrange for the proper people to run the Aladdin for Abdul.

Malnik said that he wanted to package the Aladdin sale with the Cricket Club. He said that he owned 25 percent of the club and Sam Cohen owned the other 75 percent. Moreover, he admitted that he didn't like Cohen. In any event Abdul could buy the Cricket for $42 million. Or, Malnik said, Abdul could keep him as a partner in the Cricket and pay only $30 million, maybe less, for Cohen's piece of the complex. He said that he would handle all of Abdul's casino problems in Atlantic City. He wanted Abdul immediately to put up $10 million in good faith money to be held in escrow for the Aladdin deal.

Back at the hotel that night Weinberg and Amoroso discussed Malnik's offer with Good. Malnik obviously wanted to unload the Aladdin. Nevada officials were probing the ownership of the huge hotel. Weinberg said that the mob apparently wanted to bail out while its points still had value. If Malnik, who was barred in Nevada from casino ownership, selected the Aladdin staff for Abdul, the mob would still have a voice in the casino with Abdul as a front.

The Cricket Club, Weinberg had learned, was a loser. It had been open for four years and only half of the units had been sold. Besides, argued Weinberg, there was the matter of Cliff Perlman's involvement in the Cricket Club loans. Nevada officials had told Perlman to end all ties with Malnik two years ago. If anyone learned of Perlman's continuing responsibility for the Cricket loans, Caesars' licenses could be endangered both in Nevada and Atlantic City. If Abdul bought the club, Perlman was home free.

Good was fascinated. On the surface, no crime was involved in the Malnik offer. But the Bureau was gaining valuable information on Lansky's casino interests. The information could be used later at licensing hearings in Nevada and New Jersey. There was only one problem, said Good. None of it was on tape. He told Weinberg to arrange a meeting with Malnik at some place where he could be taped. Weinberg howled.

Malnik was supercautious, he said. He had only talked to them on his own boat while the engine roared. Get it on tape, Good repeated.

Over the next month, Criden pressed for an answer to Malnik's offer and Weinberg went into a quarter stall. Malnik had not been specific enough, Weinberg complained. Abdul's accountants wanted flow sheets on Aladdin profits. There had to be more discussion of the $10 million payoff to the Detroit mob. What kind of receipt could he show Abdul for that? Weinberg urged another meeting. Criden was stubborn. Weinberg, learning that Malnik was due in New York that week, invited him through Criden to Abdul's suite at the Plaza Hotel. Criden was noncommittal.

Errichetti, by this time, had gone into his permanent sulk and rarely answered when Weinberg called. One day, however, he came to the phone and accused Weinberg of stalling Malnik. Weinberg countered that Malnik might come to the Plaza that week. The Mayor disagreed. "I think he feels you're fulla shit," said Errichetti. "And you know what, you'd better get it [the $10 million] up before anything else happens. That's the word I'm getting." Weinberg put down the phone and scratched his head. Damn Good and his tapes!

He thought about it. Malnik had admitted a dislike for Sam Cohen. Weinberg recognized the dislike as the new-guard old-guard syndrome. Quite simply, he figured that Malnik was jealous of Cohen's long ties of friendship with Lansky. Senator Williams's business partner George Katz was talking the same way in reverse. Katz, close to Cohen, kept insisting that Cohen was Lansky's top man, not Malnik. Weinberg decided to use the rivalry as a wedge to force another meeting with Malnik. First, though, he'd have to fan the fire a little.

Weinberg called Katz and confided that Malnik hated Cohen. He said that Malnik wanted Cohen out of the Cricket Club because Cohen was too cheap to run a quality place. He related a story from Malnik that Cohen screamed at club waiters for putting more than two pats of butter on a plate.

Katz: Who? Sam does that?

Weinberg: Yeah.

Katz: I don't believe it.

Weinberg: That's what he says.

Katz (later): Meyer says he doesn't even know Malnik.

Weinberg: I know he says it, but that's bullshit.

Katz: Well, I'm not going to tell you any different.

Weinberg: We were told this.

Katz: Whoever told you is full of shit.

Weinberg: He's not a partner?

Katz: He's not supposed to talk about it, whether he is or isn't.
Do you understand?

Weinberg cradled the phone, smiling. Katz would burn up the long-distance line to Florida telling Cohen about Malnik's insults. Now for his next call. This time it was to Howard Criden. He told Criden that someone very close to Lansky had told him that Sam Cohen dealt for Lansky, not Malnik. And he said his friend had told him that Cohen would sell the Cricket to Abdul at a cheaper price. Criden had been at meetings with Weinberg and Katz, so he knew who Weinberg's tipster was. Now it was his turn to be upset.

Several days later, Criden was back on the phone. Malnik had agreed to meet again. This time, Weinberg was taking no chances. He complained that Malnik's apartment and the Forge Restaurant were too busy. Malnik was always either getting phone calls or greeting customers. They needed a quiet, private place. He suggested Criden's condominium at the Hemisphere House in Hallandale. Criden agreed. Weinberg hung up jubilant. He and Amoroso could bring the bugged attaché case to the apartment without appearing conspicuous.

The meeting was set for the evening of October 27. Meanwhile, there was another development. Malnik's bank had called Abdul's friend at

Chase Manhattan. The message went back to Malnik that Abdul had an account in the millions. At this point in the investigation, Weinberg and Amoroso used the names of Abdul and Yassir interchangeably. Both were partners, they explained, operating as Abdul Enterprises, Ltd. It was a fuzzy story. But it avoided slip-ups.

Weinberg and Amoroso arrived at Criden's ocean-view condominium at the appointed time to find Criden waiting with Malnik. Gingerly, Weinberg put the attaché case on the floor next to the coffee table. Malnik played the host. He poured coffee for everyone, and began by asking Amoroso whether he wanted sugar or Sweet 'N Low.

During the next hour, mob protocol was strictly observed. Never once did Malnik or the Abscam agents mention the name of Lansky. Malnik's presence as Lansky's man was accepted and understood. Atlantic City was not on that night's agenda. That would be discussed at a later date. Malnik stuck with his sales pitch for the Aladdin and the Cricket Club. But he gave a fascinating glimpse at the power of the mob in Las Vegas. In the process, he tied Caesars Palace to Lansky by implication. And he said enough to provide fireworks for casino licensing agencies in Nevada and New Jersey.

The bottom line of Malnik's taped conversation was something that honest law enforcement agencies had known for years. There can be no successful casino gambling without the mob. It was evident in everything he said.

Malnik started with a review of the cost figures for the Aladdin. Weinberg questioned how it would be possible to account to Yassir for the secret $10 million paid to the mob point-holders from Detroit.

Weinberg: Who will be getting the ten million cash?
Malnik: There's no way I can tell you.
Weinberg: How the hell we gonna explain that to Yassir? . . .
Somebody's gonna have to accept it.

Malnik: Someone will accept it, but no one is gonna accept it
   and acknowledge it . . . [later] I mean it's as sensitive as
   hell . . . [later] I think the somebody who is gonna accept it is
   not an identifiable person to begin with, right? Let's assume
   that three people are receiving a portion of it. . . . They're not
   in the deal. They don't appear anywhere.

Malnik told Weinberg and Amoroso that the Aladdin was presently
under option to Eddie Torres, former operator of the Riviera in Las
Vegas, and his partner Del Coleman. How could Malnik keep Torres
and Coleman from exercising their option, Weinberg asked. "I can arrange it so that they can't," Malnik replied quietly.

Malnik said that after Abdul bought the Aladdin, Torres would
manage it. He would guarantee Torres. "I'm not worried about his integrity," said Malnik. "Because he'll owe the integrity to me." He added:
"There will be nobody who will steal anything from you. . . . Nobody is
gonna be taking scores out of that place. Nobody. You don't have to
worry about anybody."

The discussion turned to other costs once Abdul acquired the
Aladdin. Malnik said that there would only be one—the political slush
fund. He spoke about it carefully, almost hesitantly. In fact, he was discussing the mob's most poorly kept secret—a fund to fix Nevada politicians. Even so, Malnik played his cards closely.

Malnik: Things [the slush fund] that are customary, that are
   done. There are certain obligations that are taken care of. . . .
   None of it's mandatory, follow me?
Criden: Most of the casinos make certain contributions to a
   group. Okay?
Weinberg: Absolutely.
Criden: To various political guys in the state. Okay? If you
   wanna contribute, you get part of the benefit. . . .

The conversation drifted, but Weinberg nudged it back toward the slush fund. He was hoping to get names, but Malnik was too careful.

Weinberg: Are they [officials] cracking down out there now?
Malnik: Oh, my God. It's so extensive, the investigation, you have absolutely no idea!
Weinberg: Is there somebody you can reach out for?
Malnik: Sure.
Weinberg: Well, that could be our way then.
Malnik: There are a few things that we have going, but . . . it's still a problem. . . . You don't have everybody going . . . in unison. . . . You got a couple [of politicians] here, a couple there . . . I don't have to tell you what politicians are [laughs]. I'll take what you got as long as there's no heat. Once there's a little bit of heat . . . I don't like these guys anyway.

Malnik conceded that the Aladdin's profits were in the doldrums (it was under state trusteeship). But he was enthusiastic about the casino's possibilities. He became expansive and revealed the continuing Lansky interest in Caesars Palace.

He gushed: "What you have to do is what *we* did with Caesars Palace. *We* always, *we* never made any money because *we* always put it back into the joint. *We* always added two hundred rooms here, three hundred rooms there, till over at that joint *we* have two thousand rooms now."

Weinberg nodded in satisfaction. Gottcha, Caesars. Malnik had used the word *we* six times in talking about Caesars Palace. The same group owned the Boardwalk Regency in Atlantic City. So much, he thought, for political promises to keep casino gambling clean.

Malnik talked on about his group's ability to make or break almost any casino through control of key employees. "Just like poor credit," he said. ". . . We take a joint that's making ten million dollars a year and turn it into a loser of ten million dollars a year." As Weinberg listened, he mentally renewed his determination never to buy gambling-casino stocks. Betting football games with a bookie was safer.

The subject moved to the Cricket Club in Miami. Malnik denied that it was going broke. He said that the club had just sold condominiums to the presidents of Mexico and Guatemala. He had, however, a more ambitious plan for Abdul and Yassir. He proposed buying the next-door Lear School and the Jockey Club next to the school. The two new packages, he said, could be joined to the Cricket to create the biggest resort in Miami. Moreover, the entire package wouldn't cost more than $60 million if he were kept in as a 25 percent partner. If casino gambling were legalized in Florida, according to Malnik, the package would be worth more than $300 million.

Weinberg and Amoroso showed enthusiasm. A total of $180 million for the Aladdin and the new Cricket package was not difficult, they said, for their rich Arab employers. It sounded like a good deal. Weinberg, however, left open an escape-hatch. It all depended, he said, on how the Arabs felt about paying the secret $10 million in cash to people who would never acknowledge the money.

Malnik warned that the deal would have to move quickly. Other buyers, including entertainer Johnny Carson, were nibbling at the Aladdin. As Malnik lifted Criden's phone to make a call, he smiled: "I think [this phone] is a lot safer than mine."

It had been a productive evening. Weinberg wanted to pump Malnik some more. But the tape in the attaché case was almost exhausted. Amoroso hurried to get out with the tape intact. Weinberg asked one last question of Criden. If Abdul purchased the properties, who was going to pay Criden his part in putting the deal together?

Criden replied, "I'm not your responsibility. Let's put it this way. I'm Alvin's [Malnik] responsibility."

On the drive back to the motel, Weinberg couldn't shake the memory of Criden's final words. Criden, through his nationwide net of fellow middlemen, seemed able almost at will to produce Congressmen for bribes. He had already brought in several of them and appeared ready to produce others. But Criden was obviously Malnik's man. And Malnik was Lansky. . . . He wondered how many Congressmen Criden produced for the mob.

The old fear returned. He had scammed Lansky's protégé. The tape would make life miserable for the gambling mob—at least for a little while. The politicians would come back with their hands out as soon as the heat was off, and things would return to normal. The government would forget Mel Weinberg. But the mob wouldn't. He shuddered. It was a sultry night, but the breeze from the ocean felt cold.

Atlantic City, N.J. (AP), Nov. 11, 1980—Atlantic City's four legal casinos grossed $58.7 million or an average of $1.9 million a day, during October—pushing the Boardwalk's total win close to $1 billion. . . . Caesars Boardwalk Regency won $18.3 million, or an average of $591,851 a day during October. This is 10 percent more than the September gross and 23 percent more than the October 1979 take . . .

TAPE SIXTEEN

Weinberg: Malnik is very sharp. That's his rep every place. He said too much to us that night, but almost anybody else woulda said more. Sure, I worry about it. I ain't going into no witness protection program. That's like bein' in a prison without no doors. I've seen other guys from my walk of life, let's say. They bust their humps workin' and testifyin' for the government. They set themselves up to be dead men. Five years later nobody gives a shit about them. They're, like, embarrassin' to everybody. They're blown. They can't help anybody's careers no more. That's why so many of these government jokers like the protection program. They can send you some place in the fuckin' Utah desert and change your name and never have to see you or think of you again. Screw them. If John gets me a big bonus at the end of this and the book makes money, I'll support my family and protect myself. If not, I'll haunt their asses.

12

TAKE OUTS AND TAKE DOWNS

I'm a swindler. There's only one difference between me and the
Congressmen I met on this case. The public pays them a salary
for stealing.
                                                    —MEL WEINBERG

Weinberg was exhausted. He slouched, eyes at half-mast, in an easy chair
in the study of the Washington townhouse. A vagrant thought wormed
into his consciousness. He had forgotten to take his blood-pressure pills.
He was too tired to reach down for them and too afraid of dying not to.

Every time he straightened up from putting on his socks a blizzard of
tiny, white lights would shimmer in front of his eyes. A warning signal,
the doctor had said. Slow down. Take it easy. Strokes kill. The same tired
shit. He stirred for the first time in the last hour. Heaving a deep sigh, he
reached down to his pocket for the brown plastic pillbox. Screw strokes
too, he thought.

He washed the pills down with a swig of diet soda. Can in hand, he
sat thinking, vaguely aware of sounds from other parts of the house.
Laughter filtered down the stairway from the second floor. Good had just
come in from Long Island. He was probably crowing because he had
grabbed the only other bedroom with its own bathroom. Weinberg had

the first one. The next agents in would get the two bedrooms without baths. Laggards got the bed in the basement control room or the couch.

A rustle of noise in the kitchen. Weinberg cataloged it. Agent Ernie Haridopolos making a sandwich. Ernie was always eating. All the FBI agents were ape for sandwiches, he grimaced. Breakfast, lunch and dinner, sandwiches. He pictured the FBI academy. A course on sandwich-making tucked in between Machine-Gun Shooting 203 and Creative Ways to Screw Informants Out of Their Expenses 607. He was sick of sandwiches.

A Bureau electronics specialist walked softly into the semidarkened room. He snapped on a light near the TV and popped a fresh roll of videotape into the hidden camera. The light clicked out and the agent strode from the room. Weinberg eyed the silent TV screen. The agent, he knew, was setting up for tomorrow's visit from a Florida Congressman named Kelly. Good had promised that Kelly would be the last. Abscam, he said, was finally shutting down.

This time, Good apparently meant it. Weinberg had conflicting emotions when he got the word. He had to admit that even he couldn't keep stalling much longer. Counting the titanium loan to Senator Williams and his group, he and Tony Amoroso had promised more than a half-billion in Arab loans and payments to Abscam targets. Some of them, like Bill Rosenberg and Big George from Florida, had been waiting more than a year. Once his credibility was lost, Abscam was over anyway.

But Weinberg didn't want to give up yet. Howard Criden was producing Congressmen with machinelike regularity. He had promised to shovel Abdul all the Congressmen that it wanted, and he was keeping his word. Weinberg was also puzzled. Why hadn't he been told to push for meetings with some of the other big Congressmen that had been mentioned on the tapes? He shook his head. He could guess one of the reasons. Too many tapes were coming in at once. Sometimes there were as many as seventeen in one day. Many were long conversations. A Congressman's name could be dropped in the middle of a conversation by

Criden and be completely forgotten by Weinberg and Amoroso. The tape volume was so big that Washington was weeks, even months, behind in transcribing. He knew that some of the tapes were flown directly to Washington to be played for the FBI Director and Justice Department people. But Washington only gave orders to set a meeting with a target after Good had sent down specific names. If Good didn't have the name, he couldn't send it down.

He still had absolute confidence in Puccio and Good. They would go after anyone. But he had given names to both and never heard anything further about those names. The Pooch and Good were company men. If they disagreed with Washington, they didn't tell him about it. Still, he wondered. Some of those names seemed worthwhile.

He traced them in his mind. Jimmy Wright of Texas, the House Majority Leader, John Brademas, the Majority Whip, House Speaker Tip O'Neill, Senator Ted Kennedy, Congressmen Jim Howard, William Hughes and Frank Guarini of New Jersey. And he still wondered about Congressman James Mattox of Texas, who had been scheduled to visit the townhouse on the day they had paid Congressman Thompson. He had been called and canceled by Criden because they were running late. There had been no push for another meeting with him.

There was, Weinberg admitted, another side to the story. It was his job to handle all of the contacts with middlemen for meetings with the Congressmen. He had to go to all of the meetings with Amoroso, and afterward, he had to handle all of the stalls. He was already overloaded. Phones were ringing constantly, and he found himself flipping from one case to another. The pressure was enormous. He knew he couldn't handle any more targets before Abscam's credibility evaporated. So did Good.

Washington was a buzz word to Weinberg. As the case progressed, it became a synonym for bad news. It was Washington that was always pushing for more on Senator Williams. Washington wouldn't give him another raise. Washington wanted more receipts for his expenses. Washington wanted him to stall a meeting with a Congressman for weeks while it tried to make up its mind one way or the other. Washington, he had long ago decided, was the world's biggest collection of assholes.

Weinberg closed his eyes but he couldn't sleep. A freezing rain gusted against the windows. A copy of the *Washington Post* crumpled at his feet said that it was January 7, 1980. He thought about the jumbled events of the past few months. There had been a huge spurt of activity, the harvest of the Abscam illusion. The cast of characters had suddenly grown so large he had trouble recalling all of the names. His mind drifted backward in time. It had started with Murphy.

Congressman John Murphy of New York had been the sharpest of them all. Tough and pragmatic, Murphy had graduated first in his class at West Point and was a highly decorated hero of the Korean War. He was Chairman of the House Merchant Marine and Fisheries Committee, the man who controlled the flow of Federal money to the subsidy-hungry U.S. shipping industry. Inconclusive Federal investigations had linked him to Somoza, the Shah of Iran and the Gambino crime family.

Congressman Thompson had reached Murphy, and Criden had brought him in. Puccio was ecstatic when he heard that Murphy was coming. He was, Weinberg was told, a real biggie. Weinberg was ordered to arrange the meeting for the Hilton Inn at Kennedy instead of the townhouse. Puccio wanted to be sure that if Murphy took the bribe, the crime would take place in his jurisdiction. The Pooch wanted to handle the Murphy case personally.

The meeting had been on October 20. Murphy was glib, but careful. Amoroso and Weinberg had given him the standard pitch about the Arabs' need for asylum. He'd agreed to help. But when Amoroso had handed him the $50,000, Murphy had ordered Criden to take it. Amoroso had offered the usual Arab business investments to promote jobs in Murphy's district, which covered Staten Island and lower Manhattan. But the Congressman had a counterproposal. Some friends of his, he said, would be in contact with Abdul representatives to discuss a mutually advantageous shipping deal.

Criden later told Weinberg that Murphy had only kept $10,000 of the bribe for "walking-around money." The rest had been split among Thompson, Criden and others. The Congressman's real interest, Criden explained, was in the shipping deal. The reason became apparent at the townhouse three weeks later. Criden brought in Larry Buser, a New Jersey shipping executive, who formerly headed the gigantic American Export Lines and still served as an occasional consultant to Murphy's House committee.

Buser proposed that Abdul loan as much as $100 million to a firm that Buser and Criden would form to buy the Farrell Lines shipping company and another shipping firm owned by the Puerto Rican government. The companies would be merged and Murphy would assure passage of Federal legislation that would make the new company highly profitable. Murphy would have a secret interest in the firm, which would be fronted by Criden. Weinberg and Amoroso hinted that they could get approval for the loan if they, too, were given a secret interest. It was agreed.

Puccio wanted more. He said that although Murphy had pointed the way to deal at the first meeting, he hadn't attended the second one with Criden and Buser. At his trial, Puccio warned, Murphy could claim that he had never discussed the shipping loan with Buser and Criden and knew nothing about it. John Jacobs was concerned that Murphy hadn't actually handled the bribe money on film. He wanted an admission from the Congressman. Weinberg was ordered to arrange another meeting including Criden, Buser and Murphy.

The targets resisted. Murphy was well insulated on the shipping deal and didn't want to come into the open. Weinberg adopted what the Abscam team called the Arab hardline. Abdul and Yassir loved the deal, Weinberg told Criden, but they were not going to invest up to $100 million unless they were certain that Murphy would be one of the owners. This would guarantee that he would push through the needed legislation. Criden grudgingly agreed to bring Buser and Murphy to the townhouse a month later.

Puccio and Jacobs were excited. The Pooch, a sudden convert to am-biance, told Good to hire a Washington caterer and serve Murphy a sumptuous dinner, and Good in turn told Agent Bruce Brady to handle the arrangements. Weinberg bit his tongue. Brady was a good agent, but he monitored expense accounts for the team and Weinberg had him pegged as a skinflint.

SCENE

Weinberg views the superbly set table in the dining room of the town-house. Murphy and the others are scheduled to arrive in a few minutes. Weinberg is in shock. The table is piled with cardboard trays of cold cuts, each covered with Saran Wrap. The cold cuts are not even good cold cuts like corned beef, tongue or pastrami. They are goyem cold cuts. Liver-wurst, bologna, boiled ham and gluey squares of Kraft's processed American cheese. The caterer, Weinberg decides, must be another Congressman. He hears voices in the next room. Brady is talking to another agent. "I got everything at Grand Union for $42," Brady boasts. Weinberg groans. Then he shrugs. Murphy looks like the processed-American type. Shit!

The dinner meeting began predictably:

Weinberg: Sure you don't wanna bite to eat or somethin'? How about a sandwich?

Amoroso: And I'll put some of the other stuff out . . . get somma this mustard.

Buser and Criden again discussed the shipping deal. But they avoided mentioning Murphy's interest. Murphy for his part said little. Weinberg understood. In the parlance of corruption, Murphy's presence at the meeting was sufficient. It was a statement of his interest. Amoroso pressed Murphy to commit himself on tape, but Murphy didn't bite. He said that he would explain the situation personally to the Arabs when he met them.

Amoroso knew that Jacobs was monitoring the situation from the control room and was impatiently waiting for him to get Murphy's oral admission on the bribe money. Neither Amoroso nor Weinberg had wanted to press it. They were both worried that the question might trigger Murphy's suspicions. But both wanted to please Jacobs, who had been their Strike Force tiger.

Amoroso: I was reluctant to give you the money, because you,
   you were, you were very . . .
Murphy (stiffening): You didn't. You didn't give me any money.
Amoroso: Well, okay then . . .
Murphy: I never, I never received money from anyone . . . and
   would not accept anything . . . from you or Howard.

The foxy Congressman had sensed something amiss. Less than twenty-four hours after he had left the townhouse, he put private detectives to work on Abdul. Both Murphy and Thompson, tried together, were later convicted. But Murphy's taped denial was a key defense argument.

The next Congressman was John Jenrette, Jr., of South Carolina, a member of the important House Appropriations Committee, and one of the few Congressmen not brought in by Errichetti or Criden. He came through John Stowe, a Virginia salesman who had negotiated with Weinberg over a batch of CDs early in Abscam. In conversations with Weinberg, he had often boasted that he was close to a Congressman. One day, while stalling Stowe, Weinberg mentioned the Arabs' immigration problem. Stowe volunteered to produce Jenrette.

Known for his hard drinking, Jenrette wanted to deal through Stowe. He balked at coming to the townhouse. Appointments were made and suddenly broken. As it happened, he had reasons to be skittish. He was under investigation by the Justice Department in connection with a

South Carolina real estate deal and subsequent tampering with a Federal grand jury. Jenrette and Stowe drove through the neighborhood observing the townhouse on several occasions before they finally came.

Jenrette said he wanted the money, but he would have to wait until the next day to make his decision. His attorney, he explained, was to meet Attorney General Civiletti to learn whether the government was dropping its investigation of him. If it did, he said, he would take the $50,000 bribe. "I got larceny in my blood; I'd take it in a goddamned minute," he told Amoroso. He said that the White House was helping him out. Jenrette called back the next day and sent Stowe to the townhouse for the bribe. On the phone he later acknowledged receiving it.

Jenrette also wanted a massive loan from the Arabs to save a failing real estate venture in which he was involved. But he didn't come for the loan empty-handed. Both Jenrette and Stowe said that they could produce crusty old Senator Strom Thurmond, the South Carolina Republican. The price for Thurmond's assistance, they said, would be $100,000. Negotiations on the Thurmond meeting lasted until Abscam closed down.

According to Jenrette and Stowe, Thurmond would not come to the townhouse, but would meet Weinberg and Amoroso in his Senate office or in a hotel room. He would not discuss money. He would agree to help the Arabs as a favor for Stowe. Moreover, he would only accept the money from Stowe, they reported, and that would only be after he had introduced the bill for the Arabs in the Senate. Suspecting a trick, Amoroso wouldn't give the money over to Jenrette and Stowe, who offered to hold it for Thurmond.

SCENE

Weinberg is in the townhouse kitchen. He is at the stove making Egyptian Eyes for breakfast. He cannot stand any more sandwiches. He cuts round holes in two pieces of bread, puts the bread in a sizzling frying pan and breaks an egg into each of the holes. He watches the eggs set in the bread and neatly flips them over. Eyes downcast, he smiles. He sidesteps a mess on the floor. Bruce Brady had thrown cornhusks into the garbage disposal the night before and everything had backed up. It is still there. He sighs and reaches over to the huge pile of dirty coffee cups stacked on the sideboard. He throws one into soapy water. "Hey, be careful," says an agent who has just come in. "We borrowed this antique china from the Smithsonian. It's worth a fortune!"

Then came Congressman John Murtha of Johnstown, Pennsylvania. Criden brought Murtha to the townhouse, explaining that he had been recruited for the Arabs by Thompson and Murphy. It was one of those chain-reaction things, thought Weinberg. First the middlemen bring the Congressmen. Now the Congressmen bring each other. If Abscam didn't fold soon, he mused, they'd be holding sessions of Congress in the townhouse.

Murtha had been edgy. He wanted Arab investments in his district. He promised to help Abdul and Yassir stay in the United States. But he wouldn't take the money. Maybe later, he said. He complained that he would have to split his $50,000 with Thompson and Murphy. The much-decorated Vietnam combat hero left, promising he'd call later about the bribe. Criden complained that he had lost a payday because he couldn't cut cash that Murtha hadn't taken. Amoroso had peeled $5,000 from the bribe wad and given it to him.

Weinberg stirred in his easy chair. Sleet still tattooed the study window. He slugged from the can of diet soda. It was getting flat. Like life, he thought. He churned his mind for a cheerful thought. Up popped Joe Silvestri. The hefty, flamboyant middleman from New Jersey had been a latecomer to Abscam. A building consultant with a string of New Jersey housing projects built on state and Federal loans, Silvestri was well hooked into New Jersey politics. He had been brought to Weinberg by Mayor Errichetti. Since then, the two men had split.

Weinberg enjoyed Silvestri. Like the Mayor, he was another crook at heart. He was a big spender, a great storyteller, and he was filled with promises. The first politician that he brought in was State Senator Joe Maressa of New Jersey. After that, Silvestri was all downhill. Weinberg learned, though, that it had been Silvestri who had brought Criden and Thompson together before Thompson had taken the bribe. Criden had given Silvestri $3,500 as his cut of the $50,000.

A former New Jersey State Trooper, Maressa was with a political faction challenging Mayor Errichetti for control of the Democratic Party in southern New Jersey. He promised to help Abdul get its casino license if the Arabs hired him as their lawyer. Amoroso took a hard line. Maressa finally took $25,000 and a promise of employment at Abdul's Atlantic City casino when it was opened.

Silvestri had then brought seventy-five-year-old Congressman Edward Patten of New Jersey to the Hilton Inn at Kennedy. It had already been a busy day for Weinberg and Amoroso. Murphy had been bribed in the same hotel room a few hours before. Silvestri passed out anisette-soaked cigars and everybody lit up as the meeting with Patten got underway.

Patten was a conversational wanderer. Each time Amoroso mentioned the proposed $50,000 bribe, Patten would charge down memory lane with disjointed accounts of refugee problems starting with the Jews under Hitler and concluding with the Vietnamese boat people. At various times, Patten said he would help the Arabs, he would think about helping the Arabs, and he wasn't sure he could help the Arabs.

Somewhere between Patten's rambles about Benito Mussolini and Hungarian refugees, Weinberg sneaked a look at Amoroso. Tony caught Weinberg's look and arched his eyebrow. Patten was out of it. "Oh, God," moaned Amoroso as Patten launched into another fragmented discourse. Silvestri grinned and turned his hands palms up. Amoroso slid the $50,000 payment back into a drawer. It took another ten minutes to disengage from Patten. Silvestri later reported that Patten had been convinced that Weinberg and Amoroso were with the Mafia.

Silvestri's next try was Senator Larry Pressler of South Dakota, a former Rhodes scholar, who was running in the Republican presidential primaries. The New Jersey hustler had arranged to bring Pressler to the townhouse, explaining that the Senator desperately needed money for his campaign. The meeting was interesting, particularly in light of how Pressler later described it to the press.

The session with Pressler had occurred on November 7, 1979. Amoroso had begun with the basic pitch on the Arabs' quest for permanent refuge in the United States. Pressler stressed that he would be sympathetic to their cause. "Let me give you a little bit of my philosophy," he said, ". . . I just attended a meeting [Iran hostage crisis] . . . they're asking people for advice on what to do about the Shah and I said keep him here. . . . If you submit to blackmail once, you'll be submitting again and again. . . . You can tell your people [the Arabs] that you've got a man who voted to keep him [the Shah] here . . ."

Amoroso asked if Pressler could introduce a bill or take other positive official action to help the two Arabs. Amoroso said it would be worth $50,000, which Pressler could call a campaign contribution if he wished. Pressler carefully replied: "We do seek contributions, but we can't make any promises or any, you know, a, ah, other than to listen and to be educated, but, ah, and then to make a judgment, you know."

The Senator had to promise something for money to be in violation of the law. The intimation that he would be sympathetic was not enough. Pressler, noting that fifty-one Senators were needed for a majority, said that even if he did introduce a bill, he could not guarantee it would be passed. But he promised to have his Senate staff research all the possibilities, including those of a special bill. Amoroso suggested that they talk again after the staff research had been completed.

Pressler persisted: "In any event, it would not be proper for me to promise to do anything in return for a campaign contribution, so I would not make any promises or any . . . I mean you can judge. You can hear my general philosophy and you can make a judgment. Ah, but I can't, ah, you know, ah, you can't make a commitment to do anything in these campaigns. Indeed, I wouldn't [be] fully intellectually honest doing that, you know, until I'm fired up with the situation. So maybe that's, maybe that makes it possible for you to, you know, to help out, or to take steps and . . ."

Weinberg stared at the thirty-seven-year-old Senator. He thought: This guy wants us to give him $50,000 on trust. Amoroso said he'd prefer to talk again. Pressler left, promising to call back with his staff report. The meeting had been very friendly.

SCENE

Weinberg and Agent Steve Bursey enter the garage of the Resorts International casino in Atlantic City. It had been a helluva day. Earlier, with the help of Silvestri and Maressa, Abdul had held a gigantic cocktail party at Resorts for New Jersey legislative and city officials. The party had been mobbed. Mayor Errichetti had tossed a rival cocktail party several floors below and it had bombed. Errichetti was reportedly smoldering. After the party, Weinberg and Bursey had gone to the crap tables and tapped out. All they had left was credit cards. The two men walk to the Abdul limousine and discover a huge gash in the front tire. There is no spare. There is no evidence pointing to the culprit. But Weinberg has his own ideas. "That fuckin' Mayor won't ever give up," he laughs.

Silvestri had been a mixed bag, Weinberg reflected. He smiled, remembering the night last fall when Silvestri had promised to bring Congressman William Hughes of New Jersey for a payoff at the Holiday Inn in Toms River, New Jersey. The camera had been set up and the rest of the crew lurked in the next room while Amoroso and Weinberg sat with $50,000 waiting for Hughes and Silvestri to arrive. They never showed. Silvestri alibied that he had written down the wrong date in his calendar. Hughes later stated that he had never agreed to any meeting. There was no further follow-up by the Abscam group.

Silvestri proposed two candidates whose names nearly blew the minds of those who were monitoring the tapes. The two prospects were House Speaker Tip O'Neill and Senator Ted Kennedy, President Carter's sure primary opponent. They cooled on Kennedy when Silvestri reported that any money would have to be given as a campaign contribution.

Washington, apparently, was interested in the Speaker. Weinberg was asked to get more details on Silvestri's proposal. The hefty builder talked at first about a $100,000 payment to O'Neill in Washington. He later switched the scene of the proposed meeting to Boston. He also offered to bring in Congressman James Florio of New Jersey, Maressa's political ally. But Silvestri was like quicksilver. Here now, off on another deal five minutes later. Nothing further developed.

It was dark. The sleet had stopped. Weinberg heaved out of the chair, carrying the empty soda can into the kitchen to toss it into an over-flowing garbage bag. He wasn't shocked at corruption in the nation's Capitol, both real and rumored. To his mind, Washington was like everyplace else. Grab or be grabbed; fastest wins. He understood the game. He had played it all his life.

Congressman Richard Kelly of Zephyrhills, Florida, had begun with Bill Rosenberg. Early in the fall of 1979, Rosenberg had brought in an accountant from Smithtown, Long Island, named Stanley Weisz. While Weisz nodded agreement, Rosenberg explained that the wealthy accountant had inside connections with the Internal Revenue Service, could get Abdul forged gold certificates, and knew powerful New York politicians.

Amoroso and Weinberg were busy with other things and put Rosenberg and Weisz on hold. But Rosenberg was drooling over Weinberg's stories about the money grabbed by middlemen as their cut of the Congressional bribes. Rosenberg told Weinberg that he and Weisz could produce a Congressman for a payoff. The unctuous swindler told Weinberg to contact a mob-connected labor consultant in Florida for more details.

A flurry of phone calls later, Weinberg and Amoroso met in Florida with Gino Ciuzio, a convicted felon, who had once acted as bodyguard for Paul Sciacca, a former boss of the Joe Bonanno crime family. Authorities believed that Ciuzio was a Bonanno crime family soldier. Weinberg and Ciuzio spent the early part of the conversation trying to outvouch each other. Ciuzio kept insisting that he was from "downtown" and that he knew "nice people." Roughly translated, meaning that he was in the rackets and associated with a crime family.

Weinberg and Ciuzio swapped the names of mob luminaries, finally settling on John Del Mastro of Huntington, Weinberg's old friend from Orlando's Restaurant. A mutual vouch established, the two men discussed Del Mastro until both were convinced that they really did know the mob front man. Amoroso came on strong with his CIA cover. Weinberg vouched for Tony, and they were ready to talk business.

Ciuzio explained that he owned Congressman Kelly, a former Florida circuit court judge. The wise-cracking hoodlum painted a chilling picture of the Congressman's gradual erosion. "I'm a rare guy," said Ciuzio. "I got all the fuckin' patience. I nurtured this guy for two and a half years, then I made my move, very respectfully, nice. . . It takes a long time to get there . . . we have been holdin' hands for a long time. Now he's pregnant, ya understand? . . . He's already takin' money, so we're married."

Ciuzio, who lived near Orlando, spelled out the package. He would deliver Kelly for $250,000. The Congressman would get $100,000 of the bribe and Ciuzio, Weisz and Rosenberg would each take $50,000 as a finder's fee. Kelly would be produced and make the promise to introduce a bill on the Arabs' behalf. But no money was to be passed directly to the Congressman, insisted Ciuzio. *He* would give the money to Kelly. "You guys would like protection, too, from a fuckin' Congressman who obviously ain't gonna go to jail for you and me," he explained.

The offer had been made with Amoroso gingerly agreeing to the terms, figuring Weinberg still had several weeks to talk Ciuzio into letting Kelly accept the money directly. Ciuzio, however, stayed stubborn. The fast-talking hoodlum later did make one concession. He agreed to take $25,000 down on the $250,000 package. He said he would produce Kelly at the townhouse on January 8, 1980. Rosenberg and Weisz would come with them.

They came en masse with Kelly, a pinch-faced, balding man with a deep drawl. A Republican, he had urged the rest of Congress to let New York City sink during its financial crisis. Kelly was excited. He had just come from a meeting in the White House. Amoroso invited Kelly into the study and closed the door. It was Weinberg's job to keep the other three talking while Amoroso felt out the Congressman about taking the money.

Ciuzio was obviously worried. He walked into the men's room with Weinberg and braced him. He told Weinberg that Amoroso was not to give Kelly any money. The money was to be given to Ciuzio. "He ain't takin' no fuckin' money in his hand . . . nobody else is to take the money," the hoodlum warned. Weinberg waffled an answer and walked him back to the group. For the next half-hour, as Ciuzio nervously glanced at the closed study door, Weinberg loosed a torrent of Runyonesque chitchat. He wanted to give Tony plenty of time.

As it turned out Kelly was a piece of cake. Amoroso gave him the Arab refugee pitch. He told Kelly, as he had the other Congressmen, that the Arabs would be accused of looting their national treasuries. It didn't seem to bother Kelly. The FBI agent then began to edge into the subject of the bribe. Kelly excused himself for a moment to speak outside with Ciuzio. Amoroso sipped his cold black coffee, thinking that he had lost the Congressman.

Kelly came back. "Very good arrangement . . ." he said. "I'm glad to be associated with you. . . . Let's do it." Amoroso looked shocked. Kelly continued: "Don't stumble around, jump in there and get it [the money]." As Amoroso reached into the drawer and handed Kelly $25,000, the Congressman added, "I'm so damned poor, you wouldn't believe it; I mean if I told you how poor I was, you'd cry—I mean, tears would roll down your eyes."

The former judge, whom Ciuzio had derisively called "ten-speed in brown shoes," then carefully stuffed the bills into all of his pockets. Suddenly, it dawned on Amoroso. Kelly was stiffing his partners. His intention was to sneak the money right by them. He did precisely that.

Abscam was almost over. There was only one loose end. Congressman Peter Rodino of New Jersey, Chairman of the House Judiciary Committee. Congressman Myers had mentioned Rodino as had Congressman Lederer and Congressman Jenrette. Joe Silvestri had said he could arrange a meeting with Rodino. Even Washington was in a box. Rodino's name was all over the tapes and those tapes would be used at other trials. The government was sure to be asked what steps had been taken to check out the leads on Rodino.

Weinberg and Amoroso were told to discuss it with Silvestri. The bulky builder fussed with details for several weeks. Finally he produced a contact whom he claimed would get through to Congressman Rodino. He was Tony De Luca, a New Jersey labor man. De Luca explained that no one met Rodino directly on matters like this. The way to the Congressman, he said, was through his son-in-law Charles Stanziale, a Newark attorney. A meeting was set for mid-January.

It was held in the cocktail lounge of the Meadowlands Hilton near the gigantic sports complex in northern New Jersey. Present were Stanziale, De Luca, Weinberg and Amoroso. Stanziale and De Luca had chosen the meeting spot. Weinberg wore a body-tape. The background noises in the lounge made it difficult to record clearly. The tape, however, was reasonably audible.

Amoroso gave the standard story. The Arabs needed a bill introduced to stay in the U.S. when they came here. They were willing to pay $50,000 to Rodino for introducing the bill. It was the same offer that Silvestri had made earlier to Stanziale. Nevertheless, Stanziale had agreed to the meeting and now he offered a proposal of his own.

It would be a careful, step-by-step process. The Arabs would hire Stanziale's law firm on a consultant basis. That would be the first fee. The

law firm would check out the Arabs' portfolio (background). If everything was satisfactory, the law firm would handle the case for them. This
would involve another fee, which was to be discussed later. The Congressman's son-in-law said that eventually they might actually meet
Rodino. He gave Weinberg and Amoroso his business card and did not
report the bribe offer to authorities.

Stanziale's proposition was carefully analyzed by Washington and by
Puccio's group. It would be expensive and time-consuming to play out
the sting on the off chance that Stanziale would finally produce Rodino.
Time was running out. Tired as he was, Weinberg begged them to give
it a shot. He recalled earlier cases, like the one involving Senator Williams, where the insulation had been strong. Each time he and Amoroso
had managed to strip it away.

But two years of Abscam stalls were wearing thin. More and more
people knew about the sting. Security was increasingly difficult. Good,
Amoroso and Weinberg literally staggered with physical exhaustion. The
decision was made. Shelve Rodino. No more cases. That phase of Abscam
was done.

There was a series of strategy sessions in Puccio's office. The Philadelphia FBI wanted to expand the probe through Criden and Myers into
the City Council. Weinberg resisted going to Philadelphia. But he arranged for Criden to be introduced to an undercover FBI agent posing as
a hotel-investment specialist for Abdul.

Philadelphia was given a ten-day deadline to run its sting. Both
United States Attorney Peter Vaira and the Philadelphia FBI office were
understandably unhappy about the deadline. The Abscam tapes were
swollen with leads on the City of Brotherly Love. Both Puccio and Good
argued, however, that Weinberg could no longer stall the more than half-
billion in loans and payments due from the Arab coffers. Despite the time
limitations, Philadelphia scored bribe charges against three members of
the City Council, including Council President George Schwartz, and
added bribery counts against Myers.

The attitude of the United States Attorney's office in Newark had moved from animosity to outright hostility. Virtually the entire structure of the New Jersey political system had been exposed as corrupt by the Abscam team operating under the director of the Federal Strike Force in Brooklyn. The participation of the Newark office in Abscam had been minimal—a face-saving invention of the Department of Justice. The public was sure to question Newark's inability to clean its own house.

Robert J. Del Tufo, the United States Attorney in Newark, had remained remote. The attack against Abscam was handled by his chief assistant, Ed Plaza, and Plaza's aide, assistant U.S. Attorney Robert Weir, Jr. These were the two Federal officials who had berated Weinberg in Atlantic City for giving instructions to Senator Williams. Neither had let up on him since.

The harassment of Weinberg had gotten so bothersome in the fall of 1979 that Good had gone to Newark and in an explosive confrontation accused Plaza and Weir of jeopardizing the entire investigation. He told them they were insensitive to Weinberg's unusual position within the framework of the investigation. Weinberg, he told them, was neither a lawyer nor a trained FBI agent. He also reminded them that the Williams case was Puccio's, not Newark's.

But the activities of Plaza and Weir continued. Late in December 1979 Plaza and Weir wrote a stinging memorandum, which their boss Del Tufo forwarded to Assistant Attorney General Philip B. Heymann, who headed the criminal division of the Department of Justice. In it they questioned the validity of the Abscam technique. They charged that Weinberg had been allowed to operate without proper supervision. They claimed that he had entrapped Senator Williams and also accused him of putting words into the mouths of potential defendants.

News of the memo exploded on the Abscam team early in January. The memo would be a powerful weapon in the hands of defense attorneys.

It was unprecedented that a United States Attorney's office would write such a memo critical of a brother office in another jurisdiction. In a presidential election year it could give the highly politicized Attorney General's office a valid excuse to dump all of the cases. Most of the targets were prominent Democrats.

The word came down. The memo had made Washington very nervous.

Weinberg, naturally, was furious. "These bums [Newark] didn't do shit before we went into Atlantic City," he railed. "They're pissed because we showed 'em up. They got a lot to protect over there. They're tryin' to stop us." The entire Abscam team, Puccio, Good, Amoroso and the rest, were grim-faced. But, unlike Weinberg, they were battle-scarred veterans of the vicious backbiting that permeates the Federal law enforcement structure. Forget about it, they cautioned. The most important thing, they said, was to finish Abscam with a professional flourish.

The plan was to call in Criden, Rosenberg and Weisz for final meetings at Kennedy Airport. Amoroso would lead them through a recitation of the things they had done for Abdul as middlemen. Faced with these tapes, they might plead guilty and become government witnesses. A huge team of FBI agents would simultaneously hit the homes of the other targets, who would be informed that they were under investigation in connection with the Abscam sting. They would be asked to make statements. Abdul would surface as Abscam. The date for the massive operation was set for Saturday, February 2, 1980.

Weinberg was told to invent a story that would guarantee that Criden, Weisz and Rosenberg would come to the Hilton Inn at the airport. For Weinberg it was a labor of love. He called Criden on January 25, 1980.

Weinberg: I spoke to Tony.

Criden: Right.

Weinberg: He wants to meet you Saturday at the Hilton Hotel in Kennedy Airport. . . . Uh, he says he'll have the money for you . . . and he has something else. Uh, one of the Arabs are coming over with him. He wants to introduce you to him.

Criden: Oh, super. . . . What's . . . doing with the shipping [Murphy] thing?

Weinberg: That's one of the things he's [Amoroso] supposed to bring back with him. . . .

Criden: Oh, boy. Anything doing with the other thing, you know, the Pete Williams [titanium loan] thing?

Weinberg: Yeah, that's closing, uh, in fact that should be closing, uh, around the following week. That's gonna be okay.

Criden: Oh, that's super . . .

Weinberg cradled the phone and grinned. Criden would be there, even in a hurricane. He rubbed his chin. He was growing a beard. The stubble itched. After the trials he would shave it off again. The changes in appearance might make it tougher for people to recognize him later. He rubbed his hands. He couldn't wait until he shoved it to Rosenberg. He called the bothersome swindler on January 31 and told him to come to the hotel with Weisz. He said that he had money for both of them.

Rosenberg: How much are we talking about?

Weinberg: Well, I'm not there . . . I don't have my paper of how much you have coming here.

Rosenberg: Oh, there's . . . a lotta money.

Weinberg: We'll have at least, maybe five . . .

Rosenberg: You'll have five million?

Weinberg: Yeah.

Rosenberg: Oh, my. That would be terrific . . . [Later] I, ah, Mel, I'll have to bring a big bag then.

Weinberg: Yeah, bring a big bag.

Rosenberg: Are you safe there?

Weinberg: Oh, we aren't bringin' the money in till Saturday, Bill. Come on, we're not stupid.

Rosenberg (later): Great, Mel.

Weinberg laughed so hard after he hung up that he dropped his cigar. He could just picture Rosenberg right now, rummaging through his closets for the biggest suitcase he could find. He'd probably bring two. Laughter spent, he looked at the phone thoughtfully. He had just planted Abscam's last sting.

TAPE SEVENTEEN

Good: Mel Weinberg was the critical factor in the success of Abscam. The viability of any undercover operation depends entirely on its credibility. No undercover FBI agent could have given Abscam the type of credibility it got from Weinberg. He has been a con man for thirty years; he had been locked up; he has been dealing with organized crime figures his entire adult life. That's the kind of person who can hold up under background checks, who knows how to react to any situation. Another factor was Tom Puccio and his Strike Force. They never let us down. They were aggressive, positive. They always knew what they were going to do and they did it. The other element was the FBI. The Bureau stood to the mark all the way.

TAPE EIGHTEEN

Weinberg: I wish we coulda done more. Criden was ready to bring in more Congressmen; I think we coulda got at least a third of the whole Congress. And look at New Jersey. We hadda lot more to do there. Ain't nobody in that state gonna follow up on what we did there. The politicians want New Jersey to stay that way. You shoulda seen them at that party we gave for them at Resorts. These were the big guys runnin' the legislature and the cities. All they talked about was how much they was stealin'. It was unbelievable. But, I guess that's what the people want. Most people are crooks at heart anyway, aren't they?

13

GOTTCHA!

We are in a world in which we must choose between being a victim or an executioner—and nothing else. Such a choice is not easy. —ALBERT CAMUS

We stepped on some big toes. There's been a lotta pressure on the assholes. —MEL WEINBERG

Weinberg sat quietly in the corner of the Strike Force office and watched it all come down. It was Saturday, February 2, 1980. The phones were ringing incessantly. Ashtrays overflowed. Styrofoam cups of half-finished coffee littered the desk tops. FBI agents and assistant Strike Force attorneys barged in and out of Tom Puccio's inner sanctum. Everybody and everything was in motion.

He tugged contentedly at his cigar. The big day. Some hundred FBI agents were banging on the doors of Abscam targets from New York to Florida. The Senator, the Congressmen, the middlemen, the swindlers, all of them getting the bad news. He pictured it in his mind. Howdy, Mr. Congressman. We're FBI. We got some great home movies showing your ass in a sling.

Somehow, the newspapers were on to it. *Newsday* and the *New York*

Times would be running stories. NBC had filmed pictures of the agents at Senator Williams's house. Puccio and Good were unhappy about the papers. *Newsday* had named every one of the Congressmen and the Senator. Puccio said that the paper's reporters had been sniffing for the past week. Weinberg grinned. He liked *Newsday*. Besides, he couldn't understand the fuss. With the story out in the open, the Department of Justice was locked in. No way to kill the cases in private.

Weinberg felt good. If he had been familiar with the word, he would have described the feeling as elation. He had met and taken some of the biggest people in the country. Rich, successful people. Educated people. Him against them. The kid from the Bronx and still world champ-een. He liked the sound of it. Greed was the equalizer. The idea of big bread was a magic wand. Wave it and, presto! smart people become instant assholes. Always.

It had been a dynamite morning. First Howard Criden had come to the hotel at the airport. Puccio wanted the attorney tied more directly to the Myers and Lederer bribes, and so Amoroso set it up. When Criden arrived, the agent assured him that the sheikh was due in any minute. Further, to reassure the sheikh he told Criden that he wanted to tell Yassir everything that he had done for him. Criden had gushed. He had started with Myers and Lederer and kept on going. He boasted that he had five more Congressmen ready to come in for bribes. He said Murtha was now ready to take the money. Then FBI agent Bill Quinn had knocked on the door. Criden stopped for the expected regal entrance of Yassir. Amoroso had opened the door for Quinn and turned to Criden.

Amoroso: Howie, my name is Tony Amoroso.
Criden (**mystified**): It's okay.
Amoroso: Okay. Just so you know, okay? An FBI agent. Sorry, Howard.
Criden (**pause**): Yes, sir.
Quinn: Bill Quinn. How are you?
Criden (**pause**): Okay.

Amoroso: They're gonna talk to you.

Criden (sighs): Okay, gentlemen . . .

At Puccio's office later in the day, Criden admitted he had become vaguely suspicious during the last week. The undercover FBI agents used on the Philadelphia end of the sting looked too much like policemen. He said that he had continued, hoping he was wrong, because he was already too deeply involved to make any difference.

The netting of Rosenberg and Weisz was another matter. True to his word, Rosenberg had come with a suitcase, ready to stuff it with money. He had gone slackjawed when Amoroso told him that FBI agents wanted to talk to him. Weisz was a more interesting performer. Amoroso had given him $50,000, solidly linking him to the Kelly payoff. But when the FBI agents identified themselves and demanded the money back, he wouldn't give it up, screaming that it was his finder's fee. His lawyer finally convinced him to surrender the cash.

Now, as Weinberg blew cigar smoke he thought about Mayor Errichetti. From what an agent had said on the phone, the Mayor had clammed up when he got the news. That was no surprise. Errichetti was a stand-up man. His type of man. They would have made a helluva team. Unbeatable. Maybe a firm called W & E Investors. No. The Mayor would insist that his own initial come first.

He had last spoken to Errichetti the day after Christmas. The Mayor, for a change, had answered the phone. His voice had seemed softer, more friendly. They had reminisced. The Mayor had needled him. They'd had a couple of laughs. Sure, they had agreed, we'll get together after the holidays. Weinberg sighed. He would miss Errichetti.

One confrontation predictably was a heated one. That evening there was a nasty scene in Puccio's office. Robert Del Tufo's assistant Ed Plaza had come in from Newark to monitor the action. As usual, he came ready to fight. He had started pumping Puccio and Good and they gave neutral answers. One word had led to another and Plaza had shouted, "I hope you all fall on your faces." Good controlled a strong impulse to punch Plaza in the nose. Plaza had stomped out. Up his, Weinberg grinned.

In the rush of events the newspapers and television made Abscam a household word. It was, they said, the biggest scandal in the history of Congress. After exploring the plight of the Congressmen, the media became interested in Weinberg, now under guard twenty-four hours a day. On one of his trips home to Florida Weinberg received a telegram from New York *Daily News* columnists Jimmy Breslin and Mike Daly. It read:

IF YOU CALL ME COLLECT ON THE TELEPHONE, I WILL PUT YOUR NAME IN MY STORY IN A VERY BIG NEWSPAPER IN NEW YORK.

He grinned. Just what he needed. But he was flattered. Breslin was big time. He folded the telegram and kept it as a souvenir.

There was the usual rush for credit. It was the day of the bosses. Civiletti, Heymann and Nathan took their bows in Washington. The *New York Times* and the New York *Daily News* incorrectly lionized Neil Welch, retiring boss of the New York FBI office, as the man who supervised the Abscam investigation. A fine agent, Welch had had almost nothing to do with the case. It was impossible to ignore the role of Weinberg and Amoroso. Their names dominated the tapes. Puccio kept the limelight as prosecutor of the major cases.

Totally ignored was the role of FBI Supervisor John Good, the man who started Abscam, ran it, protected it, and brought it to a successful conclusion. So were the names of others who had actually done the work: FBI Agents Myron Fuller, Jack McCarthy, Steve Bursey, Ernie Haridopolos, Bruce Brady, Gunnar Askeland, Bob Fitzpatrick, Margo Denedy, Ed Woods, Mike Wilson and Tom McShane. Little was made of the courage displayed by FBI Director William Webster. Nothing was said about Strike Force attorney John Jacobs.

Many of the Senators and Congressmen mentioned on the tapes as potential targets were interviewed by FBI agents. Their stories varied.

Some were flabbergasted. They said they had never been approached to meet with Abscam agents. Others said that they had refused invitations to attend Abscam meetings. The invitations, some said, had come from lawyers and known middlemen like Silvestri.

Many of these officials were undoubtedly telling the truth. Criden and Errichetti had occasionally overestimated their ability to produce a given Congressman. Silvestri was a flagrant name-dropper. Neither Criden, Errichetti nor Silvestri, however, cooperated with the government. As a result, it may never be possible to know how many of the Senators and Congressmen mentioned on the tapes refused Abscam meetings only because they would not come from behind their middlemen and take the bribes directly. Another question left unanswered is why *none* of the unsuccessful bribe offers were reported to authorities.

On his trips to New York in the weeks following the arrests Weinberg stayed under an assumed name at the Holiday Inn on the Long Island Expressway in Plainview. He scanned all the daily papers and flicked the TV from one news show to another. The sting had become special to him; this was his scam, his most perfect creation.

Most of the comments were favorable. The others were predictable.

House Speaker Tip O'Neill told a reporter, "It was a setup, a goddamn setup."

Senator Bill Bradley of New Jersey said, "I deplore the fact that the rights of those being investigated have not been protected; and I deplore the rush to condemn, to joke and be cynical."

Joseph Lordi, Chairman of the New Jersey Casino Control Commission, told an audience that he opposed "the reprehensible handling of the Abscam probe by the FBI. Never in all my years in public office in New Jersey have I seen anything like what has happened this week."

Ira Glasser, an official of the American Civil Liberties Union, fired off a letter to Attorney General Civiletti questioning how much evidence of wrongdoing had been available before the targets for the undercover investigations had been selected.

Congressman John F. Seiberling of Ohio said that Congress needed to look into "the idea of giving some people of dubious moral standards free rein to entice anyone they can entice to commit a crime." His concern was echoed by Congressman Peter Rodino.

At a hearing of Rodino's House Judiciary Committee, FBI Director Webster stoutly defended the use of special undercover agents like Weinberg. He said that the FBI had used similar sting techniques in the past. Rodino disagreed. "It's an entirely different kind of case, a different kind of setting," said the New Jersey Congressman. "[It is] fraught with so much peril of jeopardizing reputations."

U.S. Senator Larry Pressler of South Dakota told the press that he too had been a visitor to the Washington townhouse. He said that Weinberg and Amoroso appeared to be businessmen interested in helping some Arab friends stay in the United States. He said that they vaguely mentioned something about contributions. He added: "After two or three minutes, I stood up and said the purpose of the meeting was different than I was led to believe. I repeated three times the word illegal." He implied that he had stalked out.

The *Washington Post,* scooped on the Abscam story by *Newsday* and the *Times,* complained in an editorial: "No citizen, member of Congress or not, should be required to prove his integrity by resisting temptation . . ."

There were other developments. Rosenberg pleaded guilty. Congressman Murtha agreed to testify for the government. Congress replaced Murtha on the House Ethics Committee with Congressman Wyche Fowler of Georgia. Congressman Patten decided not to seek reelection. And New Jersey State Senator Joseph Maressa gave a unique explanation of why he had taken Abscam money. He said, "The Arabian Nights portrait these two agents painted was such that I felt like it would be patriotic to take some of the OPEC money and get it back to the United States."

Congressional committees spent weeks flexing their muscles and then quietly subsided. So did headlined promises of a massive housecleaning in

New Jersey. The Casino Control Commission got some new board members, following the sudden resignation of Vice-Chairman Kenneth MacDonald. State Democratic Chairman Richard Coffee remained at the helm of his party. And Caesars Boardwalk Regency was promised a permanent license on the casual condition that Cliff Perlman and his brother divest their interests in the corporation. Earlier, Resorts International had gotten its permanent gambling license after the commission decided that the firm and its officials had no ties to Meyer Lansky.

The Department of Justice, meanwhile, concentrated on finding and punishing those responsible for leaking Abscam information to the press. Richard Blumenthal, the United States Attorney from Connecticut, was appointed to conduct the probe. Swarms of FBI agents descended on Good, Amoroso, Puccio and other members of the Abscam team. All of them volunteered to take lie detector tests and spent hours answering questions. Weinberg was interviewed twice. He agreed to take a polygraph test at the first interview. At the second he flatly refused.

Media columnist Tom Collins reported in *Newsday:* "The question in many journalists' minds is a simple one: Who is going to wind up in jail: reporters or Congressmen?" He might well have thrown the entire Abscam team into his equation.

As spring 1980 advanced, the defense strategy emerged clearly. The defendants had either been entrapped or victimized by investigative overstep. And the chief government witness against them was a known swindler and liar named Mel Weinberg. Defense lawyers began playing hardball. As usual, Weinberg was in the middle.

Reports filtered into the Department of Justice that Weinberg had hustled some of the targets for expensive gifts, claiming that he would forward them to Abdul and Yassir. Most of these claims came from defense lawyers and were reported to Washington by Del Tufo's office in Newark. New Jersey garbageman George Katz said that he had given Weinberg three expensive gold watches. The victim who complained loudest, however, was Mayor Errichetti. He claimed to have given

Weinberg a stereo, a video cassette recorder, a TV set and a microwave oven. The story was first headlined in the *Philadelphia Bulletin*.

Another plague of FBI agents descended on Weinberg. The three watches were produced from the FBI property room in Hauppauge. Weinberg had turned them over to Good after he received them from Katz. Sure, he had asked Katz for them, he said. He wanted Katz to believe that he and Amoroso were the kind of people who would cheat their own employers if the deal was right. Why wouldn't someone in his position do that? He denied taking anything from Errichetti, and produced a bill of sale from a local department store for the microwave oven found in his home.

"Washington's spendin' more time on me than it is on the Congressmen," he complained to Good. "Suppose I had scammed the Mayor for a TV, what the hell difference would it make? Either these bums took bribes or they didn't, and we know that they did. I don't see them offerin' to give the money back to the government. Why doesn't Washington bother them?" Good spent almost every night with Weinberg. He explained that the government prosecutors had to be prepared for any defense argument.

The Department of Justice assigned the various Abscam cases to four U.S. Attorneys' offices. Thomas Puccio got Errichetti, Williams, Myers, Lederer, Thompson and Murphy. He also got the case involving Carpentier and the bribed immigration agent. Washington got Kelly and Jenrette. Philadelphia got the three City Councilmen. Robert Del Tufo got Atlantic City, MacDonald, Maressa, Silvestri and Katz in connection with reported bribes to Errichetti and Mayor Gibson. The other three offices immediately demanded Weinberg's help in preparing their cases. Puccio was accused of keeping Weinberg under wraps for himself.

A meeting of the four offices was called for June in Washington by Assistant Attorney General Philip Heymann. Several problems were to be thrashed out. Of foremost concern was access to Weinberg. The prosecutors from Philadelphia and Washington, who would be handling the cases in those cities, had never even met him. If Weinberg was going to be their star witness, they wanted to look at him and talk to him.

There was also the problem of the tapes. They were everywhere, and many had not yet even been transcribed. Many of the tapes were in Puccio's office; others were in Hauppauge, still others were in Florida. Some of the cases had moved from city to city as they unfolded. A tape that was important to one of Puccio's cases in New York was equally important to a case in Washington. Some of the tapes were vital to cases in three or four of the jurisdictions. Few copies had been made. Collecting, sorting, copying and transcribing the tapes would be a nightmare.

The leaders of the FBI Abscam team were ordered to the meeting. Good was told to bring Weinberg. The feisty con man gloated. Finally, he was coming face to face with Washington.

They gathered in the glistening J. Edgar Hoover Building, the FBI's national headquarters. Weinberg was impressed. Where was the room where they meat-axed expense accounts, he asked Good. The FBI supervisor humored him. "All around you," he said, extending his arms. "John, I believe yah," Weinberg snorted.

They entered the conference room and took seats. Amoroso sat on one side of Weinberg, Good on the other. Good's Washington supervisor, Michael Wilson, sat nearby. The rest of the people in the room stared at Weinberg as though he were an odd insect that had slipped through the porch screen. Screw you too, he thought, as he stared back benignly.

Assistant Attorney General Heymann peptalked teamwork, coordination and the imperatives of professionalism. Then he turned the gavel over to his assistant Irving Nathan and left the room. So much for Heymann, thought Weinberg. He decided that Nathan, who was young, smart and arrogant, personified his image of a wise-assed Washington lawyer. It was instant dislike.

The session lasted for a week. It was tough work. Again and again, Weinberg struggled to express the abstracts of the Abscam operation. It was one big sting, but thousands of little stings too. No case had any clear beginning. An idea would start in a conversation with one person. Word would pass from one middleman to the other, one target to the next. He had heaped fuel on the fire as it spread.

As he tried to explain the vast network of stings his audience would understand only parts of the illusion. Weinberg was frustrated in his efforts: as though he were describing a tapestry to people who were only interested in looking at threads. Gradually, however, they made the connections.

He listened, fascinated, as Justice Department officials discussed the elements of entrapment. It was more a discussion of what was not entrapment, than what was. Temptation was allowable. It all came down to the person being tempted. Would he have been disposed to commit this or a similar crime? That was the key question. If the government virtually wrestled a person into committing a crime, that was entrapment. None of Abscam's targets, the team members argued, had been talked into committing a crime that they didn't want to commit. None had said no. The only push, they explained, had been to have the defendants do personally what they had offered to do through middlemen. The crime was the same either way.

Weinberg was asked about calls that were not taped and others that were only partially taped. Patiently, he explained about the tape malfunctions. Other times, he said, he had simply run out of tapes. Each call had to be recorded on a separate tape. On days when he got eight or ten calls at his home, his supply of tapes would be exhausted. Whenever he could tape, he said, he did. Hadn't he taped his controversial instructions to Senator Williams?

Irving Nathan asked Weinberg about a book Weinberg supposedly had been commissioned to write. Was he writing one? Weinberg truthfully replied that he was not personally writing a book. The questions then came rapid-fire. Weinberg admitted that he was involved in a book project. Nathan announced that the government did not want him to write a book. With that Weinberg blew. What in hell, he asked, had the government done for him? He wasn't a government employee, and consequently, he didn't have to take orders from Nathan. The matter was dropped.

Shortly after the coordination session, the hostility between the Abscam team and Ed Plaza of Robert Del Tufo's office in Newark erupted into another bitter quarrel. It happened on June 18, 1980, at the office of the United States Attorney in Washington, where Plaza and his assistant Robert Weir had come to interview Weinberg and Amoroso. Good was present.

Weinberg refused to talk with them, as did Amoroso. Good bluntly told Plaza: "You've been breaking our balls since the beginning of this case. You don't believe in this case. You've been lying to us; you've been telling untrue stories. You've been after Mel's ass. We don't trust you. We don't want to talk to you."

Plaza replied, "That's a lie." Weir then asked Good to put his cards on the table. Good didn't hesitate. He pointedly asked why Newark had not yet impaneled a grand jury to begin hearing evidence on the Abscam cases it had been assigned by the Justice Department. All of the other U.S. Attorneys' offices, he said, had already gotten indictments. The implications of Newark's passivity were clear.

The meeting broke up and the three team members stalked out as Plaza and Weir placed a call to Heymann. But the Department of Justice took the cases away from Newark. The Attorney General sent a member of his own Washington staff to take over the Abscam cases assigned to Del Tufo's office. Del Tufo resigned the next month. But Plaza and Weir stayed on. Later they would appear as witnesses for defense attorneys attempting to overthrow the Abscam convictions.

In July, there was a dress rehearsal in Philadelphia for the coming Abscam trials. The Philadelphia Councilmen had made a motion before a Federal judge to throw out their indictments charging that the government had violated their rights by orchestrating the Abscam press leaks. Reporters and editors from *Newsday*, the *New York Times*, NBC and the *Philadelphia Inquirer* were subpoenaed to the hearing. So were Good, Weinberg and a bevy of government officials.

Scheduled to go on trial in Brooklyn the following month were Congressman Myers, Mayor Errichetti, attorney Howard Criden and Criden's law partner, Philadelphia Councilman Louis Johanson. Errichetti's lawyer was Ray Brown, the attorney who had completely changed the focus of a New Jersey murder case and won acquittal for his client after maneuvering a *New York Times* reporter into a contempt sentence for refusing to reveal his sources of information. The Philadelphia hearing smacked strangely of Brown's strategy.

The only real casualty of the hearing was Jan Schaffer, a plucky *Inquirer* reporter, who was given a six-month contempt sentence for refusing to answer a question that might reveal her sources. Weinberg's debut as an Abscam witness was not exactly a triumph. He seemed ill at ease, a person in search of a posture. At one moment he was cocky, at the next hesitant. Richard Ben-Veniste, Criden's lawyer, adroitly skipped from subject to subject, testing Weinberg's defenses for the bigger trial to come.

Weinberg was totally unprepared. He had been at home with Marie in Florida under the impression that he would not actually be called to testify in Philadelphia. The night before, a call had come from New York. He would testify the next day. Marie hurriedly packed an overnight bag and he left the house immediately with two FBI agents. At that late hour connections into Philadelphia were made with difficulty.

Both government and defense witnesses are usually prepared by their lawyers before testifying. From these prep questions, witnesses get an idea of what to expect on the stand. There was no session with Assistant U.S. Attorneys of the Philadelphia office before Weinberg took the stand the next day. They sat at the prosecution table voicing few objections to Ben-Veniste's wide-ranging examination. The judge was crusty, frequently demanding that Weinberg answer questions more explicitly. Alone on the stand he felt abandoned.

For the usually ebullient Weinberg, it was a low point. Over the following days he was unusually subdued, wondering if the fix had already been made in Washington. Was his side setting him up to be the Abscam fall guy?

Thomas Puccio reassured Weinberg emphatically. The government was determined to make the charges stick. Puccio himself would try the cases in Brooklyn. Good and Amoroso virtually lived in Weinberg's hotel room early that August as he studied transcripts of the Myers case. They dined with him almost every night, reinforcing his ego, helping him anticipate defense tactics. Weinberg's brash confidence flowered again in the sunshine of their attention.

His restoration was complete when he read in the newspapers that defense lawyers were predicting they would wipe the courtroom floor with him. They would hammer at his background as a professional swindler. They intended to prove that he had been a thief and liar all of his life. When they finished, they said, no juror would ever believe him. It was a well-planned strategy, designed to put a witness on the defensive.

What the defense lawyers failed to understand, though, was Weinberg's excessive pride in his criminal career. Crooks who boast about their crimes quickly wind up in jail. That had been Weinberg's lifelong cross, as though a painter had been forced to hide a masterpiece in a locked closet. Now Weinberg would get a chance to display his to the entire world. He couldn't wait to take the witness chair.

Every eye in the Brooklyn Federal Courtroom was on Weinberg as he came through the doors on that August morning of 1980 and walked to the stand.

Pete Bowles caught the scene in *Newsday*: "Melvin Weinberg, the government's chief undercover informant in the Abscam operation, walked into Federal court yesterday wearing a three-piece, cream-colored suit, patent leather shoes, a gold bracelet, two pinkie rings and a smile of confidence."

Weinberg gazed over at Federal Court Judge George C. Pratt. A tall, thoughtful jurist with a keen mind, Pratt was generally regarded as a rising star on the Federal bench. He would preside over the bulk of the Abscam trials for the next year.

Thomas Puccio gently took Weinberg through the prosecution's case.

Amoroso had already introduced the videotape of the Myers payoff as evidence. Weinberg for his part described the various taped conversations he had had with Mayor Errichetti and Howard Criden. Skillfully, Puccio linked them to the bribe, a careful orchestration. For the record, he also asked Weinberg about his old conviction in Pittsburgh. It went quickly.

Then the defense lawyers took over and hammered at Weinberg for the next three and a half days. The game plan was evident in their questions. To establish entrapment, they introduced the tape in which Weinberg coached Senator Williams in the hotel lobby. Hadn't he done the same with Myers and the other defendants? He replied that he hadn't. They pointed to gaps on the tapes and to conversations for which there were no tapes. Hadn't he erased and destroyed tapes that would have shown him coaching the defendants to commit crimes? No, he had not.

They led him through the various salary and bonus payments he had gotten from the government. Wasn't he really a bounty hunter, paid by the scalp? He could barely conceal a smile as he denied it. Wasn't he going to get rich on a book? He admitted that he hoped so. His answers were cool and exact. The witness seemed completely at ease.

Then they launched into his criminal career, asking him about his early days of window smashing, the Yaqui Indian deal, the South American trip, Swiss Bank Associates and London Investors. They painted a picture of a committed swindler and he admitted to it. Twice, Ben-Veniste asked him why he was smiling.

Defense attorney John Duffy had fired the first salvo:

Duffy: Do you know what a con man is?

Weinberg: A con man is someone who will try to con ya outta somethin'.

Duffy: Maybe I can help. Is he a fellow who lies?

Weinberg: A con man tries to tell the truth as much as possible. Otherwise he will get in trouble.

Duffy: Are you a con man?

Weinberg: I don't know. They say I am.

Duffy: Have you spent most of your adult life living by your wits, sir?

Weinberg: That's correct.

Duffy: Living off of money that you got from other people under false pretenses?

Weinberg: That's correct.

Duffy: Is it fair to say that a confidence man will lie, cheat and swindle whenever it serves his purpose to do so?

Weinberg: That is correct.

Duffy: To further his own interests?

Weinberg: That is correct.

Duffy: And you say you have been known as a confidence man?

Weinberg: That's correct.

Next to question Weinberg was Ben-Veniste, a former Watergate prosecutor and the tiger of the defense. Weinberg admitted that London Investors had been a scam and that he had franchised it out.

Ben-Veniste: In the London Investors scam, you had actually franchised that scam to con men all over the world?

Weinberg: We franchised it, but not to con men.

Ben-Veniste: Not to other con men, but for other con men to use the same scam?

Weinberg: That's correct.

Ben-Veniste: Right. You were like the MacDonald's of con men?

Weinberg: That's correct.

Weinberg was excused from the stand and the case dragged on. The Mayor's nephew-driver Joseph Di Lorenzo testified that he had delivered TV sets, a stereo and a video recorder to Weinberg at his uncle's request. Under cross-examination from Puccio, he said that he never asked Errichetti about the contents of attaché cases the Mayor had carried from the Abdul office. During a court recess, the youthful Camden Energy Director remarked to a stranger, "If I asked my uncle a question like that, he'd smack me in the mouth."

Both sides made their summations. The defense argument was best posed by Duffy. He told the jury: "It's Mel versus Ozzie [Myers]; that's what it boils down to." Judge Pratt gave his charge on Saturday, August 30, 1980, and the jury retired. Weinberg returned to his motel, a Holiday Inn near New York's LaGuardia Airport.

Weinberg sat that night at a table in the hotel dining room with FBI Agent Steve Bursey and two friends from Long Island. He puffed on his cigar and confidently predicted a guilty verdict. The Myers case was Abscam's strongest. Without it the others would surely fail.

But as the evening waned without a verdict, he showed tension. He toyed with the food on his plate and bit more deeply into his cigar. Twice he left the table to call the Strike Force office in Brooklyn. "Nothin' yet," he reported at 9:35 P.M. He sat down again and talked. "Both sides took their best shot on this one," he said. "If we win, I think the rest of them will fold. But if we lose this one, we got big problems. It took big balls for the FBI to take on Congress. There could be a lotta blood on the floor."

Shortly after 10:30 P.M., Weinberg went up to his room. He tossed the jacket of his three-piece Pierre Cardin suit onto the king-sized bed and called Puccio's office again. "Nothing', huh?" He hung up and slouched on the bed. The bureau was piled high with tape transcripts. He was supposed to study them for future trials. He waved toward the transcripts. "Well, if the verdict comes in bad, at least I won't have to read all this shit," he said.

Shortly after midnight, the phone rang. Weinberg had been watching a movie rerun on television. He grabbed the phone. "Yeah?" he barked. There was a pause as he listened. He broke into a grin. "All of them? On the big ones? Great. Thanks." He turned to his visitors: "Guilty," he said. "What did I tell ya."

Weinberg was wrong about future guilty pleas. The five remaining

Congressmen would all go to trial. Weinberg and Amoroso would testify each time. And all five would be found guilty. The Williams case would not be tried until April 1981.

Weinberg was the prime defense target at each of the Congressmen's trials. He blunted the attacks with an unexpected blend of candor and humor. Myers, Jenrette and Thompson all tried to explain away the damaging videotapes with the excuse that they had been drunk when the bribes were passed. Given the lush-quotient of Congress, the excuse was plausible, but juries didn't buy it. Kelly argued that he had taken the money as part of his secret investigation of hoodlum Ciuzio and others. The jurors convicted him anyway.

Several days after the Myers trial, Weinberg was back in Florida. He had come home to Marie. Now he stood with his son on a pier near his house. Nestled alongside was his boat, a trim sports cruiser. A friend was there to talk for a few minutes before father and son went fishing.

Suppose, he was asked, the convictions were overturned by a higher court. Would he feel that Abscam had been a waste? "Nah," he answered. "We showed what was really goin' on. The tapes are the record. Nobody can change that. New Jersey stinks and so does Congress. The courts can find all the technical shit they want, but it don't affect the bottom line. Nothin's gonna change though, because that's the way people are."

He said that he couldn't resume his career as a swindler. "I'm too well known," he grinned. "I'd have to go awful fuckin' deep in the woods to find a sucker who ain't heard of me. Besides, knowin' too much makes ya nervous. I'd always be lookin' for empty screwholes in doors. And if some poor bastard came to me with an attaché case, I'd probably smack him in the nose and toss it out the window." He paused for a minute as he prepared to shove off. "But then again," he shrugged, "who knows?"

The boat swung away from the pier and nosed into the bay. As the cruiser moved away, its name stood out in bold letters painted on the stern:

UP YOURS II

LATER

One year later. Senator Harrison Williams was convicted and resigned from the Senate just hours before his probable expulsion. George Katz, the New Jersey garbage contractor and mob confidant, died before he could be tried. The Justice Department could not confirm his taped statements about chilling the tax case against Newark Mayor Kenneth Gibson. Former Newark U.S. Attorney Robert J. Del Tufo swore under oath that he had asked the Justice Department to indict the Mayor for income-tax evasion. The Justice Department confirmed Del Tufo's statement, adding that the decision not to prosecute Gibson was made in Washington. Convicted middleman Howard Criden declined to take the stand at his own trial but gave an affidavit to attorneys for the Perlman brothers, stating that he was fibbing when he boasted on tape about knowledge of ties between Meyer Lansky and casino operator Cliff Perlman. The Perlman brothers, meanwhile, arranged to dispose of their interest in Atlantic City's Boardwalk Regency Casino after the state casino-control commission refused to issue the casino a permanent license.

Scores of defense lawyers decried Abscam, accusing the government of entrapment, investigative overkill, and other procedural peccadilloes.

The courts have consistently rejected these charges, but they have won ready acceptance from a strange amalgam of right-wing radicals, religious cultists, and those few who feel it is more important to be perceived as liberal than informed. Their primary target, then and now, is Mel Weinberg, certified crook.

Congress has shown little curiosity about those unindicted Congressmen who now admit that they were offered bribes and then failed to report the offers to authorities. But Congress is about to launch an investigation of the FBI's Abscam tactics to ensure, I am convinced, that no Congressman ever again will be nailed with his hand in the cookie jar.

Marie Weinberg hung herself in Tequesta, Florida, in early 1982. She had been cut down twenty years before by Weinberg and a friend, when she had attempted to commit suicide in exactly the same way. A psychiatric evaluation at the time stated that Marie had strong suicidal tendencies, tended to romanticize events, and had a schizoid (split) personality.

I had talked to Marie frequently while preparing this book. She told me often that she was aware that Weinberg kept company with other women. She accepted this and the fact that the book would deal with it. Shortly after the book's publication in the spring of 1981, Marie wrote me that she had enjoyed it tremendously. She was handling everything well. But, as the battle to destroy Abscam intensified, I believe that someone took Marie by the hand, brought her to the apartment that Mel shared with Lady Diane, later revealed as Evelyn Knight, and forced Marie to confront a reality that she desperately wanted to ignore. She later told me that people she would identify only as "they" had shown her certificates purporting that Weinberg had secretly divorced her and married Evelyn in Haiti. Marie would not be convinced otherwise. At about this time, it is known that Marie was in frequent contact with a private detective hired by Senator Williams and a reporter for columnist Jack Anderson, a relentless critic of Abscam, and that her phone conversations were taped.

Marie signed an affidavit prepared for her and several defendants

filed it with the courts in an attempt to discredit Mel's trial testimony.
Marie was told that she would have to testify before the U.S. Senate at
the Williams expulsion hearing. And, somehow, somewhere, she got the
impression that Weinberg would seek custody of their adopted child.
What had begun as a hurt woman's flirtation with her estranged husband's enemies had suddenly gone wildly out of control. It was a feeling
that she had described to her psychiatrist in 1962, a sense that her life
was being patterned by others, that she was a puppet dangling from
strings.

March 24, 1982
Robert W. Greene